26th Conference on Computational Linguistics and Speech Processing

(ROCLING 2014)

Zhongli, Taiwan
25 – 26 September 2014

Editors:

C. Chang
H. Wang
J. Chien
H. Kao
S. Wu

ISBN: 978-1-63439-624-0

Printed from e-media with permission by:

Curran Associates, Inc.
57 Morehouse Lane
Red Hook, NY 12571

Some format issues inherent in the e-media version may also appear in this print version.

Printed by Curran Associates, Inc. (2015)

Association for Computational Linguistics
209 N. Eighth Street
Stroudsburg, Pennsylvania 18360

Phone: 1-570-476-8006
Fax: 1-570-476-0860

acl@aclweb.org

Additional copies of this publication are available from:

Curran Associates, Inc.
57 Morehouse Lane
Red Hook, NY 12571 USA
Phone: 845-758-0400
Fax: 845-758-2634
Email: curran@proceedings.com
Web: www.proceedings.com

Proceedings of the Twenty-Sixth Conference on Computational Linguistics and Speech Processing

ROCLING XXVI (2014)

September 25-26, 2014

National Central University, Zhongli, Taiwan

Sponsored by:
Association for Computational Linguistics and Chinese Language Processing
National Central University

Co- Sponsored by:
Academic Sponsor
Institute of Information Science, Academia Sinica

Government Sponsors
Ministry of Education
Ministry of Science and Technology

Industry Sponsors
ASUSTeK Computer Inc.
Cyberon Corporation
Chunghwa Telecom Laboratories
Industrial Technology Research Institute
Fortemedia

Welcome Message from Chairs

On behalf of the program committee, it is our pleasure to welcome you to the National Central University, Jhongli, Taiwan, for the 26th Conference on Computational Linguisitics and Speech Processing (ROCLING), the flagship conference on computational linguistics, natural language processing, and speech processing in Taiwan. ROCLING is the annual conference of the Computational Linguisitcs and Chinese Language Processing (ACLCLP) which is held in autumn in different cities and universities in Taiwan. This year we received 25 submissions, each of which was reviewed by two to four reviewers on the basis of originality, novelty, technical soundness, and relevance to the conference. Totally, we accept 16 oral papers and 5 poster papers which cover the areas of speech and speaker recognition, text mining, speech processing and synthesis, and natural language processing. We are grateful to the contribution of the reviewers for their extraordinary efforts and valuable comments.

ROCLING 2014 features two distinguished lectures from the renowned speakers in speech processing as well as natural language processing. Dr. Frank Soong (Principal Researcher/Research Manager of MSRA) will lecture on "Search for the Elementary Particles in Human Speech - Clues for the Common Units Across Different Speakers and Languages" and Dr. Hang Li (Chief Scientist of Huawei Technologies) will speak on "Semantic Matching: The Next Big Thing for Natural Language Processing?". This ROCLING also features two Doctoral Consortiums, one Industry Track and one Academic Demo Track which provide forums and show-and-tells for PhD students, industrial and academic researchers and developers.

Finally, we appreciate your enthusiastic participation and support. Wishes a successful and fruitful ROCLING 2014 in Jhongli.

Chia-Hui Chang
Hsin-Min Wang
General Chairs

Jen-Tzung Chien
Hung-Yu Kao
Program Committee Chairs

Organizing Committee

Honorary Chair

Jing-Yang Jou, National Central University

General Chairs

Chia-Hui Chang, National Central University

Hsin-Min Wang, Academia Sinica

Advisory Committee

Jason S. Chang, National Tsing Hua University

Hsin-Hsi Chen, National Taiwan University

Keh-Jiann Chen, Academia Sinica

Sin-Horng Chen, National Chiao Tung University

Wen-Lian Hsu, Academia Sinica

Chu-Ren Huang, Hong Kong Polytechnic University

Chin-Hui Lee, Georgia Institute of Technology

Lin-shan Lee, National Taiwan University

Hai-zhou Li, Institute for Infocomm Research

Chin-Yew Lin, Microsoft Research Asia

Helen Meng, Chinese University of Hong Kong

Jian Su, Institute for Infocomm Research

Keh-Yih Su, Behavior Design Corporation

Hsiao-Chuan Wang, National Tsing Hua University

Jhing-Fa Wang, National Chen Kung University

Chung-Hsien Wu, National Chen Kung University

Steering Committee

Chia-Ping Chen, National Sun Yat-Sen University

Jing-Shin Chang, National Chi Nan University

Berlin Chen, National Taiwan Normal University

Kuang-Hua Chen, National Taiwan University

Hung-Yan Gu, National Taiwan University of Science and Technology

Zhao-Ming Gao, National Taiwan University

Jyh-Shing Jang, National Taiwan University

Yuan-Fu Liao, National Taipei University of Technology

Chao-Lin Liu, National Chengchi University

Wen-Hsiang Lu, National Cheng Kung University

Shu-Chuan Tseng, Academia Sinica

Yuen-Hsien Tseng, National Taiwan Normal University

Yih-Ru Wang, National Chiao Tung University

Program Committee Chairs

Jen-Tzung Chien, National Chiao-Tung University

Hung-Yu Kao, National Cheng-Kung University

Publicity Chair

Richard Tzong-Han Tsai, National Central University

Local Arrangement Chair

Jia-Ching Wang, National Central University

Publication Chair

Shih-Hung Wu, Chaoyang University

Industry Track Chair

Wen-Hsiang Lu, National Cheng-Kung University

Academic Demo Track Chair

Yeou-Jiunn Chen, Southern Taiwan University

Doctoral Consortium Chairs

Richard Tzong-Han Tsai, National Central University

Yu Tsao, Academia Sinica

Keynote 1 -
Search for the "Elementary Particles" in Human Speech – Clues for the Common Units Across Different Speakers and Languages

Frank Soong

Principal Researcher / Research Manager of MSRA

Thursday, September 25

10:00 ~ 11:00

Location: International Conference Center

Biography

Frank Soong is a Principal Researcher and Research Manager of the Speech Group, where speech modeling, recognition, synthesis research is conducted. He received his BS, MS and Ph. D, all in EE from the National Taiwan University, the University of Rhode Island and Stanford University, respectively. He joined Bell Labs Research, Murray Hill, NJ, USA in 1982, worked there for 20 years and retired as a Distinguished Member of Technical Staff in 2001. In Bell Labs, he had worked on various aspects of acoustics and speech processing, including: speech coding, speech and speaker recognition, stochastic modeling of speech signals, efficient search algorithms, discriminative training, dereverberation of audio and speech signals, microphone array processing, acoustic echo cancellation, hands-free noisy speech recognition. He was also responsible for transferring recognition technology from research to AT&T voice-activated cell phones which were rated by the Mobile Office Magazine as the best among competing products evaluated. He was the co-recipient of the Bell Labs President Gold Award for developing the Bell Labs Automatic Speech Recognition (BLASR) software package. He visited Japan twice as a visiting researcher: first from 1987 to 1988, to the NTT Electro-Communication Labs, Musashino, Tokyo; then from 2002-2004, to the Spoken Language Translation Labs, ATR, Kyoto. In 2004, he joined Microsoft Research Asia (MSRA), Beijing, China to lead the Speech Research Group. He is a visiting professor of the Chinese University of Hong Kong (CUHK) and the co-director of CUHK-MSRA Joint Research Lab, recently promoted to a National Key Lab of Ministry of Education, China. He was the co-chair of the 1991 IEEE International Arden House Speech Recognition Workshop. He is a committee member of the

IEEE Speech and Language Processing Technical Committee of the Signal Processing Society and has served as an associate editor of the Transactions of Speech and Audio Processing. He published extensively and coauthored more than 200 technical papers in the speech and signal processing fields. He is an IEEE Fellow.

Abstract

In this talk, we will raise an interesting or even intriguing question: Can we find the `elementary particles_ of a person˘s speech in one language and use them for speech/speaker recognition and rendering his/her voice in a different language? A positive yes_ can make `elementary particles_ useful for many applications, e.g. mixed code TTS, second language learning, speech-to-speech translation, etc. We try to answer the question by limiting ourselves first to how to train a TTS in a different language with speech collected from a monolingual speaker. Additionally, a speech corpus in the targeted new language is recorded by a reference speaker. We then use our `trajectory tiling algorithm,_ invented for synthesizing high quality, unit selection TTS, to `tile_ the trajectories of the sentences in the reference speaker˘s corpus with the most appropriate speech segments in the monolingual speaker˘s data. To make the tiling proper across two different (reference and monolingual) speakers, the difference between them needs to be equalized with appropriate vocal tract length normalization, e.g., a bilinear warping function or formant mapping. All tiled, sentences are then used to train a new HMM-based TTS of the monolingual speaker but in the reference speaker˘s language. Different length units of the :elementary particles_ have been tried and a label-less frame length (10 ms) segments have been found to yield the best TTS quality. Some preliminary results also show that training a speech recognizer with speech data of different languages tends to improve the ASR performance in each individual language. Also, in addition to the fact that audio `elementary particles_ of human speech in different languages can be discovered as frame-level speech segments, the mouth shapes of a mono-lingual speaker have also been found adequate for rendering the lips movement of talking heads in different languages. Various demos will be shown to illustrate our findings in talking head lips rendering, speaker recognition in different languages, speech recognition model trained with the help of data collected in different languages.

Keynote 2 -
Semantic Matching: The Next Big Thing for Natural Language Processing?

Hang Li
Chief Scientist of Huawei Technologies

Friday, September 26
09:00 ¯ 10:00
Location: International Conference Center

Biography

Hang Li is chief scientist of the Noah's Ark Lab at Huawei. He is also adjunct professor of Peking University and Nanjing University. His research areas include information retrieval, natural language processing, statistical machine learning, and data mining. He graduated from Kyoto University in 1988 and earned his PhD from the University of Tokyo in 1998. He worked at the NEC lab in Japan during 1991 and 2001, and Microsoft Research Asia during 2001 and 2012. He joined Huawei Technologies in 2012. Hang has more than 100 publications at top international journals and conferences, including SIGIR, WWW, WSDM, ACL, EMNLP, ICML, NIPS, and SIGKDD. He and his colleagues' papers received the SIGKDD°08 best application paper award, the SIGIR'08 best student paper award, and the ACL'12 best student paper award. Hang has also been working on the development of several products. These include Microsoft SQL Server 2005, Microsoft Office 2007 and Office 2010, Microsoft Live Search 2008, Microsoft Bing 2009 and Bing 2010. He has also been very active in the research communities and served or is serving the top conferences and journals. For example, in 2012, he is track co-chair of the web search track of WWW'12; senior program committee members or area chairs of WSDM'12, KDD'12, CIKM'12, ACML'12, AIRS'12; co-chair of KDD'12 summer school, etc.; and an editorial board member on the Journal of the American Society for Information Science, ACM Transaction on Intelligent Systems and Technology, and the Journal of Computer Science & Technology.

Abstract

Most of natural language processing (NLP) tasks, such as information retrieval, question answering, and machine translation, are based on matching between language expressions. This approach works quite well in practice; its limitation is also obvious, however. Sometimes mismatch between language expressions can occur. We argue that `semantic matching˘ is an effective approach to overcome the challenge, that is to conduct more semantic analysis and perform matching between language expressions at semantic level. In this talk, I will first point out why semantic matching can help significantly enhance the performance of NLP. I will then justify my argument with some examples. More specifically, I will introduce our recent work on using machine learning techniques to construct models for semantic matching. These include latent space model for query document matching in search, string re-writing kernel for question answering, and deep matching model for short text conversation.

Proceedings of the Twenty-Sixth Conference on Computational Linguistics and Speech Processing ROCLING XXVI (2014)

TABLE OF CONTENTS

Oral Session 1: Speech and Speaker Recognition

Oral Session 2: Speech Processing and Synthesis

Oral Session 3:Text mining

Oral Session 4:Natural Language Processing

Poster Session:

運用概念模型化技術於中文大詞彙連續語音辨識之語言模型調適

Leveraging Concept Modeling Techniques for Language Model Adaptation in Mandarin Large Vocabulary Continuous Speech Recognition

郝柏翰　Po-Han Hao 國立臺灣
師範大學資訊工程學系
60047082s@ntnu.edu.tw

陳思澄　Ssu-Cheng Chen 國立
臺灣師範大學資訊工程學系
60247071s@ntnu.edu.tw

陳柏琳　Berlin Chen 國立臺灣
師範大學資訊工程學系
berlin@ntnu.edu.tw

摘要

語言模型已被廣泛地使用在各種自然語言相關的研究議題上；譬如，在語音辨識上，語言模型是關鍵的組成，其主要的功能通常是藉由已解碼的歷史詞序列資訊來預測下一個詞彙為何的可能性最大，以協助語音辨識系統從眾多混淆的候選詞序列假設中找出最有可能的結果[1, 2]。本論文旨在於發展新穎動態語言模型調適技術，用以輔助並彌補傳統 N 連(N-gram)語言模型不足之處。為此，我們本提出所謂的概念語言模型(Concept Language Model, CLM)，其主要假設是認為每一句的語句都是用來代表語者內心隱含而欲傳達的概念，並藉由語言(及語音)來具體表達相對應的語意內容。而概念模型最主要的目的則是希望能夠獲取使用者欲表達的概念，並假設在語音辨識過程中，同一概念之中歷史詞序列中所有詞彙以及待預測詞彙具有共同出現的關係，進而藉此關係達到預測待預測詞彙出現機率的目的。

在實作上，概念模型會使用(搜尋)與初步語音辨識結果相關的同領域文件(或調適語料)內表述的若干概念，用以近似語者內心欲傳達的真正含意，並基於此來建立概念語言模型。而概念語言模型的建立是分兩個面向來探討，它們分別是「詞彙」面向與「文件群聚」面向。首先，在實作上，概念模型會使用(搜尋)與初步語音辨識結果近似同領域文件(或調適語料)內表述的若干概念，用以近似語者內心欲傳達的真正含意，並基於此來建立概念語言模型。而概念語言模型的建立是分兩個面向來探討，它們分別是「詞彙」面向與「文件群聚」面向。首先，我們發展所謂的詞概念語言模型(Word-based Concept Language Model)，並應用於語言模型調適。在建構詞概念語言模型時，我們期望能夠針對每一語句不同的語意內容(第一階段語音辨識結果，以詞圖[3]表示)，在調適語料的若干相關的文件中挑選一組具有代表性的概念關鍵詞組，藉以描述任一對歷史詞序列中所有詞彙與待預測詞彙之間的相依關係。其次，我們亦發展所謂的群聚概念語言模型(Cluster-based Concept Language Model)，假設在調適語料的文件集內之文件可以由一組概念類別度來獲得語句可能的概念分布，並做為語言模型預測的根據。實作上，概念類別的求取可透過一般分群演算法諸如 *K*-Means 演算法[4]而求得；而根據每一語句的語意內容與各個概念類別的相關性，挑選一組具有代表性的概念類別組，藉以描述任一對歷史詞序列中所有詞彙與待預測詞彙之間的共同出現關係，並獲得對於待測詞彙之預測機率。再者，我們嘗試以不同方式來估測此種概念語言模型，並將不同程度的鄰近資訊(Proximity Information)融入概念語言模型以放寬其既有詞袋(Bag-of-Words)假設[3]的限制。

本論文是基於公視電視新聞語料庫來進行大詞彙連續語音辨識(Large Vocabulary Continuous Speech Recognition, LVCSR)實驗，以比較本論文所提出語言模型調適技術與其它當今常用技術之效能，包括了觸發對模型(Trigger-Pair Model)、機率式潛藏語意分析(Probabilistic Latent Semantic Analysis)以及狄利克里分配(Latent Dirichlet Allocation)[5]等。實驗結果顯示我們的語言模型調適技在以字錯誤率(Character Error Rate, CER)評估標準之下，其它當今常用的語言模型調適技術相較，有相當具競爭性的表現，並且對於僅使用 *N* 連語言模型的基礎語音辨識系統能有明顯的效能提升。

關鍵詞：語音辨識、語言模型、概念模型、鄰近資訊

致謝：本論文之研究承蒙教育部¯國立臺灣師範大學邁向頂尖大學計畫(102J1A0800)與行政院科技部研究計畫(MOST 103-2221-E-003-016-MY2, NSC 103-2911-I-003-301, NSC 101-2221-E-003-024-MY3 、 NSC 101-2511-S-003-057-MY3 、 NSC 101-2511-S-003-047-MY3 和 NSC 102-2221-E-003-014- MY3)之經費支持，謹此致謝。

參考文獻：

[1] R.Rosenfeld, `Two decades of statistical language modeling: Where do we go from here,_ *Proceedings of IEEE*, vol. 88, no. 8, 2000, pp. 1270¯1278, 2000.

[2] J. R. Bellegarda, `Statistical language model adaptation: review and perspectives,_ *Speech Communication*, vol. 42, no. 11, pp. 93¯108, 2004.

[3] S. Ortmanns, H. Ney and X. Aubert, `A word graph algorithm for large vocabulary continuous speech recognition,_ *Computer Speech and Language*, vol. 11, 43-72, 1997.

[4] R. Baeza-Yates and B. Ribeiro-Neto, *Modern Information Retrieval: the Concepts and Technology behind Search*, Addison-Wesley Professional, 2011.

[5] D. Blei and J. Lafferty, `Topic models,_ in A. Srivastava and M. Sahami, (eds.), *Text Mining: Theory and Applications*, Taylor and Francis, 2009.

探究新穎語句模型化技術於節錄式語音摘要

Investigating Novel Sentence Modeling Techniques for Extractive Speech Summarization

劉士弘 Shih-Hung Liu, 陳冠宇 Kuan-Yu Chen,
謝育倫 Yu-Lun Hsieh, 王新民 Hsin-Min Wang, 許聞廉 Wen-Lian Hsu
中央研究院資訊科學研究所
{journey, kychen, morphe, whm, hsu}@iis.sinica.edu.tw

陳柏琳 Berlin Chen 國立臺灣師
範大學資訊工程學系
berlin@ntnu.edu.tw

摘要

近幾年來，基於語言模型化(Language Modeling, LM)架構之摘要方法已初步在節錄式語音摘要任務上展現具競爭性的效能。在此架構下，對於被摘要文件每一句候選語句之語句模型的建立，可透過虛擬相關回饋(Pseudo Relevance Feedback, PRF)策略來獲得較可靠的參數估測。一般來說，虛擬相關回饋在執行上可分為兩個階段：1)相關資訊(或者說虛擬相關文件)的選取；2)語句模型化與參數重新估測。首先，有別於現有基於語言模型化架構之摘要方法都聚焦在語句模型參數的重新估測，本論文深入探討與應用各種適合於節錄式語音文件摘要的虛擬相關文件選取技術，用以強化語句模型的參數估測。再者，本論文更進一步地考量使用每一語句的非相關性(Non-relevance)資訊對於虛擬相關文件選取的影響。同時，我們亦額外嘗試基於重疊分群(Overlapped Clustering)概念來有效地選取重要的虛擬相關文件。最後，本論文探索使用三混合模型(Tri-Mixture Model)來表示每一語句，期盼其能更精確地表示一句語句之獨特詞彙使用和語意相關資訊。本論文的語音文件摘要實驗語料是採用公開的公視廣播新聞(MATBN)；實驗結果顯示，相較於其它現有虛擬相關文件選取技術，我們所發展的虛擬相關文件選取技術能提供相當不錯的摘要效能改善。

關鍵詞：節錄式自動摘要、虛擬相關回饋、語句模型、非相關資訊、重疊分群

一、緒論

隨著網際網路的普及與蓬勃發展，大量含有語音資訊的多媒體內涵快速地傳遞並分享於全球各地，像是電視新聞、課程演講、會議錄音和語音郵件等。由於這些多媒體內涵透過自動語音辨識(Automatic Speech Recognition, ASR)處理後都可以表示成語音文件及其對應的自動轉寫(Automatic Transcripts)供瀏覽使用，節錄式語音摘要(Extractive Speech Summarization)在過去十年逐漸成為熱門研究議題[17][25]。節錄式語音摘要目標在於根據一定的摘要比例，從語音文件中選取重要語句並組合成摘要，以期能夠扼要的表示語音文件主要的主題或語意資訊；藉此，使用者能迅速地瀏覽大量多媒體內涵並能充分理解其中主題或語意資訊。

當前主流的節錄式語音摘要方法大致可分為三類：(1)基於文件結構或語句位置資訊來選取重要語句；(2)基於特定詞彙或語意資訊之非監督式(Unsupervised)摘要方法；(3)需要使用人工摘要標註來訓練模型之監督式(Supervised)摘要方法。第一類摘要方法大都是簡單地從文件的緒論(Introductoion)或結論(Conclusion)所在段落擷取出若干語句來組成摘要[1]；此類方法僅適用在特定具有一致結構的文字或語音文件上，因此在實際應用上有其侷限性。另一方面，第二類摘要方法通常將自動摘要任務視為如何排序並挑選具代表性(或重要性)語句之問題，其方法通常是以非監督式方式產生出一種語句層次的摘要特徵或重要分數以供語句排序使用。而第二類摘要方法又可進一步地分成三小類：(I) 以向量(Vector) 為基礎的方法， 包含 有向量空間 模型(Vector Space Model, VSM)[8]、潛藏語意分析(Latent Semantic Analysis, LSA)[8][13]及最大邊際關聯(Maximal Marginal Relevance, MMR)[2]等；(II)以圖(Graph)為基礎的方法，具代表性的有馬可夫隨機漫走(Markov Random Walk, MRW)[30]、詞彙排序(LexRank)[7][23]及最小支配集(Minimal Dominating Set)[28]等；(III)以組合最佳(Combinatorial Optimization)為基礎的方法，包括有次模(Submodularity)[14]以及線性整數規劃(Linear Integer Programming)[22]等。最後，第三類監督式摘要方法通常將自動摘要之任務視為二元分類問題(Binary Classification)，亦即將語句區分為摘要語句或非摘要語句。在訓練階段，必須事先準備好一些訓練文件以及其對應的人工標註過摘要資訊，然後結合各種詞彙、語意或音韻等特徵來表示語句，並且透過各種分類器的學習機制進行摘要(分類)模型的訓練；在測試階段，對於將被摘要之文件，此類方法將文件裡的每一句語句進行二元分類，即可依所設定摘要比例來取摘要語句以產生出摘要。在此類方法中，較著名的包括簡單貝氏分類器(Na¾e-Bayes Classifier)[11]、高斯混合模型(Gaussian Mixture Model, GMM)[24]、隱藏式馬可夫模型(Hidden Markov Model, HMM)[6]、支援向量機(Support Vector Machines, SVM)[10]與條件隨機場域(Conditional Random Fields, CRF)[29]等。由於監督式摘要方法所使用的模型在訓練時必須使用一定數量文件及其對應經人工標註過摘要資訊，所以當它們被應用到新的摘要任務或應用領域時，相較上述兩類摘要方法而言，是會耗費許多人力與時間的。值得一提的是，自動摘要研究也可從其它不同面相來進行探討，包括了來源、需求、方式、用途等，有興趣的讀者可參考相關文獻[17][20][21][25]進行更深入的瞭解。

有別於上述的摘要方法，近期有一些基於語言模型化(Language Modeling, LM)架構之摘要方法被提出，並且初步在節錄式文字或語音摘要任務上展現不錯的效能。在此架構下，對於被摘要文件每一句候選語句之語句模型的建立，可透過虛擬相關回饋(Pseudo Relevance Feedback, PRF)策略來獲得更加可靠的參數估測。一般來說，虛擬相關回饋在執行上可分為兩個階段：1)相關資訊(或者明確地說，虛擬相關文件)的選取；2)語句模型化與參數重新估測。本論文同樣也基於語言模型化架構來發展語音摘要方法，其貢獻主要有三方面。首先，有別於現有基於語言模型化架構之摘要方法都聚焦在語句模型參數的重新估測，本論文深入探討與應用各種適合於節錄式語音文件摘要的虛擬相關文件選取技術，用以強化語句模型的參數估測。其次，本論文更進一步地考量使用每一語句的非相關性(Non-relevance)資訊對於虛擬相關文件選取的影響。同時，我們亦額外嘗試基於重疊分群(Overlapped Clustering)概念來有效地選取重要的虛擬相關文件做為語句模型的參數估測之依據。最後，本論文探索使用三混合模型(Tri-Mixture Model)來表示每一語句，期盼其能更精確地表示一句語句之獨特詞彙使用和語意相關資訊。

本論文後續安排如下：第二節首先介紹使用語言模型於節錄式語音摘要任務之原理，然後闡述虛擬相關回饋的觀念及其現有虛擬相關文件選取技術；第三節將介紹本論文提出之新穎式虛擬相關文件選取技術；第四節則介紹現有各種關聯模型，並且說明如何結合語句關聯性資訊來改進語句模型之估測，使其得以更精準地代表語句的語意內容；第五節介紹實驗語料與設定以及摘要評估之方法；第六節說明實驗結果及其分析；

最後，第七節為結論與未來研究方向。

二、使用語言模型於語音文件摘要

在過去近二十年來，各種語言模型在資訊檢索任務中已被廣泛地應用，並且有不錯的實務成效[34]。近期在語音摘要領域，亦開始有一些基於語言模型化架構的非監督式摘要方法被提出。本節將先簡介兩種常見的、基於語言模型化架構的摘要方法：其一為使用語句語言模型生成文件的文件相似度量值(Document Likelihood Measure, DLM)的摘要方法[3]；另外為使用庫爾貝克-萊伯勒離散度量值(Kullback-Leibler Divergence Measure, KL)[13][15]來計算文件模型和語句模型間之距離的摘要方法。接著，我們將闡述如何利用虛擬相關回饋(Pseudo Relevance Feedback)概念來獲得更可靠的語句模型估測，並介紹數個在資訊檢索領域已被發展出的新穎虛擬相關文件選取技術。

2.1、文件相似度量值

我們可以把語音文件摘要任務視為是資訊檢索的問題。一般來說，資訊檢索(Information Retrieval, IR)旨在尋找相關文件(Relevant Document)來回應使用者所送出的查詢(Query)或資訊需求(Information Need)。同樣地，在從事語音文件摘要時，我們可將每一篇被摘要文件視為是查詢，而文件中的每一句語句(Sentence)視為候選資訊單元(Candidate Information Unit)；據此，我們可以假設在被摘要文件中，與文件本身愈相關的語句就愈有可能是可用來代表文件主旨或主題之摘要語句。

當給定一篇被摘要文件 D 時，文件中每一句語句 S 的事後機率 $P(S|D)$ 可以用來表示語句 S 對於文件 D 的重要性。當使用語言模型來計算 $P(S|D)$ 時，我們透過貝氏定理(Bayes˜Theorem)將 $P(S|D)$ 展開成[3]：

$$P(S|D)=\frac{P(D|S)P(S)}{P(D)}, \tag{1}$$

其中 $P(D)$ 是文件 D 的事前機率，由於 $P(D)$ 不影響語句的排序結果，故可省略不討論；另一方面，$P(S)$ 是語句 S 的事前機率，可以使用各式非監督式方法或監督式方法來求得[3]。在此先假設語句的事前機率為一個均勻分布(Uniform Distribution)，所以 $P(S)$ 亦可省略。最後，$P(D|S)$ 是語句 S 所形成的語言模型生成文件 D 之機率(或稱作文件相似度)，可以用來表示文件 D 與語句 S 之間的相似關係，如果語句 S 生成文件 D 的機率值愈高，代表語句 S 與文件 D 愈為相似(語句愈能代表文件 D)，即愈有可能是摘要語句。我們可以更進一步地假設文件 D 中詞彙與詞彙之間是獨立的，並且不考慮每一個詞彙在文件 D 中發生的順序關係(即詞袋假設(Bag-of-Word Assumption))，則語句 S 生成文件 D 的文件相似度量值(Document Likelihood Measure, DLM) $P(D|S)$ 可拆解成文件 D 中每一的詞彙 w 個別發生的條件機率之連乘積：

$$P(D|S)=\prod_{w\in D}P(w|S)^{C(w,D)}, \tag{2}$$

此種方法是為語句 S 建立一個語句模型(Sentence Model) $P(w|S)$，w 是一個出現在文件 D 中的詞彙，$C(w,D)$ 是詞彙 w 出現在文件 D 中的次數。其中，我們可利用最大化相似度估測(Maximum Likelihood Estimation, MLE)的方式來建立每一個語句的語句模型：

$$P(w|S)=\frac{C(w,S)}{|S|}, \tag{3}$$

在(3)中，$C(w,S)$ 表示詞彙 w 在語句 S 中出現的次數，$|S|$ 則表示語句 S 所含的總詞數。

值得注意的是，由於語句 S 通常僅由少數字詞所組成，因此容易遭遇資料稀疏(Data Sparseness)的問題，這會使得語句模型使用最大化相似度估測時，不僅可能無法準確地估測每一個詞彙在語句中真正的機率分佈，也可能因為某些詞彙的條件機率值為零，導致語句 S 產生文件 D 的機率值為零。為了減輕上述的現象，本論文使用 Jelinek-Mercer 平滑化(Smoothing)技術藉由使用以大量文字語料訓練而成的背景單連語言模型(Background Unigram Language Model)來調適語句模型[33]，故 $P(D|S)$ 可進一步地表示成：

$$P(D|S)=\prod_{w\in D}[\lambda\cdot P(w|S)+(1-\lambda)\cdot P(w|BG)]^{C(w,D)}, \quad (4)$$

其中， $P(w|BG)$是詞彙 w 由背景單連語言模型所產生的機率值。

2.2、庫爾貝克-萊伯勒離散度量值

語言模型使用於文件摘要的研究中，除了可被用於計算語句生成文件的可能性外，另一種方式為藉由庫爾貝克-萊伯勒離散度量值(Kullback-Leibler Divergence Measure, KL)，來評估文件中每一個語句的重要性。當使用庫爾貝克-萊伯勒離散度量值於摘要任務中，被摘要文件 D 和 D 中的每一個語句 S 都將分別被描述為一個單連語言模型；當相對於被摘要文件 D 的文件模型(Document Model)，語句模型的離散度量值愈小時，則代表語句與文件愈相關，亦即語句 S 愈重要。在此摘要架構下，排序語句重要性的公式如下[15]：

$$KL(D\|S)=\sum_{w\in V}P(w|D)\log\frac{P(w|D)}{P(w|S)}, \quad (5)$$

其中，V (Vocabulary)表示一個由語言裡所有可能的語彙所形成的集合。本論文的研究中，文件模型 $P(w|D)$ 的建立方式與語句模型相同(參照式(3))。當我們更進一步地對(5)作分析時，可以發現當文件模型僅使用最大化相似度估測(MLE)的前提下，採用庫爾貝克-萊伯勒離散度量值所得到的語句排序將與使用文件可能性(Document Likelihood)測量方式(即文件相似度量值)所得到的結果是相同的[4]。

由於使用庫爾貝克-萊伯勒離散度量值時，不僅每一句語句被表示成語句模型，每一篇被摘要文件 D 亦被視為一個文件(機率生成)模型，而文件模型在經由各式語言模型調適與平滑化的技巧下，可以有系統地、適當地調適文件模型的機率分佈；因此相較於文件相似度量值(DLM)只能針對語句模型進行調適，庫爾貝克-萊伯勒離散度量值(KL)能透過不同模型參數估測技術的使用來求取語句模型和文件模型，以獲得更佳的自動摘要效能。

2.3、虛擬相關回饋

通常，文件中的語句僅由少許的詞彙所組成，當語句模型使用最大化相似度估測時，容易遭遇資料稀疏的問題；再者，由這語句 S 中些許的表面詞彙是遠不夠正確估算語句 S 與被摘要文件 D 之間的相似度(或低估了此相似度)，所以藉由背景語言模型進行語句模型之調適為最常見的方法之一(參照式(4))。

為了有效解決語句的資料稀疏及相似度被低估的問題，我們可利用在資訊檢索(Information Retrieval)領域被廣泛應用的虛擬相關回饋(Pseudo Relevant Feedback, PRF)技術來強化語句模型(重新估測或對其做調適)[5]。為此目的，當虛擬相關回饋運用於文件摘要領域中時，會將每一語句 S 當成是一個查詢(Query)，然後輸入到一個資訊檢索系統中，找出一些與語句 S 最可能相關的文件，而這些文件就稱之為虛擬相關文件

(Pseudo Relevant Documents)；一個最簡單的方式即是選取排名最前面(檢索分數最高)的幾篇文件(Top-ranked Documents)。有了這些虛擬相關文件後，就可以利用它們來增進語句模型以解決語句資料稀疏及其相似度低估之問題。

當使用虛擬相關回饋技術時，通常會遭遇到兩個挑戰。第一為如何選取、純化(Purify)虛擬相關文件，意即如何去除虛擬相關文件的冗餘性(Redundancy)和摒除非相關資訊(Non-relevant Information)。第二則是如何有效地運用虛擬相關文件來重新估測語句模型或進一步調適。對於第二個挑戰，已經有許多學者提出各種不同的關聯模型方法，常見的有關聯模型(Relevance Model, RM)[12]和簡單混合模型(Simple Mixture Model, SMM)[32]等(我們將在第四節介紹上述各種關聯模型)。然而對於第一個挑戰的研究，雖亦有少數學者提出一些虛擬相關文件選取方法，但相較於第二個挑戰的研究，仍顯較匱乏。

關於虛擬相關文件的選取方式，過去在資訊檢索領域有學者陸續提出間隔式最高 K (Gapped Top K)選取法[27]、群中心(Cluster Centroid)選取法[27]以及主動式-關聯多元密度(Active-RDD)選取法[31]，其中 RDD 三個英文字母分別代表關聯(Relevance)、多元(Diversity)以及密度(Density)，下面將簡單介紹上述虛擬相關文件選取方法。

間隔式最高 K 選取法就是在最高排序文件中每間隔 J(例如兩個間隔，J 為 2)挑選出 K 個相關文件出來當作是最高排序文件，簡單的例子如下：假設最高排序文件有 10 篇，我們每間隔 2 篇要挑出最高 3 篇出來，則第一、第四及第七篇會被挑選出來當作是最高排序文件。間隔式最高 K 選取法的主要思想是要挑選出具有多元性的文件，但其實此選取方法也是相當不穩定的。群中心選取法則是先將最高排序文件作分群(Clustering)，分群方法可以是任意的，常用的分群方法為 K 中心(K-means)分群法，然後再從分出來的每一群中挑選出一篇最相關的文件，以此構成新的最高排序文件，由分群的觀念可知，群中心選取法旨在選取出具有多元性的文件，與間隔式最高 K 選取法相較，群中心選取法是一個比較穩定的選取方法。主動式-關聯多元密度選取法為同時考量最高排序文件中的關聯性、多元性以及密度性的一種貪婪(Greedy)選取法[31]。以上選取方法常見於資訊檢索領域中，有興趣的讀者可參考相關文獻[5]，本論文是首次將上述方法運用在(語音)文件摘要任務中並做深入探討。

三、新穎式虛擬相關文件選取

基於主動式-關聯多元密度選取法，除了考量到虛擬相關文件(最高排序文件)中的關聯性、多元性以及密度性之外，我們認為非相關性(Non-relevance)資訊(在這裡是指語句的非相關性資訊)也是相當重要的線索，可以用來幫助重新選取更好的虛擬相關文件，因此本論文提出額外考量非相關資訊以改進主動式-關聯多元密度選取法，稱之為主動式-關聯多元密度非相關(Active-RDDN)選取法。另一方面，本論文也提出使用重疊分群(Overlapped Cluster)的概念來幫助重新選取更有效的虛擬相關文件，茲介紹如下：

3.1、主動式-關聯多元密度非相關選取

假設語句 S 已經輸入到資訊檢索系統中並得到了最高排序文件 $\mathbf{D_{Top}}=\{D_1,D_2,\ldots,D_M\}$，那主動式-關聯多元密度非相關選取則是從最高排序文件中迭代地(Iteratively)同時考慮四種重要因素(關聯性、多元性、密度性以及非相關資訊)來重新選取更具代表性的文件集。具體地說，最高排序文件中的每個候選(Candidate)文件 D_m 都會有著同時考量四種因素的一個線性結合的分數，其選取公式如下：

$$D^* = \underset{D_m \in \mathbf{D}_{\mathrm{Top}} - \mathbf{D}_{\mathrm{P}}}{\arg\max} \Big[(1-\alpha-\beta-\gamma)\cdot M_{Rel}(S,D_m) + \alpha\cdot M_{NR}(S,D_m) + \beta\cdot M_{Diversity}(D_m) + \gamma\cdot M_{Density}(D_m)\Big], \tag{6}$$

其中 $\mathbf{D}_{\mathrm{P}}$ 為已經選入的文件集，$M_{Rel}(S,D_m)$、$M_{NR}(S,D_m)$、$M_{Diversity}(D_m)$及 $M_{Density}(D_m)$分別代表候選文件 D_m 的關聯性量值、非相關資訊性量值、多元性量值、以及密度性量值，而 α、β、γ 為可調參數且其總和為 1(即 $\alpha+\beta+\gamma=1$)。值得一提的是，式(6)與早期用於資訊檢索及摘要領域的經典公式最大邊際關聯(Maximal Marginal Relevance, MMR)相似[2]。另外，關聯性量值 $M_{Rel}(S, D_m)$可定義為文件 D_m 語句 S 的負庫爾貝克-萊伯勒離散度量值(即-$KL(D_m \| S)$)。下面將分別介紹非相關資訊量值、多元性量值、以及密度性量值。

3.1.1、非相關性資訊量值

對於一個語句 S，其非相關性(Non-relevance)資訊通常可以從第一次資訊檢索時排在最後面的一些文件(最低排序(Low-Ranked)文件)來代表，那麼語句 S 的非相關模型 $P(w|NR_S)$ 便可由最低排序文件來估測，而非相關性資訊量值可由下面式子表示：

$$M_{NR}(S,D_m) = KL(NR_S \| D_m), \tag{7}$$

其中 NR_S 表示語句 S 的非相關性資訊，亦即最低排序文件。若非相關性資訊量值越小，表示候選文件 D_m 與對應於語句 S 的非相關性資訊很相像，則不應該被選取當成代表性文件；反之，則表示候選文件 D_m 與語句 S 的非相關資訊離較遠，應該有機會被選取起來當成代表性文件。實際上，虛擬相關文件(最高排序文件)相對於最低排序文件是相當少量的，所以實作上我們可利用全部的文件集來估測語句 S 的非相關模型，更明確的說，就是利用背景語言模型 $P(w|BG)$來當作是語句 S 的非相關模型 $P(w|NR_S)$。

3.1.2、多元性量值

在資訊檢索領域中，多元性(Diversification)的考量已備受矚目，相較於傳統只考量關聯性的查詢使得有太多重複及冗餘查詢結果，額外考慮多元性是希望能提供查詢者多元且多樣性的查詢結果，以滿足不同需求的使用者。而在虛擬相關回饋下，若最高排序文件的重複性文件太多，則會導致後面的關聯模型估測有太多的冗餘資訊，導致模型估測不良，所以多元性量值考量的點就是希望選取過的文件或與已選文件相近的文件不要再被選取進來，亦即去除最高排序文件的冗餘性，使得其後面的關聯模型估測更精準。多元性量值就是從已選的文件 $\mathbf{D}_{\mathrm{P}}$ 中找出與候選文件 D_m 有最小對稱離散度量的值，可由下列表示：

$$M_{Diversity}(D_m) = \min_{D_j \in \mathbf{D}_{\mathrm{P}}} \frac{1}{2}\cdot\Big[KL(D_j \| D_m) + KL(D_m \| D_j)\Big], \tag{8}$$

3.1.3、密度性量值

另一方面，最高排序文件中的結構(Structural)資訊可以被當成是一個線索來幫助選取代表性文件，其主要目的是希望在考量多元性資訊的同時，也應避免選取到過度極端的文件，因為過度極端文件很可能是錯誤的資訊。為了實現這個想法，我們可以利用計算最高排序文件中的候選文件 D_m 與其他候選文件 D_h 的負平均對稱(Negative Average Symmetric)離散度量值來達成，其公式如下所示：

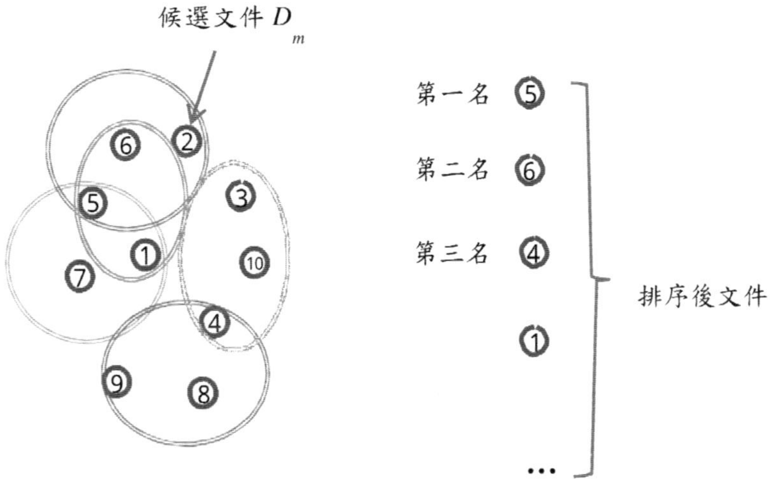

(a) (b)

圖一、使用重疊分群概念的候選文件選取示意圖，

(a)利用 k-NN 為每個候選文件 D_m 找出重疊分群，並計算其重疊分群個數。

(b)依據每一候選文件 D_m 的重疊分群個數做排序。

$$M_{Density}(D_m)=\frac{-1}{|\mathbf{D}_{\mathrm{Top}}|-1}\cdot\sum_{\substack{D_h\in\mathbf{D}_{\mathrm{Top}}\\ D_h\neq D_m}}\left[KL(D_h\,\|D_m)+KL(D_m\,\|D_h)\right], \tag{9}$$

其中 $|\mathbf{D}_{\mathrm{Top}}|$為最高排序文件之個數。若負平均對稱離散度量值越大，表示此候選文件 D_m 與最高排序文件中的其他候選文件 D_h 很接近，亦即可能是最高排序文件中心點(密度大的文件)，所以此候選文件 D_m 可能是個重要的文件，應該要被選入；反之，就會離中心點較遠(密度較低)，有可能會是不重要的文件，就不應該被選入。

3.2、重疊分群

本論文提出使用重疊分群(Overlapped Cluster)的概念來重新選取更好的虛擬相關文件(即 $\mathbf{D}_P$)以利接下來各種不同的關聯模型估測。其重疊分群選取方法為一個三步驟的演算法，示意圖如圖一所示，其演算法描述如下：

1. 第一步驟：計算最高排序文件中兩兩候選文件的相似度，在此是將候選文件表達成向量空間模型(Vector Space Model)並使用餘弦相似度(Cosine Similarity)量值來做計算。
2. 第二步驟：利用 k-最近鄰居(k-NN)來為每個候選文件 D_m 找出 k 個最接近的相關文件，並形成一個群(每個候選文件都會形成一個分群，而此分群中會有 k+1 個文件)。
3. 第三步驟：對於每個候選文件 D_m 都去計算重疊分群的個數(以圖一例子來說明，候選文件編號 5 被三個分群所包圍，所以其重疊分群個數為 3)，並且按照重疊分群個數來對每個候選文件作排序，排序後即可得到新的最高排序文件。

重疊分群的概念在資訊檢索領域中已有些許研究[18]，它是利用最高排序文件的結構資訊來幫助訓練語言模型，而本論文的思想是要利用重疊分群的概念來找出支配(Dominate)文件，若一個候選文件的重疊分群個數很多的話，表示它是很重要的且能夠支配其他候選文件，則應該要被選為代表性文件。本論文是首次將重疊分群的概念用在(語音)文件摘要任務上。

四、各種關聯模型之簡介

當我們透過資訊檢索系統已取得虛擬相關文件(最高排序文件，即 $\mathbf{D}_{\mathbf{Top}}$)，或進一步地使用上一節提出之方法來改善虛擬相關文件後(即 $\mathbf{D}_{\mathbf{P}}$)，接下來就要做模型估測，底下介紹常見的模型包含有關聯模型(Relevance Model, RM)、簡單混合模型(Simple Mixture Model, SMM)以及三混合模型(Tri-Mixture Model, TriMM)。

4.1、關聯模型

關聯模型的基本假設是認為每一語句 S 皆是被用來描述一個概念、想法或主題，我們稱之為語句的關聯類別(Relevance Class) R_S。在本論文中，我們的目標是想進一步地模型化關聯類別所代表的資訊，藉此來豐富語句模型所能傳達的語意內容或主題特性。然而，實際上每一語句 S 的關聯類別 R_S 是非常難以求得的；為此，我們透過虛擬相關回饋(Pseudo Relevant Feedback)來尋找與關聯類別可能相關的一些文件，並藉由這些文件來近似關聯類別 R_S。更明確地，在實作上我們將虛擬相關文件(最高排序文件)$\mathbf{D}_{\mathbf{Top}}$=$\{D_1,D_2,\ldots,D_M\}$或透過上一節所介紹的選取方法來產生較佳的虛擬相關文件 $\mathbf{D}_{\mathbf{P}}$ 用以代表關聯類別 R_S。接著，透過檢視詞彙 w 與語句 S 在這些虛擬相關文件中同時出現之關係，可計算出詞彙與語句的聯合機率[12]：

$$P_{\mathrm{RM}}(w,S)=\sum_{D_m\in\mathbf{D}_{\mathrm{P}}}P(w,S\mid D_m)P(D_m), \tag{10}$$

當我們進一步地假設在給定某一篇虛擬相關文件時，詞彙與語句是獨立的，並且語句內的詞彙也是獨立且不考慮其先後次序(即所謂的詞袋假設)，則透過虛擬相關回饋所估測的語句模型為：

$$P_{\mathrm{RM}}(w\mid S)=\frac{\sum_{D_m\in\mathbf{D}_{\mathrm{P}}}\prod_{w'\in S}P(w'\mid D_m)P(w\mid D_m)P(D_m)}{\sum_{D_{m'}\in\mathbf{D}_{\mathrm{P}}}\prod_{w''\in S}P(w''\mid D_{m'})P(D_{m'})}, \tag{11}$$

我們稱之為關聯模型(Relevance Model, RM)。關聯模型的優點在於藉由虛擬相關文件的資訊，可以更清楚地知道語句所蘊含的資訊、所欲表達的內涵，所以相較於傳統使用最大化相似度估測的語句模型，可更準確地表達語句的語意內容或主題特性，以提升摘要的成效。

4.2、簡單混合模型

簡單混合模型的基本想法是假設由虛擬相關回饋技術所得到的虛擬相關文件是相關的且能從最高排序文件中估測比較好的簡單混合模型 $P_{\mathrm{SMM}}(w|S)$，更明確地說，簡單混合模型是假設虛擬相關文件 $\mathbf{D}_{\mathbf{P}}$ 裡的詞彙 w 是源自於二種成分混合模型(Two-Component Mixture Model)，其一為簡單混合模型 $P_{\mathrm{SMM}}(w|S)$，另一為背景語言模型 $P(w|BG)$。簡單混合模型的估測是藉由期望值最大化(Expectation Maximization, EM)演算法來最大化虛擬相關文件的對數相似度(Log-Likelihood)以進行模型的估測，其虛擬相關文件的對數相似度的定義如下[32]：

$$\begin{aligned}LL_{\mathbf{D}_{\mathrm{P}}}=&\sum_{D_m\in\mathbf{D}_{\mathrm{P}}}\sum_{w\in V}c(w,D_m)\\&\cdot\log[(1-\alpha)\cdot P_{\mathrm{SMM}}(w\mid S)+\alpha\cdot P(w\mid BG)],\end{aligned} \tag{12}$$

其中 α 為平衡參數，用來控制模型估測時是要比較偏好簡單混合模型或是背景語言模型，$c(w,D_m)$為詞彙 w 在虛擬相關文件 D_m 的次數，式(12)的最大化可透過期望值最大化迭代更新式來達成：
期望值步驟：

$$\tau_w^{(l)} = \frac{\alpha \cdot P_{\text{SMM}}^{(l)}(w|S)}{\alpha \cdot P_{\text{SMM}}^{(l)}(w|S) + (1-\alpha) \cdot P(w|BG)}, \tag{13}$$

最大化步驟：

$$P_{\mathbf{SMM}}^{(l+1)}(w|S) = \frac{\sum_{D_m \in \mathbf{D_P}} c(w, D_m) \cdot \tau_w^{(l)}}{\sum_{w' \in V} \sum_{D'_m \in \mathbf{D_P}} c(w', D'_m) \cdot \tau_w^{(l)}}, \tag{14}$$

其中 l 表示期望值最大化的第 l 次迭代。這個簡單混合模型的估測會加強具有獨特性(Specificity)的詞彙之機率，例如某詞彙沒有在背景語言模型中有好解釋(Well-Explained)則會被加強其機率，這樣使得此模型為更具有鑑別(Discriminant)能力的語句模型；反之，若是沒有獨特性的詞彙，則其機率就會被背景語言模型所吸收。

4.3、三混合模型

另一方面，本論文嘗試將三混合模型(Tri-Mixture Model)[9]用於語音摘要任務。三混合模型可視為是複雜化後的簡單混合模型；它更進一步的假設虛擬相關文件 $\mathbf{D_P}$ 裡的詞彙 w 是源自於三種成分模型(Component Models)，其一為文件模型 $P(w|D_m)$，其二為三混合模型 $P_{\text{TriMM}}(w|S)$，最後為背景語言模型 $P(w|BG)$。三混合模型的估測也是藉由期望值最大化演算法來最大化虛擬相關文件的對數相似度以進行模型的估測，其虛擬相關文件的對數相似度的定義如下[9]：

$$LL_{\mathbf{D}_\text{P}} = \sum_{D_m \in \mathbf{D}_\text{P}} \sum_{w \in V} c(w, D_m) \cdot \log[(1-\lambda-\mu) \cdot P_{\text{TriMM}}(w|S) + \lambda \cdot P(w|D_m) + \mu \cdot P(w|BG)], \tag{15}$$

其中 λ 和 μ 為平衡參數，用來控制模型估測時是要比較偏好三混合模型或文件模型亦或是背景語言模型，$c(w,D_m)$為詞彙 w 在虛擬相關文件 D_m 的次數，式(15)的最大化可透過期望值最大化迭代更新式來達成：
期望值步驟：

$$\begin{cases} r_{w,D_m} = \dfrac{c(w,D_m) \cdot (1-\lambda-\mu) \cdot P_{\text{TriMM}}(w|S)}{(1-\lambda-\mu) \cdot P_{\text{TriMM}}(w|S) + \mu \cdot P(w|BG) + \lambda \cdot P(w|D_m)} \\ e_{w,D_m} = \dfrac{c(w,D_r) \cdot \lambda \cdot P(w|D_m)}{(1-\lambda-\mu) \cdot P_{\text{TriMM}}(w|S) + \mu \cdot P(w|BG) + \lambda \cdot P(w|D_m)} \end{cases}, \tag{16}$$

最大化步驟：

$$\begin{cases} \hat{P}_{\mathbf{TriMM}}(w|S) = \sum_{D_m \in \mathbf{D_P}} \dfrac{r_{w,D_m}}{\sum_w r_{w,D_m}} \\ \hat{P}(w|D_m) = \dfrac{e_{w,D_m}}{\sum_w e_{w,D_m}} \end{cases}, \tag{17}$$

運用此三混合模型來調適語句模型時，庫爾貝克-萊伯勒離散度量值的公式(參照式(5))可進一步地表示成：

$$KL(D \| S) = \sum_{w \in V} P(w|D) \log \frac{P(w|D)}{\gamma \cdot P(w|S) + (1-\gamma) \cdot P_{\text{TriMM}}(w|S)}, \quad (18)$$

其中$0 \le \gamma < 1$，當$\gamma = 0$代表使用三混合模型取代原本的語句模型。

關聯模型、簡單混合模型及三混合模型在資訊檢索領域中已被廣泛應用[12][32][9]，但在摘要任務中卻是相對較少研究的，值得一提的是，雖然關聯模型、簡單混合模型已初步被應用在摘要任務上[4][19]，但三混合模型卻是本論文首次引入到(語音)文字摘要任務中。

五、實驗語料及評估方法

5.1、實驗語料

本論文實驗語料庫為公視新聞語料(Mandarin Chinese Broadcast News Corpus, MATBN)，是由中央研究院資訊科學研究所耗時三年與公共電視台合作錄製並整理的中文新聞語料，其錄製內容為每天一個小時的公視晚間新聞深度報導。我們抽取其中由2001 年 11 月到 2002 年 8 月總共 205 則新聞報導，區分成訓練集(共 185 則新聞)以及測試集(共 20 則新聞)兩部分，其詳細的統計資訊如表一所示。全部 205 則語音文件長度約為 7.5 小時，我們先做人工切音，切出真正含有講話內容的音訊段落，再經由語音辨識器自動產生出的語音辨識結果稱之為語音文件(Spoken Document, SD)，因此語音文件中只包含有語音辨識錯誤之雜訊；另一方面，我們將此 205 則語音文件藉由人工聽寫的方式，產生出沒有辨識錯誤的正確文字語料，我們稱之為文字文件(Text Document, TD)，每則文字文件再經由三位專家標記摘要語句，我們將此標記的人工摘要做為語音文件與文字文件的正確摘要答案。藉由比較語音文件和文字文件的摘要效能，我們可以觀察語音辨識錯誤對於各種摘要方法之影響。本研究的背景語言模型訓練語料取材自2001 到 2002 年的中央社新聞文字語料(Central News Agency, CNA)，並且以 SRI 語言模型工具訓練出經平滑化的單連語言模型，我們假設此單連語言模型為明確度中的非相關資訊之來源。另外，本論文蒐集 2002 年中央通訊社的約十萬則同時期新聞文字文件做為建立關聯模型時的檢索標的[4]，關於語句 S 的虛擬相關文件(最高排序文件)篇數為20(也就是$|\mathbf{D}_{\mathbf{Top}}|$=20)，而經由各種不同虛擬相關文件選取方法的篇數為 3(亦即$|\mathbf{D}_{\mathbf{P}}|$=3)。

5.2、評估方法

自動摘要的評估方法主要有兩種，一為主觀人為評估，另一為客觀自動評估；前者為請幾位測試人員來為系統所產生的摘要做評估，給分的範圍為 1-5 分，後者則是預先請幾位測試者依據事先定義好的摘要比例挑選出適合的摘要語句，系統所產生的摘要句子將與測試者所挑選出的句子計算召回率導向的要點評估(Recall-Oriented Understudy for Gisting Evaluation, ROUGE)[16]。由於主觀人為評估非常耗時耗力，所以目前多數自動摘要方法皆採用召回率導向的要點評估做為文件摘要的評估方式，本論文亦採用此種評估方式。ROUGE 方法是計算自動摘要結果與人工摘要之間的重疊單位元(Units)數目占參考摘要(Reference Summary)長度(單位元總個數)的比例。估計的單位可以是 N-連詞(N-gram)、詞序列(Word Sequences)，如：最長相同詞序列或詞成對(Word Pairs)。由於此方法是採用單位元比對的方式，不會產生語句邊界定義的問題，並且適合於多份人工摘要的評估。其評估的分數有三種，ROUGE-1(Unigram，簡寫為 R-1)、

表一、實驗語料統計資訊

	訓練集	測試集
語料時間	2001/11/07-2002/01/22	2002/01/23-2002/08/22
文件個數	185	20
文件平均持續幾秒	129.4	141.2
文件平均詞個數	326.0	290.3
文件平均語句個數	20.0	23.3
文件平均字錯誤率 (Character Error Rate, CER)	28.8%	29.8%
文件平均詞錯誤率 (Word Error Rate, WER)	38.0%	39.4%

ROUGE-2(Bigram,簡寫為 R-2)和 ROUGE-L(Longest Common Subsequence,簡寫為 R-L)分數，ROUGE-1 是評估自動摘要的訊息量，ROUGE-2 是評估自動摘要的流暢性，ROUGE-L 是最長共同字串，本論文希望觀察摘要的流暢性，因此，實驗數據主要是以 ROUGE-2 分數為主。本論文所設定的摘要比例為 10%，其定義為摘要所含詞彙數占整篇文件詞彙數的比例，也就是以詞彙做為判斷摘要比例的單元。在挑選摘要語句過程中，若選到某語句中的某個詞彙時就已經剛好達到摘要比例，為了保持語句語意完整性，此語句剩下的詞彙也會被挑選成為摘要。

六、實驗結果

本論文主要著重在虛擬相關文件選取方法之發展與改進，是屬於非監督式摘要方法的範疇，因此所比較的對象以非監督式摘要方法為主；除此之外，本論文亦嘗試與現今最被廣為使用的監督式機器學習方法做比較，即支持向量機(SVM)[10]。

6.1、基礎實驗

首先，我們比較庫爾貝克-萊伯勒離散度(KL)與數個非監督式摘要方法之摘要成效，包含有最長語句摘要(Longest Sentence, LS)、首句摘要(LEAD)[26]、向量空間模型(Vector Space Model, VSM)[8]、潛藏語意分析(Latent Semantic Analysis, LSA)[8]、最大邊際關聯(Maximal Marginal Relevance, MMR)[2]以及整數線性規劃(Integer Linear Programming, ILP)[22]。一般來說，文件中長句可能蘊含有較豐富的主題資訊，因此依據文件中語句長度做排序後，依序選取最長語句做為摘要結果是一種簡單的摘要方法。除此之外，也有學者研究發現，文件常以開門見山法的方式來提點出主題，因此文件開頭的前幾個語句經常是具代表性的語句，首句摘要即是以此概念出發，選取前幾句語句來形成整個文件的摘要。最長語句摘要(LS)及首句摘要(LEAD)都僅適用在一部分具有特殊結構的文件上，因此它們的缺點就是有其侷限性。另外，向量空間模型是把文件和語句分別視為一個向量，並使用詞頻-反文件頻(TF-IDF)特徵來計算每一維度的權重值，文件與語句間的關聯性是藉由餘弦相似度量值來估測，當語句分數較高時，則越有機會成為此文件的摘要。潛藏語意分析是在向量空間的假設下更進一步地使用奇異值分解(Singular Value Decomposition, SVD)來找到可能的潛藏語意空間，使之能在考量潛藏語意的情況下進行文件與語句的關聯性量測。最大邊際關聯可視為是向量空間模型的一個延伸，在做語句排序時考量了冗餘性以達到更好的摘要結果。整數線性規劃是一個全域(Global)

表二、基礎實驗結果

		F-score		
		ROUGE-1	ROUGE-2	ROUGE-L
TD	LS	0.225	0.098	0.183
	LEAD	0.310	0.194	0.276
	VSM	0.347	0.228	0.290
	LSA	0.362	0.233	0.316
	MMR	0.368	0.248	0.322
	KL	0.411	0.298	0.361
	ILP	**0.442**	**0.337**	**0.401**
SD	LS	0.181	0.044	0.138
	LEAD	0.255	0.117	0.221
	VSM	0.342	0.189	0.287
	LSA	0.345	0.201	0.301
	MMR	**0.366**	**0.215**	**0.315**
	KL	0.364	0.210	0.307
	ILP	0.348	0.209	0.306

的限制性最佳化(Constraint Optimization)的語句選取方法[22]。 表二為本論文之基礎實驗結果。首先，在 TD 的實驗中，KL 的摘要效果比 LS、LEAD、VSM、LSA、MMR 等非監督式摘要方法來得好些；因 LS 與 LEAD 僅適用於特殊文章結構上，所以若被摘要文件不具有某種特殊的文章結構，其摘要效能就會有限。相較之下，KL 是較具一般性的摘要方法，因此比較不會受限於文章的結構之影響，故摘要效能比 LS 以及 LEAD 來得彰顯。KL 與 VSM 皆使用淺層的詞彙(詞頻)資訊，但由於 KL 是計算語句模型與文件模型之間的距離關係，對於代表語句與文件的語言模型，我們較容易透過各種技術來進行模型的估計與調適，進而獲得較好的摘要成果。MMR 在選取時多考慮了冗餘資訊，所以摘要效果也比 VSM 來得好些。LSA 在潛藏語意空間計算文件與語句的餘弦相似度量值，其結果顯示也會較 VSM 好。整數線性規劃是一個全域選擇方法，所以在 TD 上可以得到最好的摘要效能。另一方面，在 SD 的實驗中，KL 同樣較優於 LS、LEAD 之摘要方法，但 VSM 的結果則稍微較 KL 好一點，我們認為這可能是因為 VSM 比較不受到語音辨認錯誤的影響。原以為 ILP 也會在 SD 中得到最好的摘要效能，結果反而是 MMR 得到最好的摘要效能，可能的原因是 ILP 受到語音辨識錯誤的影響比較大，造成其摘要結果不彰。

通常語音文件主要會有語音辨識錯誤和語句邊界偵測錯誤的問題，但我們有先經人工切音，因此摒除了語句邊界偵測錯誤的問題，藉由比較 TD 與 SD 之實驗結果，我們可以觀察語音辨識錯誤率對摘要結果的影響性。比較各式方法，SD 比 TD 下降了 1.9%~8.8%的 ROUGE-2 摘要效能，由此可知語音辨識錯誤率對摘要效能是有顯著的影響性。為了減緩語音辨認錯誤的問題，在未來我們將嘗試使用音節(Syllable)為單位來建立語句以及文件模型；或利用詞圖(Word Graph)、混淆網路(Confusion Network)來含括更多的可能正確候選詞彙以裨益模型估測；更可利用韻律資訊(Prosodic Information)等聲學線索來輔助減緩語音辨認錯誤對摘要效能的影響。

表三、關聯模型之實驗結果(使用最高排序文件前三篇(Top3))

		F-score		
		ROUGE-1	ROUGE-2	ROUGE-L
TD	KL	0.411	0.298	0.361
	RM	0.450	0.336	0.400
	SMM	0.436	0.325	0.385
	TriMM	**0.457**	**0.350**	**0.404**
SD	KL	0.364	0.210	0.307
	RM	0.374	0.226	0.321
	SMM	0.375	0.221	0.314
	TriMM	**0.379**	**0.228**	**0.325**

6.2、基礎關聯模型之實驗

使用關聯模型於語句模型之建立時，需要做一次的資訊檢索來為每個語句找出虛擬相關文件，由同時期的新聞文字文件(共 101,268 篇)中為每一語句選取出 20 篇虛擬相關文件，但為了要與後續虛擬相關文件選取方法作公平的比較，因此此基礎關聯模型實驗是取前三篇(Top3)來進行關聯模型之估測與相關實驗[4]。由於文件中的語句通常相對簡短，因此當使用最大化相似度估測建立語句模型時，容易遭遇資料稀疏的問題，不容易獲得精準的模型，故我們期望考慮額外的關聯資訊於語音文件摘要，亦即藉由虛擬相關文件來重新估測並建立語句的語言模型，能獲得進一步地摘要成效。重新估測後的關聯模型則可與原本的語句模型相結合或取代之，相結合的參數調整在本實驗中是採用經驗設定(Empirical Setting)。實驗結果如表三所示，在 TD 與 SD 之摘要成效上，使用關聯模型(RM)、簡單混合模型(SMM)及三混合模型(TriMM)皆能比基礎的 KL 實驗較好，尤其是三混合模型(TriMM)相較於 KL 在 TD 及 SD 的 ROUGE-2 結果上能有 5.2%與 1.8%的改進。接著，我們比較不同關聯模型的摘要成效，首先是關聯模型(RM)與簡單混合模型(SMM)的比較，從表三的實驗結果得知關聯模型在 TD 上表現比簡單混合模型來得好，但在 SD 似乎在 ROUGE-1 就沒比簡單混合模型好，不過 SD 的 ROUGE-2 跟 ROUGE-L 都還是比簡單混合模型的效果好。關聯模型的假設是強調詞彙 w 與語句 S 在這些虛擬相關文件中同時出現之關係(參照式(10))來估測模型，而簡單混合模型是強調訓練好的模型能讓有獨特性的詞彙得到更多的機率值因而讓模型具有鑑別能力，兩者皆有其好處。最後，三混合模型(TriMM)因複雜化了簡單混合模型(SMM)，額外多考量文件模型的影響力，因此相較於關聯模型及簡單混合模型能得到更佳的摘要效能，三混合模型相較於關聯模型在 TD 上有明顯的進步，於 ROUGE-2 結果能有 1.4%的改進，但在 SD 上，於 ROUGE-2 結果只有微量的 0.2%改善。

在關聯模型的相關實驗中，語音辨識錯誤也是影響摘要效能非常嚴重，在三混合模型的數據中，SD 比 TD 劇烈下降了 12.2%的 ROUGE-2 摘要效能，在未來研究中，我們認為可以以次詞索引(Subword Indexing)的方式來建立關聯模型以減緩語音辨識錯誤之影響。

表四、各種虛擬相關文件選取方法於關聯模型之實驗結果

F-score		RM			SMM			TriMM		
		R-1	R-2	R-L	R-1	R-2	R-L	R-1	R-2	R-L
TD	Top3	0.450	0.336	0.400	0.436	0.325	0.385	0.457	0.350	0.404
	Gapped *K*	0.451	0.338	0.401	0.433	0.317	0.385	0.454	0.343	0.406
	Centroid	0.449	0.334	0.402	0.439	0.331	0.389	0.456	0.353	0.407
	Active-RDD	0.460	0.341	0.408	0.449	0.342	0.400	0.463	0.355	0.414
	Active-RDDN	0.464	0.352	0.411	0.455	**0.346**	0.405	0.466	**0.367**	0.421
	Overlapped	**0.470**	**0.354**	**0.416**	**0.460**	0.341	**0.410**	**0.471**	0.362	**0.422**
SD	Top3	0.374	0.226	0.321	0.375	0.221	0.314	0.379	0.228	0.325
	Gapped *K*	0.374	0.228	0.322	0.371	0.218	0.313	0.376	0.225	0.315
	Centroid	0.374	0.227	0.314	0.377	0.227	0.320	0.380	0.233	0.328
	Active-RDD	0.379	0.228	0.332	0.378	0.229	0.321	0.388	0.242	0.335
	Active-RDDN	0.383	0.239	0.330	0.380	0.226	0.327	0.391	0.244	0.339
	Overlapped	**0.386**	**0.239**	**0.334**	**0.382**	**0.236**	**0.332**	**0.396**	**0.250**	**0.345**

6.3、各種虛擬相關文件選取方法於關聯模型之實驗

本小節的實驗是由第一次虛擬相關文件(最高排序文件) $\mathbf{D}_{\mathbf{Top}}$ 中($|\mathbf{D}_{\mathbf{top}}|$=20)再精鍊選取出較佳的虛擬相關文件 $\mathbf{D}_{\mathbf{P}}$ ($|\mathbf{D}_{\mathbf{P}}|$=3)，我們比較所提出兩種新穎的選取方法(即主動式-關聯多元密度非相關(Active-RDDN)和重疊分群(Overlapped))與其他現有選取方法(即間隔式最高 *K* 選取法(Gapped *K*)、群中心選取法(Centroid)以及主動式-關聯多元密度(Active-RDD))於各種關聯模型(RM、SMM 及 TriMM)之摘要效能比較，實驗結果如表四所示，與基礎關聯模型只使用前三篇(Top3)虛擬相關文件的結果相較(參照表三)，大部分透過虛擬相關文件選取方法都會比只使用 Top3 的摘要結果還要來得好，除了 Gapped *K* 無論在 TD 和 SD 中，使用 SMM 與 TriMM 都會有比 Top3 差的摘要效能，因為 Gapped *K* 是一個較不穩定的虛擬相關文件選取方法，在本實驗中有比較差的結果是可以預期的。群中心選取法(Centroid)表現尚可，在 TD 及 SD 中，於各種關聯模型(RM、SMM 及 TriMM)下，比 Top3 及 Gapped *K* 都要來得好。Active-RDD 因在選取虛擬相關文件時同時考量了關聯性(Relevance)、多元性(Diversity)以及密度性(Density)，用於不同的關聯模型訓練時，相對於 Top3、Gapped *K* 以及 Centroid，無論在 TD 或 SD 中，都可以得到更好的摘要結果。Active-RDDN 在多考量了非相關(Non-relevance)資訊的情況下，其實驗結果都會比現有的選取方法較佳，相對於 Active-RDD、Centroid、Gapped *K* 以及 Top3 無論在 TD 或 SD 中，各種關聯模型(RM、SMM 及 TriMM)下都會得到比較好的摘要結果，所以證實非相關資訊確實一個有用的選取線索。最後本論文所提出的重疊分群(Overlapped)選取方法無論在 TD 或 SD 中，於各種關聯模型下(RM、SMM 及 TriMM)都可以得到最好的摘要效果，驗證了重疊分群在利用虛擬相關文件中結構化資訊確實可以找到具代表性的文件以利各種關聯模型的模型訓練或參數估測。

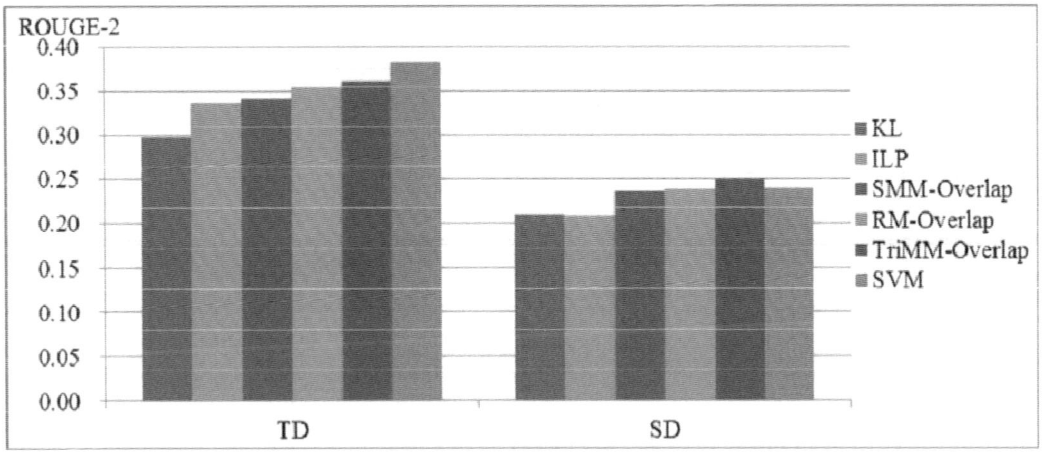

圖二、SVM 與其他非監督式摘要方法之比較

6.4、與監督式模型之比較

除了各式非監督式摘要方法外，本論文亦嘗試比較支持向量機(SVM)於文件摘要之成效，比較的對象有基礎 KL 以及使用重疊分群選取方法於不同的關聯模型中(RM-Overlap、SMM-Overlap 和 TriMM-Overlap)。支持向量機是現今常見的監督式機器學習方法之一，近年來已有學者將其運用至文件摘要領域之中[10]。本論文使用訓練集的 185 篇文件進行支持向量機模型的訓練語料，我們為文件中的每一語句抽取 35 維特徵[13]，包括有韻律特徵(Prosodic Features)、語彙特徵(Lexical Features)、結構特徵(Structural Features)以及基本的模型特徵(Model Features)等資訊，其核心函數設定為半徑式函數(Radial Basis Function)，其中 SVM 的參數設定都是使用預設值。

實驗結果如圖二所示。一如預期地，SVM 與其他各式非監督式模型相比較，在 TD 實驗上(其 ROUGE-2 為 0.383)是表現最好的方法，這是由於監督式機器學習藉由使用人工標注的摘要句子進行模型之訓練，其使用的資訊較非監督式機器學習方法多且正確，因此其摘要的效果也較非監督式機器學習來的好。值得一提的是，使用重疊分群虛擬相關文件選取方法於三混合模型中(TriMM-Overlap)，摘要之成效在 SD 上可比監督式機器學習方法的 SVM 來的好一些，此一實驗結果令人感到驚訝，因為本論文所探討之各式摘要方法僅考慮了文件與語句中的單一種特徵值，即藉由詞彙分佈資訊來挑選語句，而支持向量機不僅使用了 35 種特徵值，更需要使用人工標註的正確答案進行模型的訓練。我們認為，此結果之原因可能是由於支持向量機之摘要技術在語音辨識錯誤的情況下（在此實驗中，訓練集與測試集的詞錯誤率達 40%），未必能真的有效學習分辨摘要與非摘要語句。

七、結論與未來方向

本論文基於語言模型化架構來發展語音摘要方法，其貢獻主要有三方面。第一，有別於現有基於語言模型化架構之摘要方法都聚焦在語句模型參數的重新估測，本論文首次深入探討與應用各種新穎虛擬相關文件選取技術於節錄式語音文件摘要任務，用以強化語句模型的參數估測。第二，本論文更進一步地考量使用每一語句的非相關性(Non-relevance)資訊對於虛擬相關文件選取的影響。同時，我們亦額外嘗試基於重疊分群(Overlapped Clustering)概念來有效地選取重要的虛擬相關文件。第三，本論文探索使用三混合模型(Tri-Mixture Model)來表示每一語句，期盼其能更精確地表示語句之詞彙使用和語意相關資訊。一系列的實驗結果顯示，本論文所提出之方法的確能較其它現有的非監督式摘要方法有更加的摘要效能表現。 未來，我們的研究將有三個主要的方向：

首先，本論文所提出之虛擬相關文件選取

方法是建構在向量空間或語言模型空間上，並沒有考慮到語意空間的相似度量，我們將進一步的研究是否可以在潛藏語意空間中來選取較好的虛擬相關文件，以期獲得更好的摘要成效；其次，目前所發展的關聯模型僅運用於重建語句的語言模型，我們將嘗試使用被摘要文件的關聯資訊來重新估測並建立文件的語言模型；最後，我們希望能將非監督式方法所形成的特徵結合於更加複雜且有效的監督式機器學習方法(如 CRF 或深度類神經網絡(Deep Neural Network Learning, DNN)等)中，並融合其它語音文件所獨有之特徵(諸如音韻與語者特徵等)，期望訓練後的模型能夠在語音文件摘要上獲得更好的表現。

致謝

本論文之研究承蒙教育部-國立臺灣師範大學邁向頂尖大學計畫(102J1A0800)與行政院科技部研究計畫(MOST 103-2221-E-003-016-MY2, NSC 103-2911-I-003-301, NSC 101-2221-E-003-024-MY3 、 NSC 101-2511-S-003-057-MY3 、 NSC 101-2511-S-003-047-MY3 和 NSC 102-2221-E-003-014- MY3)之經費支持，謹此致謝。

參考文獻

[1] P. Baxendale, *Machine-made Index for Technical Literature – an Experiment,* IBM Journal of Research and Development, Vol. 2, No. 4, pp. 354-361, 1958

[2] J. Carbonell and J. Goldstein, *The Use of MMR Diversity-based Reranking for Reordering Documents and Producing Summaries,* Proceedings of the 21th Annual International ACM SIGIR Conference on Research and Development in Information Retrieval (SIGIR), pp. 335-336, 1998

[3] Y.-T. Chen, B. Chen and H.-M. Wang, *A Probabilistic Generative Framework for Extractive Broadcast News Speech Summarization,* IEEE Transactions on Audio, Speech and Language Processing, Vol. 17, No. 1, pp. 95-106, 2009

[4] B. Chen, H.-C. Chang, K.-Y. Chen, *Sentence Modeling for Extractive Speech Summarization*, Proceedings of the International Conference on Multimedia & Expo (ICME), 2013

[5] B. Chen, Y.-W. Chen and K.-Y Chen, Enhancing Query Formulation for Spoken Document Retrieval, Journal of Information Science and Engineering, Vol. 30, No. 3, pp. 553-569, 2014

[6] J.-M. Conroy and D.-P. O'Leary, *Text Summarization via Hidden Markov Models,* Proceedings of the 24th Annual International ACM SIGIR Conference on Research and Development in Information Retrieval (SIGIR), pp. 406-407, 2001

[7] G. Erkan and D. R. Radev, *LexRank: Graph-based Lexical Centrality as Salience in Text Summarization*, Journal of Artificial Intelligent Research, Vol. 22, No. 1, pp.457-479, 2004

[8] Y. Gong and X. Liu, *Generic Text Summarization using Relevance Measure and Latent Semantic Analysis,* Proceedings of the International ACM SIGIR Conference on Research and Development in Information Retrieval (SIGIR), pp. 19-25, 2001

[9] D. Hiemstra, S. Robertson, and H. Zaragoza, *Parsimonious Language Models for Information Retrieval*, Proceedings of the international ACM SIGIR conference on Research and development in information retrieval (SIGIR), pp. 178¯185, 2004

[10] A. Kolcz, V. Prabakarmurthi and J. Kalita, *Summarization as Feature Selection for Text Categorization*, Proceedings of the International Conference on Information and Knowledge Management (CIKM), pp. 365¯370, 2001

[11] J. Kupiec, *A Trainable Document Summarizer,* Proceedings of the Annual International ACM SIGIR Conference on Research and Development in Information Retrieval (SIGIR), pp. 68¯73, 1995

[12] V. Lavrenko and W.-B. Croft, *Relevance -based Language Models,* Proceedings of the 24th Annual International ACM SIGIR Conference on Research and Development in Information Retrieval (SIGIR), pp. 120¯127, 2001

[13] S.-H. Lin and B. Chen, *Improved Speech Summarization with Multiple-hypothesis Representations and Kullback-Leibler Divergence Measures,* Proceeding of the 10th Annual Conference of the International Speech Communication Association (Interspeech), pp. 1847¯1850, 2009

[14] H. Lin and J. Bilmes, *Multi-document Summarization via Budgeted Maximization of Submodular Functions*, Proceeding of NAACL HLT, pp. 912¯920, 2010

[15] S.-H. Lin, Y.-M. Yeh and B. Chen, *Leveraging Kullback-Leibler Divergence Measures and Information-rich Cues for Speech Summarization,* IEEE Transactions on Audio, Speech and Language Processing. Vol. 19, No. 4, pp. 871¯882, 2011

[16] C.-Y. Lin, *ROUGE: Recall-oriented Understudy for Gisting Evaluation.* 2003 [Online]. Available: http://haydn.isi.edu/ROUGE/.

[17] Y. Liu and D. Hakkani-Tur, *Speech Summarization*, in G. Turand R. D. Mori [Ed], Spoken Language Understanding: Systems for Extracting Semantic Information from Speech, Wiley, 2011

[18] X. Liu and W. B. Croft, *Cluster-based Retrieval Using Language Models*, Proceedings of the International ACM SIGIR conference on Research and Development in Information Retrieval (SIGIR), pp. 186¯193, 2004

[19] S.-H. Liu, K.-Y. Chen, Y.-L. Hsieh, B. Chen, H.-M. Wang, H.-C. Yen, W.-L. Hsu, *Effective Pseudo-relevance Feedback for Language Modeling in Extractive Speech Summarization*, Proceedings of the IEEE International Conference on Acoustics, Speech, and Signal Processing (ICASSP), 2014

[20] S.-H. Liu, K.-Y. Chen, B. Chen, H.-M. Wang, W.-L. Hsu, *Improving Sentence Modeling Techniques for Extractive Speech Summarization*, ROCLING XXV: Conference on Computational Linguistics and Speech Processing, 2013

[21] I. Mani and M.-T. Maybury, *Advances in Automatic Text Summarization,* Cambridge: MIT Press, 1999

[22] R. McDonald, *A Study of Global Inference Algorithms in Multi-document Summarization*, Proceedings of European Conference on Information Retrieval (ECIR), pp. 557¯564, 2007.

[23] R. Mihalcea and P. Tarau, *TextRank Bringing Order into Texts,* Proceedings of Empirical Method in Natural Language Processing (EMNLP), pp. 404¯411, 2004

[24] G. Murray, S. Renals, and J. Carletta, *Extractive Summarization of Meeting Recordings,* Proceedings of the Conference of the International Speech Communication Association (Interspeech), pp. 593¯596, 2005

[25] A. Nenkova and K. McKeown, *Automatic Summarization*, Foundations and Trends in Information Retrieval, Vol. 5, No. 2¯3: 103¯233, 2011

[26] G. Penn and X. Zhu, *A Critical Reassessment of Evaluation Baselines for Speech Summarization,* Proceedings of Annual Meeting of the Association for Computational Linguistics, pp. 470¯478, 2008

[27] X. Shen and C. Zhai, *Active Feedback in Ad Hoc Information Retrieval*, Proceedings of ACM SIGIR Conference on Research and Development in Information Retrieval (SIGIR), pp. 55–66, 2005

[28] C. Shen and T. Li, *Multi-document Summarization via the Minimum Dominating Set*, Proceedings of the International Conference on Computational Linguistics (COLING), pp. 984¯92, 2010

[29] D. Shen, J.-T. Sun, H. Li, Q. Yang, and Z. Chen, *Document Summarization using Conditional Random Fields,* Proceedings of International Joint Conference on Artificial Intelligence (IJCAI), pp. 2862¯2867, 2007

[30] X. Wan and J. Yang, *Multi-document Summarization using Cluster-based Link Analysis,* Proceedings of the Annual International ACM SIGIR Conference on Research and Development in Information Retrieval (SIGIR), pp. 299¯306, 2008

[31] Z. Xu, R. Akella and Y. Zhang, *Incorporating Diversity and Density in Active Learning for Relevance Feedback*, Proceedings of European Conference on Information Retrieval (ECIR), pp. 245¯257, 2007

[32] C.-X. Zhai and J. Lafferty, *Model-based feedback in the language modeling approach to information retrieval*, Proceeding of the International Conference on Information and Knowledge Management (CIKM), pp. 403¯410, 2001

[33] C.-X. Zhai and J. Lafferty, *A Study of Smoothing Methods for Language Models Applied to Ad Hoc Information Retrieval,* Proceedings of the Annual International ACM SIGIR Conference on Research and Development in Information Retrieval (SIGIR), pp. 334-342, 2011

[34] C.-X. Zhai, *Statistical Language Models for Information Retrieval: A Critical Review,* Foundations and Trends in Information Retrieval, Vol. 2, No.3, pp.137¯213, 2008

[35] J. Zhang and P. Fung, *Speech Summarization without Lexical Features for Mandarin Broadcast News,* Proceedings of NAACL HLT, Companion Volume, pp. 213¯216, 2007

The 2014 Conference on Computational Linguistics and Speech Processing
ROCLING 2014, pp. 21-30

台灣情緒語料庫建置與辨識

Bo-Chang Chiou and Chia-Ping Chen

摘要

現在已有許多公開情緒語料庫被實驗於語音情緒辨識的研究上，但是並沒有一個語料庫以台灣常用的語言所錄製。語音情緒辨識會因為語音中不同的文本和語言等資訊影響最後的辨識結果，因此公開的外國語言語料庫不一定適用於台灣語言的情緒辨識研究中。為了解決語料庫的問題我們自行錄製的台灣語言情緒語料庫，採用了最普遍的國語、台語以及客家語三種語言。我們的語料庫仿照德語公開語料庫 EMO-DB 錄製，對每種語言採用十位語者、十句文本以及七種情緒，每個語言收錄七百句，並且在錄製完後進行人工辨識，以一定的人工辨識率做為篩選條件，以確保一定的辨別度。錄製完後以一個龐大的聲學特徵集搭配支持向量機作為後端分類器，以此實驗做為三種語言的基準辨識率。

關鍵字: 語音情緒辨識, 情緒語料庫建置

一、緒論

在人類社會中言語溝通扮演著非常重要的角色，人們透過語言來交流和傳遞訊息，基於此理念下發展出許多人機介面科技(human-computer Interaction, HCI)，如蘋果公司的"Siri"便是此語音領域的代表作之一，將人類從鍵盤滑鼠輸入限制到能不需手動(Touchless)的聲控操作。而人類的交流不只單單透過語言文字，還有情感的交流，情感表達能包含人們所處的狀態，因此有了情感運算的研究。情感運算橫跨許多領域如電腦科學、心理學、認知哲學與工程學等，在語音領域相關為語音情緒辨識及情緒語音合成。基本的情感辨識透過分析人的臉部表情以及聲音來做辨識，更進一步則同時分析對話語意作為分辨依據。

[1]這本小書開始了情感運算的時代，此書定義了情感運算，從一個資訊工程研究者的角度來描述與說明情感運算的應用及重要性，解釋基本的訊號處理與機器學習分類的觀念。情感運算為一個龐大的研究議題，其中橫跨多個領域如資訊科學、心理學、感知科學和工程學等等。[2]對語音情緒辨識做了大略的概論，首先整理了研究中普遍常見的情緒語料庫，探討基本特徵參數如音高(Pitch)、能量(Energy)、基頻(Fundamental Frequency, F0)和梅爾倒頻譜係數(Mel Frequency Cepstral Coefficients, MFCC)等，後端則實驗高斯混合模型(Gaussian Mixture Model, GMM)、支持向量機(Support Vector Machine, SVM)、隱藏式馬可夫模型(Hidden Markov Model, HMM)和類神經網絡(Artificial Neural Networks, ANN)。

研究語音情緒辨識就必須具有情緒語音語料庫用於實驗，而語料庫的收錄會直接影響研究的實驗結果，目前常用的公開情緒語料庫如德語的 Berlin Database of Speech Emotion (EMO-DB)[3]、FAU Aibo[4]和 Vera-Am-Mittag(VAM)[5]。[6]提及在收集情感資料時，人們處於實驗室等非平常習慣的場合所收集到的情感資料實際上會與真實世界表達出的有所差異，因此情緒語音語料庫的錄製大致能分為兩類；第一類為引導性錄音，此類多在實驗室或者是錄音室中錄製，如德語的 EMO-DB，其透過在錄音室錄製並且有三位語言學專家在旁監督與指導，如此可以確保錄製出乾淨並且情緒表達度和差異性高的情緒語料。此種錄製方式較需要語者的表達能力，在語者表達能力較差的情況下無法在錄音室錄製出含有足夠情緒表達的語句;相對的第二種則是自發性的情緒表達語句，如 FAU Aibo 和 VAM，FAU Aibo 透過錄製小孩子與機器人的互動，便可以直接收集到小孩子自然表達的情緒語句。而 VAM 則是從談話性節目中節錄片段再從中挑選出情感較為活躍的句子，如此收錄的語料庫也較自然呈現。

在語音情緒辨識中提出作為基準實驗的有兩者。由於情感辨識相對於語音辨識及語者辨識為較新的領域，因此較早並沒有一個公認的基準可供參考比較，所以 INTERSPEECH 2009 Emotion Challenge[7]便採用了具有明確訓練集及測試集的 FAU Aibo 情緒語料庫，在前端使用過零率(zero crossing rate, ZCR)、能量、基頻、泛音噪音比(harmonics-to-noise, HNR)和梅爾倒頻譜系數。為了解決 FAU Aibo 五類資料量中有兩類佔了近 80%的資料數量嚴重不平均的狀況，使用 SMOTE(Synthetic Minority Oversampling Technology)[8]方法來增加數量較少的類別的樣本數，後端則以隱藏式馬可夫模型以及支持向量機做為辨識器，以此做為 FAU Aibo 的一個實驗基準。[9]實驗 9 個情緒語料庫分別為 Airplane Behaviour Corpus (ABC)、Audiovisual Interest Corpus (AVIC)、Danish Emotional Speech (DES)、EMO-DB、eNTERFACE、Sensitive Artificial Listener (SAL)、SmartKom、Speech Under Simulated and Actual Stress (SUSAS)、和 VAM 等資料庫，這些語料庫分別有不同的錄音條件，包含引導式錄音、自發性語音與各種的錄音環境等等。實驗分為兩種，第一種為擷取一般音框特徵並搭配隱藏式馬可夫模型/高斯混合模型做為後端辨識器，另一種為截取大量的聲學資訊並經由泛函將音框特徵轉換為句子特徵，如此以方便對應至後端支持向量機的訓練與辨識，此篇可視為各情緒語料庫採用聲學模型時的基準實驗參考。

目前常見的公開語音情緒辨識的語料庫並沒有以台灣本土語言錄置而成，而語音中包含了語言、語者、文本、腔調等等的資訊，這些皆會影響語音情緒辨識的準確度。因此為了提供一個較適合用於台灣語言的情緒語料庫，我們自行錄製了台灣最普遍的國語、台語及客家語三種語言的情緒語料庫。我們仿造 EMO-DB 錄製方式錄製，其中相同的七種情緒、五位男性五位女性共十位語者以及十句文本，錄製完後進行人工辨識測驗。最後再採用與[9]相同的基準實驗設定，作為我們語料庫的基準辨識率。

以下為整篇論文的架構，第一節為緒論，第二節詳細介紹我們仿造的德語語料庫 EMO-DB，第三節詳列我們自行錄製的台灣語料庫資訊，第四節為台灣語料庫的基準實驗，最後為我們的結論。

二、現有公開語料庫

我們錄製的語料庫參考已廣泛實驗於語音情緒研究的德語語料庫 Berlin Database of Emotion Speech(EMO-DB)。EMO-DB 由 10 位德語母語語者所錄製而成，經由麥克風錄製 48kHz 後降為 16kHz。錄音環境在隔音良好及具有高品質錄音設備的錄音室，因此表達的情緒並非自然呈現。語者由 3 位語言學專家從 40 位新聞播報員中挑選，在面試時每人對每種情緒透過麥克風錄製一句測試句，再將這些句子交予三位語言專家，專家根據自然度及可辨識度挑選出男女各 5 位作為錄音語者。語料庫共採用 7 種情緒分別為中性、生氣、害怕、開心、傷心、噁心和無聊，文本設計為五句長句及五句短句，文本內容為日常生活中的句子並且不帶有任何情緒詞彙，如此使語者在錄音時能較自然的表達語句，且在情緒表達過程中不會受到文本的內容而影響。錄製時語者對相同一句分別以七種情緒表達，因此每位語者至少收錄 70 句，整個語料庫至少包含 700 句，最後全部共錄製約 800 句，其中有部分句子保留二至三個版本。為了確保語句的品質，請 20 位測試者以隨機輪播的方式將每一句做七選一的人工辨識，並且對句子的自然度以 1 至 100 評分，測驗結束後捨棄辨識率低於 80%和自然度低於 60%的句子，篩選後七種情緒的句數分別為生氣 127 句、無聊 81 句、噁心 46 句、害怕 69 句、開心 71 句、傷心 62 句和中性 79 句共 535 句。

三、台灣情緒語料庫

為了研究跨語言的情緒語音辨識實驗，我們仿照了 EMO-DB 的設計方式錄製了自己的情緒語料庫，分別用相同的七種情緒表達五句長句以及五句短句，每種語言各錄製 700 句，表一列出我們的十句文本，表二與表三分別為台語與客家語的發音文本。我們選擇台灣常見的三種語言-國語、台語及客家語-作為我們的台灣錄製語言，由於客家語有不同腔調，因此我們挑選語者時選擇最為普遍的四縣腔與海陸腔作為我們的錄製腔調。錄音環境為中山大學電資大樓 F5017B 實驗室，錄音麥克風使用 ATH-AT9942，錄音介面卡為 Sound Blaster X-Fi Surround 5.1，取樣率為 16KHz，錄音時語者與麥克風間距約 20 公分。檔案命名格式為 7 碼，分別為第一碼語言 ID、第二三碼語者 ID，第四碼情緒 ID，第五六七碼文本 ID，如 H03At01 音檔則為客家語、語者 03、情緒為生氣和 t01 文本。接著分別對三種語言各找 5 位男性以及 5 位女性作為錄音者。相同的我們在錄製完後也請了 10 位測試者做人工辨識，但我們的測驗中並沒有自然度的評分。我們從中保留辨識率 60%以上的句子，表四列出三種語言挑選後各情緒所剩餘的句數，圖一表示三種情緒各個人工辨識率的句數，由圖中可看出多數錄製的人工準確度在 60%以上，所以我們的情緒語料庫具有一定的情緒辨別度。所有的錄音者和測試者皆為大學生或是研究生，並且非語言學或者音樂學系學生。

表一、台灣情緒語料庫 10 句文本

文本 ID	文本
t01	你的早餐放在桌上
t02	晚上他有一個約會
t03	最近常常睡不飽
t04	等下一起去餐廳吃飯
t05	過年要買一件新衣服
t06	這禮拜放假，要跟朋友一起出去玩
t07	昨天早上出門的時候，外套被鉤子勾到
t08	今天一整天都沒吃東西好餓喔
t09	這班火車人很多，很多人都沒位子坐
t10	早上去騎腳踏車，下午散步去買東西

表二、台語對應文本

文本 ID	文本
t01	你的早頓放在桌頂
t02	暗時依有一個約會
t03	最近定定睏不飽
t04	等咧做伙去餐廳食飯
t05	過年愛買一件新衫
t06	這禮拜放假，欲佮朋友做伙出去企桃
t07	昨透早欲出門的時陣，外套被鉤仔鉤到
t08	今仔日規工攏無食物件就夭
t09	這班火車人足濟，真濟人攏無位湯坐
t10	透早去騎腳踏車，下晡散步去買物件

表三、客家語對應文本

文本 ID	文本
t01	(ㄋㄧㄚˇ)(ㄍㄟ)兕九(ㄅㄩㄥ)兜揍轟
t02	(ㄤ)補壓(ㄍㄧˇ)武依炸右(ㄈㄧ)
t03	追(ㄎㄧㄥ)寵寵雖某報
t04	(den)哈(ㄎㄧㄥ)哈(ㄏㄧ)蠢堂(ㄕ˙)翻
t05	勾輾(ㄛㄧ)埋億良伈賞夫
t06	(ㄌㄧㄚ)禮掰(ㄅㄧㄥ)(ㄌㄧㄠ)，(ㄛㄧ)老品 (ㄧㄩ)(ㄎㄧㄥ)哈粗(ㄏㄧ)(ㄌㄧㄠ)
t07	醜比則損(ㄛㄧ)處(ㄇㄨㄣˇ)(ㄟ)死(ㄏㄧㄡ)，歪掏(ㄅ ㄨㄣˇ)(ㄍㄧㄡ)(ㄟˇ)(ㄍㄧㄡ)豆
t08	(ㄍㄧㄣˇ)(ㄅㄨㄧ)逆(ㄍㄨㄧ)逆(ㄟˇ)朱某奢懂席喊 窯喔
t09	(ㄌㄧㄚ)(ㄅㄧㄥ)(ㄈㄡ)查擰懂(ㄉㄡ)， 懂(ㄉㄡ)擰朱某(ㄨㄧ)(ㄟ)後仇
t10	則損(ㄏㄧ)(ㄎㄧˇ)師朗查，(ㄏㄚˇ)租三(ㄅㄨ) (ㄏㄧ)買懂席

表四、台灣情緒語料庫各語言篩選後句數

情緒	國語	台語	客家語	跨語言總數
生氣	58	73	62	193
無聊	66	55	59	180
噁心	46	55	54	155
害怕	57	61	64	182
開心	67	58	48	173
傷心	57	56	52	165
中性	87	64	62	213
總數	438	422	401	1261

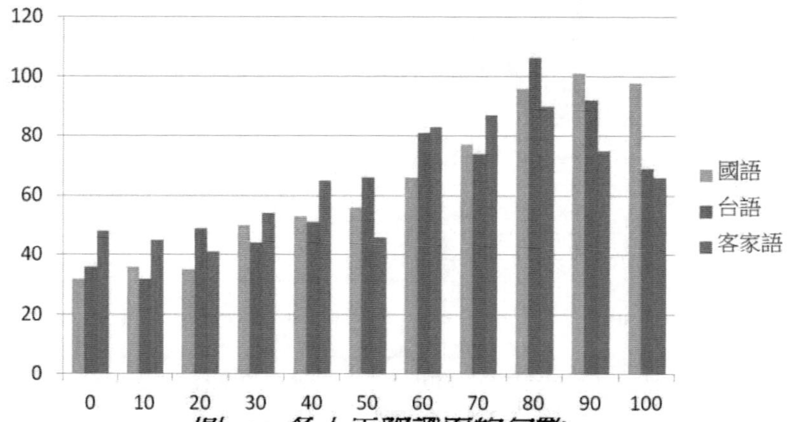

圖一、各人工辨識率的句數

四、基準實驗

4.1 實驗設定

我們實驗中採用 openEAR 0.1.0[10]與 Weka 3.6.9[11]兩套工具用於特徵參數擷取和訓練分類器。輸入的音訊處理採用 25 毫秒的漢明窗(Hamming window)並且處理過程中每次偏移 10 毫秒。在訓練分類器之前使用極值正規法(Min-Max normalization)將特徵參數縮放為 0 至 1，公式定義為算式(1)，V 與 V'分別為正規化前與正規化後的值。後端以支持向量機做為分類器，支持向量機的核心函式(kernel function)為基於序列最小化演算法(Sequential Minimal Optimization)的多項式核心(Polynomial Kernel)，Kernel 函式為算式(2)，p 設為 1。實驗方式以每次從語料庫中挑出一位語者作為測試語者，而其他語者當作訓練語者(Leave-One-Speaker-Out, LOSO)，經過 10 次訓練與辨識後統計結果便為此語料庫的辨識率。

$$V' = \frac{\mathrm{Max}_V - V}{\mathrm{Max}_V - Min_V} \tag{1}$$

$$K(x, y) = < x, y >^p \tag{2}$$

4.2 基準特徵集

本論文使用聲學特徵作為實驗的特徵參數，表五和表六分別列出大型特徵集所包含的低階參數(low-level descriptor, LLD)以及泛函(functional)。首先從音訊中擷取每個音框為 56 維的特徵，再透過泛函將這些音框特徵轉換為一個句子一組的特徵向量，56 個低階參數和 39 個泛函再計算一階與二階動態特徵後共得到 6552 個特徵參數，此便為我們的基準特徵集。

表五、56 個低階參數

Feature Group	Feature in Group	# of LLD
Raw signal	Zero-crossing-rate	1
Signal energy	Logarithm	1
Pitch	Fundamental frequency F0 in Hz via Cepstrum and Autocorrelation (ACF). Exponentially smoothed F0 envelope.	2
Voice Quality	Probability of voicing	1
Spectral	Energy in bands 0-250 Hz, 0-650 Hz, 250-650 Hz, 1-4 kHz 25%, 50%, 75%, 90% roll-off point, centroid, flux, and rel. pos. of spectrum max. and min. & 12 Mel-spectrum & Band 1-26 & 26 Cepstral & MFCC 0-12 & 13	12
Mel-spectrum	Band 1-26	26
Cepstral	MFCC 0-12	13

表六、39 個泛函

Functionals, etc.	# of fun.
Respective rel. position of max./min. value	2
Range (max.-min.)	1
Max. and min. value - arithmetic mean	2
Arithmetic mean, Quadratic mean	2
Number of non-zero values	1
Geometric, and quadratic mean of non-zero values	2
Mean of absolute values, Mean of non-zero abs. values	2
Quartiles and inter-quartile ranges	6
95% and 98% percentile	2
Std. deviation, variance, kurtosis, skewness	4
Centroid	1
Zero-crossing rate	1
# of peaks, mean dist. btwn. peaks, arth. mean of peaks, arth. Mean of peaks - overall arth. Mean	4
Linear regression coefficients and corresp. approximation error	4
Quadratic regression coefficients and corresp. approximation error	5

動態特徵計算為 delta regression，係數差公式採用 Hidden Markov Model Tool Kit 定義如算式(3)，其中 W 設為 2。

$$\Delta x_t = \frac{\sum_{i=1}^{W}(x_{t+i}-x_{t-i})\cdot i}{2\sum_{i=1}^{W} i^2} \tag{3}$$

4.3 實驗

根據表五與表六的 6552 維大型特徵集搭配支持向量機作為國語、台語和客家語三種語言的基準實驗，對每個語言的 10 位語者進行 LOSO 實驗後分別得到國語 68.5%、台語 50.7%和客家語 58.5%辨識率。表七至表九分別列出國語、台語和客家語三種語言的詳細辨識結果。

從表七至表九中可看出雖然在人工辨識上可得到至少 60%的辨識率，但在基準實驗中許多情緒的辨識率不及 60%。此實驗結果也反映出錄音狀況，七種情緒中以生氣、無聊和害怕三種情緒的辨識率較佳，此三種情緒對錄音者來說較好表達；而錄音者普遍認為噁心只單純利用語調來表達並不夠直覺，因此在錄音的情緒表達上會相對較差，三種語言的最高辨識率僅 50%；另在錄音過程中傷心和無聊兩種情緒對語者表達來說會有相似的狀況，實驗也可看出傷心的辨識結果有不少部分被分類為無聊，因此造成傷心的辨識率普遍較低。在台語的中性僅 17.2%的準確率，推測因各個語者在表達方式上的差異性過大造成分類器無法順利辨識，主要為語速與聲調的差異，而人工辨識時人們可以由語者的特性去推敲出其情緒，但辨識器上卻無法做出此判斷，所以造成辨識率不理想的狀況。

表七、國語基準實驗混淆矩陣

答案 / 結果	生氣	無聊	噁心	害怕	開心	中性	傷心	準確率
生氣	44	1	2	0	8	0	3	75.9
無聊	0	59	0	0	0	4	3	89.4
噁心	6	4	21	0	7	4	4	45.7
害怕	2	0	0	45	6	2	2	78.9
開心	7	0	4	6	40	1	9	59.7
傷心	1	10	7	2	3	31	3	54.4
中性	5	4	4	3	10	1	60	69.0

表八、台語基準實驗混淆矩陣

結果＼答案	生氣	無聊	噁心	害怕	開心	中性	傷心	準確率
生氣	45	1	8	0	14	0	5	61.6
無聊	0	43	0	0	0	7	5	78.2
噁心	6	4	27	2	4	8	4	49.1
害怕	7	1	4	39	6	2	2	63.9
開心	12	5	4	3	24	1	9	41.4
傷心	0	16	8	3	1	25	3	44.6
中性	16	13	6	6	10	2	11	17.2

表九、客家語基準實驗混淆矩陣.

結果＼答案	生氣	無聊	噁心	害怕	開心	中性	傷心	準確率
生氣	44	1	2	0	6	1	4	72.6
無聊	0	59	0	0	0	6	1	86.7
噁心	6	4	21	0	2	3	5	50.0
害怕	2	0	0	45	6	3	6	64.1
開心	7	0	4	6	16	2	8	33.3
傷心	1	10	7	2	1	15	2	28.8
中性	5	4	4	3	5	0	39	62.9

五、結論

在此篇論文中我們建立了一個台灣語言的情緒語料庫，其中以台灣常見的國語、台語和客家語三種語言錄製而成。我們仿照公開語料庫 EMO-DB 錄製，共包含了生氣、無聊、噁心、害怕、開心、中性和傷心共七種，每種語言的語者為十位，分別為五位男性以及五位女性，文本共十句，每位語者以七種情緒來表達同一句文本。在錄製後進行人工辨識的檢驗，以人工辨識率 60%作為篩選基準，以此確保我們語料具有一定的辨別度，篩選後三種語言的所剩句數為國語 438 句、台語 422 句和客家語 401 句。另我們使用了一個龐大的聲學特徵集並搭配支持向量機做為我們的基準實驗，其中分別在三種語言可以得到國語 68.5%、台語 50.7%和客家語 58.5%的辨識率，便為三個語言的基準辨識率。此資料庫及實驗數據可做為未來台灣語音情緒辨識使用及參考。在未來若可以我們希望能夠更提升語料庫的品質，如改善台語的中性辨識率過低的狀況，對於篩選後句數剩餘過少的語者進行重錄或以新的語者資料代替，提升品質的同時也增加語料庫的總句數。

參考文獻

[1] R. W. Picard, Affective computing. MIT Press, 1997.

[2] M. El Ayadi, M. S. Kamel, and F. Karray, "Survey on speech emotion recognition: features, classification schemes, and databases," in Pattern Recognition, vol. 44, pp. 572–587, Mar. 2011.

[3] F. Burkhardt, A. Paeschke, M. Rolfes, W. F. Sendlmeier, and B. Weiss, "A database of german emotional speech," in Proceedings of INTERSPEECH, pp. 1517–1520, 2005.

[4] S. Steidl, *Automatic classification of emotion related user states in spontaneous children's speech*. PhD thesis, University of Erlangen-Nuremberg, 2009.

[5] M. Grimm, K. Kroschel, and S. Narayanan, "The Vera am Mittag german audio-visual emotional speech database," in Proceedings of IEEE International Conference on Multimedia and Expo, pp. 865–868, 2008.

[6] D. McDuff, R. Kaliouby, and R. Picard, "Crowdsourcing facial responses to online videos," in IEEE Transactions on Affective Computing, vol. 3, pp. 456–468, 2012.

[7] B. Schuller, S. Steidl, and A. Batliner, "The INTERSPEECH 2009 emotion challenge," in Proceedings of INTERSPEECH, pp. 312–315, 2009.

[8] G. Weiss and F. Provost, "The effect of class distribution on classifier learning: An empirical study," tech. rep., Department of Computer Science, Rutgers University, 2001.

[9] B. Schuller, B. Vlasenko, F. Eyben, G. Rigoll, and A. Wendemuth, "Acoustic emotion recognition: A benchmark comparison of performances," in Proceedings of IEEE Workshop on of Automatic Speech Recognition Understanding (ASRU), pp. 552–557, 2009.

[10] F. Eyben, M. Wollmer, and B. Schuller, "OpenEAR introducing the munich open-source emotion and affect recognition toolkit," in Proceedings of ACII International Conference on Affective Computing and Intelligent Interaction and Workshops, 2009, pp. 1–6.

[11] I. H. Witten, E. Frank, L. Trigg, M. Hall, G. Holmes, and S. J. Cunningham, "Weka: Practical machine learning tools and techniques with java implementations," 1999.

基於稀疏表示之語者識別

Sparse Representation Based Speaker Identification

王光耀　Kuang-Yao Wang
國立中央大學資訊工程學系
Department of Computer Science and information Engineering
National Central University

王家慶　Jia-Ching Wang
國立中央大學資訊工程學系
Department of Computer Science and information Engineering
National Central University
jcw@csie.ncu.edu.tw

摘要

稀疏表示分類器(Sparse Representation Classifier, SRC)是一種基於影像稀疏表示(Sparse Representation)的機器學習方法。在影像以及人臉辨識上的研究上，稀疏表示分類器具有非常好的辨識效果以及強健性。有鑑於 SRC 在影像辨識上的高鑑別能力，近幾年已有許多基於稀疏表示的語者識別(Speaker Identification)方法相繼被提出。本論文提出一套基於稀疏表示的辨識系統，我們提出以機率型主成份分析(Probabilistic Principle Component Analysis, PPCA)建構超級向量(Supervector)，並加入檢定的方式調整特徵值選取，使語者高斯混合模型(Gaussian Mixture Model, GMM)中每個高斯的維度可以針對資料的不同作調整。接著，我們在稀疏字典上加強，透過低秩矩陣還原(Low-Rank Matrix Recovery)以及核化降維(Kernel Dimension Reduction)對說話內容(Session)以及通道(Channel)變異補償，使字典增加鑑別性。最後利用稀疏表示分類器進行分類。根據實驗結果顯示，不論是參數的改進、字典的處理，對辨識率都有一定程度的提升。此外，與傳統的 *i*-vector 語者識別系統相比，提出的系統則具有更佳的辨識率表現。

關鍵詞：稀疏表示、語者識別、核化稀疏表示、超級向量

一、簡介

以生物特徵作為辨識基礎的研究已經有長達數十年的歷史，包含人臉、語音和指紋。其中聲音因具有取得容易、非侵入性、運算量少、輸入具有便利性等優點，語者識別一直是近年來熱門的主題。語者識別利用語者語音的特性來識別使用者身份，大致上的研究方向分成語音特徵擷取以及分類演算法兩部分，其中以分類演算法的研究最多，

包含的層面也最廣，包括語者模型的建立、分類機制、因為周邊環境的影響所需的補償辦法等研究。目前來說高斯混和模型 [1][2]和支持向量機(Support Vector Machine, SVM)[3]是經典的分類方法。特徵參數方面，會將一段語音切割成數個音框，音框代表此語者在短時間內的發聲特徵，幾種常見的有梅爾倒頻譜係數(Mel-scale Frequency Cepstral Coefficients, MFCC)[5]、感知線性預測係數(Perceptual Linear Prediction Coefficients, PLPC)[6])等。

基於 GMM 超級向量(GMM-Supervector)[7-10]的辨識方法是一種綜合 GMM 模型表示以及 SVM 分類方法優點的語者識別演算法。GMM 超級向量是一種語者模型的向量表示法，通用背景模型(Universal Background Model, UBM)經過輸入語音調適後成為 GMM 語者模型，其中各個高斯成份(Components) 的期望值被串在一起形成一個超級向量。此向量表示可以用來代表整個語音檔的特徵向量，最後，再以 SVM 作為分類方法來達到辨識語者的目的。然而語者識別系統會因為錄製工具和背景不同，造成通道差異、說話內容差異和環境差異的干擾，導致辨識系統的辨識率低落。擾動屬性投影(Nuisance Attribute Projection, NAP)是一種有效補償通道干擾的方式[7][11]，藉由設計一個最佳化問題使干擾最小，配合著前面提到的方法，更有效地提高辨識系統的強健性。在 NAP 之後陸續有聯合因素分析(Joint Factor Analysis , JFA)[12][13]、*i*-vector[14-16]等技術被用來補償上述提到的差異，透過對語音參數的拆解，將一些語者不相關的資訊刪除，得到去除干擾後最能代表語者的特徵。

近年來對於複雜的資訊(例如訊號、圖像)，往往希望可以用較簡化的方式呈現，特別在訊號處理的部分，分析時經常先將資料轉換至不同的定義域，並且假設其在轉換後，會呈現稀疏分布[24]。在近期稀疏表示的發展中，SRC 在[25][26]中被提出，SRC 是一個 Nonparametric 學習方法，不需訓練過程但是需要訓練資料，以及可以直接參考訓練資料對策是資料進行分類的動作。實驗結果顯示出在人臉辨識的應用上，SRC 有著比 KNN (K-Nearest Neighbors)[27]以及 Nearest Subspace(NS)[28][29]更好的辨識率。近幾年也有少數研究將 SRC 應用於語者驗證[16-19]的問題上，然而此方面的研究仍屬於剛起步的階段，仍有許多問題值得我們探討。

本論文提出一套基於核化稀疏表示的語者識別系統，文章的編排共分成七個部分: 第一部分為簡介，第二部分為參數擷取，我們以 PPCA 建構超級向量(PPCA 超級向量)取代 GMM 超級向量[20][31]，並且以巴雷特檢定(Bartlett Test)的方式調整特徵值的選取，第三部分則是描述如何利用特徵參數建立稀疏表示分類器。第四部分描述我們提出的兩種變異補償方法，低秩矩陣還原以及核化稀疏表示分類器(Kernel Sparse Representation Classifier, KSRC)。第五部分為實驗部分，展示提出之改良方法是否具有其必要性。最後在第六部分則是結論。

二、參數擷取

在本論文中，我們利用機率型主成分分析建構超級向量[20][33]，並以提出巴雷特檢定(Bartlett Test)主成分的個數。傳統上，超級向量是由高斯混和模型建構而成，這裡加入主成分分析的概念，並希望能以機率分布模型的形式與高斯模型對應，使得資料點由原本高斯混和模型轉成 PPCA 混和模型，再透過 Latent Factor 的轉換，形成新的超級向量，稱作 PPCA 超級向量[20][21][33]，其中，主軸的挑選，我們引入巴雷特檢定(Bartlett Test)[22][23]的概念，建立假說，找到臨界的特徵值。而目前語者識別問題中，*i*-vector 是表現最好的參數之一。藉由訓練出總體變異矩陣，將原本的超級向量轉到更低維的空間，使 *i*-vector 更加表現出語者及通道的資訊，因此，我們將 PPCA 超級向量轉換到總體變異空間上，希望得到更具鑑別力的 *i*-vector 使辨識效能提升。

2.1 基於機率型主成分分析之因素分析模型

傳統的 GMM 超級向量，並沒有考量到其聲學特徵參數有高度的冗餘性[21][31]，因此應該採用更低的子空間來表示。在[21][31]中比較成份分析(Factor Analysis)與主成分分析(PCA)的關聯性，觀察成份分析的數學式：

$$\mathbf{x} = \mathbf{W}\mathbf{z} + \boldsymbol{\mu} + \boldsymbol{\varepsilon} \tag{1}$$

其中 **x** 代表高維的資料，**z** 代表低維變數，又稱 Latent Factor。回想主成分分析的數學式，找出主成分 **V** 使資料降維：

$$\mathbf{x} = \boldsymbol{\mu} + \mathbf{V}\mathbf{z} \tag{2}$$

我們可將成份分析視成對資料 **x** 做 PCA 加上一個噪音項，並且導入機率的概念解釋。

在式(1)中，**x** 是 $K \times 1$ 的原始資料， W 為 $K \times J$ 的轉換矩陣，其中 $J < K$ ，而 Latent Factor **z** 假設為一高斯分布 $N(0, \mathrm{I})$，噪音 $\boldsymbol{\varepsilon} \sim N(0, \sigma^2 \mathrm{I})$，根據以上的假設可以知道原始資料 x 能建模(Model)成 $N(\boldsymbol{\mu}, \sigma^2\mathbf{I} + \mathbf{W}\mathbf{W}^{\mathrm{T}})$ ，稱作 PPCA 模型。當遇到更複雜的資料時，希望藉由混合多組 PPCA 模型，如下式：

$$p(\mathbf{x}) = \sum_{c=1}^{M} w_c \, p(\mathbf{x}|c) \tag{3}$$

$$p(\mathbf{x}|c) = N(\boldsymbol{\mu}_c, \sigma_c^{\,2}\mathbf{I} + \mathbf{W}_c\mathbf{W}_c^{\mathrm{T}}) \tag{4}$$

其中 M 是高斯成份的個數，這可以跟高斯混合模型做對應，一般表示資料以多個高斯模型描述，這裡的基本單位以 PPCA 模型取代。

因此，我們希望找出 $\mathbf{W}_c$ 及 σ_c 來推算 Latent Factor，方法是利用最大概似估計(Maximum Likelihood Estimation, MLE)，因為已經知道 **x** 的分布，所以藉由 MLE 得到的 $\mathbf{W}_c$ 及 σ_c 可進而推出 Latent Factor $\mathbf{z}_c$

$$\mathbf{z}_c = (\mathbf{W}_c^{\,T}\mathbf{W}_c + \sigma_c^{\,2}\mathbf{I})^{-1}\mathbf{W}_c^{\,T}(\mathbf{x} - \boldsymbol{\mu}_c) \tag{5}$$

當原始資料 **x** 進入系統後，會先以 PPCA 混合模型，並且透過式(5)的轉換得到屬於每個高斯成份的 Latent Factor。當所有的參數都做了 PPCA 後，則原始以 MFCC 為基礎的 UBM 也必須調整，形成以 Latent Factor 為參數下構建的新 UBM：

$$p(\mathbf{z}|c)=\sum_{c=1}^{M} w_c N(\boldsymbol{\mu}_{z,c},\boldsymbol{\Sigma}_{z,c})=\sum_{c=1}^{M} w_c N(0,\mathbf{I}-\sigma_c{}^2\boldsymbol{\Lambda}_c{}^{-1}) \quad (6)$$

$$\text{其中}\ \boldsymbol{\mu}_{z,c}=E\{(\mathbf{W}_c{}^T\mathbf{W}_c+\sigma_c{}^2\mathbf{I})^{-1}\mathbf{W}_c{}^T(\mathbf{x}-\boldsymbol{\mu}_c)\}=0 \quad (7)$$

$$\begin{aligned}\boldsymbol{\Sigma}_{z,c}&=E\{\mathbf{z}_c\mathbf{z}_c{}^T\}-\boldsymbol{\mu}_{z,c}\boldsymbol{\mu}_{z,c}{}^T\\&=(\mathbf{W}_c{}^T\mathbf{W}_c+\sigma_c{}^2\mathbf{I})^{-1}\mathbf{W}_c{}^T E\{(\mathbf{x}-\boldsymbol{\mu}_c)(\mathbf{x}-\boldsymbol{\mu}_c)^T\}\mathbf{W}_c(\mathbf{W}_c{}^T\mathbf{W}_c+\sigma_c{}^2\mathbf{I})^{-T}\\&=\boldsymbol{\Lambda}_c{}^{-1}(\boldsymbol{\Lambda}_c-\sigma_c{}^2\mathbf{I})^{T/2}\boldsymbol{\Lambda}_c(\boldsymbol{\Lambda}_c-\sigma_c{}^2\mathbf{I})^{1/2}\boldsymbol{\Lambda}_c{}^{-T}=\mathbf{I}-\sigma_c{}^2\boldsymbol{\Lambda}_c{}^{-1}\end{aligned} \quad (8)$$

2.2 巴雷特檢定

在上個小節中提到的 PPCA 中，有一個問題是需要討論的，那就是主軸個數的挑選。我們假設後面不要的特徵值，其數值小到足以視為相同，因此，定義假說 $H_0:\lambda_{k+1}=\lambda_{K+2}=...=\lambda_n$，希望迴圈由 n-1 往前找到門檻值 k。而如果我們將特徵值的大小視為高斯分布，則巴雷特檢定[22][23]可以整理成相似度的檢驗，如下式：

$$T=\frac{\prod_{q=k+1}^{n}\lambda_q}{\left(\dfrac{\sum_{q=k+1}^{n}\lambda_q}{n-k}\right)^{n-k}} \quad (9)$$

當觀測資料數 m 夠多的話，可將 T 視為一個 X^2 分布，且將上式近似於下式：

$$T\approx\left(m-(2n-11)/6\right)\left((n-k)\log\overline{\lambda}-\sum_{q=k+1}^{n}\log\lambda_q\right) \quad (10)$$

其中 $\overline{\lambda}$ 是後 n-k 個特徵值的平均，在檢定過程中，當 $T>X^2{}_{\alpha,n}$ 時，則否決假說 H_0，檢定終止，q 即為我們挑選的主軸個數，其中 α 為 X^2 的顯著水平。

2.3 *i*-vector

啟發於早期 JFA 在語者識別上的應用，Dehak *et al.* 提出的一個新的分析方法 *i*-vector [14-16]，不像 JFA 將語者和通道分開，*i*-vector 僅用一個總體變異性空間，他發現 JFA 中的通道部分仍包含了能用來識別語者的資訊，所以將 JFA 中分開的變異部分，合併成一個單一的總體變異性空間超級向量，藉由合併錄音方式的變異性，提升其辨識性，表示如下：

$$\boldsymbol{\mu}=\mathbf{m}+\mathbf{Tw} \tag{11}$$

m 是 UBM 超級向量，與 JFA 中使用的相同；**T** 代表的是所有變異性的矩陣；*i*-vector 代表的是總體變異性元素 **w**。

最後，總結參數擷取的整體架構，參數擷取包含三個部分，第一，由 Universal Background Data 首先訓練出 UBM，並透過 PPCA 將 UBM 轉換成以 Latent Factor 為參數的 UBM，第二，當輸入語音進入系統後，擷取其 Latent Factor，接著，對新的 UBM 調適產生 PPCA 超級向量。最後，在基於 PPCA 超級向量參數下訓練總變異矩陣，並將輸入語音轉換成 *i*-vector。

三、稀疏表示分類器

我們利用稀疏表示具鑑別力的特性，應用於語者識別問題上，利用 *i*-vector 作為特徵參數，以固定維度的向量表示語音訊號。假設有 C 個不同語者類別的訓練資料，每一筆訓練資料為一個 *i*-vector，我們需要建構一個跨類別的(Global)字典 $\mathbf{D}\in\mathbb{R}^{P\times Q}$,，作法是將所有語者類別的字典組在一起

$$\mathbf{D}=[\mathbf{D}_1\ \mathbf{D}_2 \ldots\ldots \mathbf{D}_C] \tag{12}$$

其中，$\mathbf{D}_j$表示第j個類別的字典，由類別j的 *i*-vector 串接而成。此外，P 代表參數維度，Q 是訓練資料個數。在測試資料 y 與字典 D 已知的情況下，我們希望求出稀疏係數 $\mathbf{x}=[x_1\ x_2 \ldots x_k]$，使原訊號與重建訊號之間的誤差能越小越好，且 **x** 要符合稀疏特性，如下式：

$$\min_x \|\mathbf{y}-\mathbf{Dx}\|_2^2+\lambda\|\mathbf{x}\|_1 \tag{13}$$

在解出稀疏係數 x 後，決策上，將 k 類別各自的字典 $\mathbf{D}_j$ 及係數 $\mathbf{x}_j$ 還原 **y**，並與 **y** 計算誤差，獲得最小誤差者即為所屬類別：

$$j^*=\arg\min_j \|\mathbf{y}-\mathbf{D}_j\mathbf{x}_j\|_2^2 \tag{14}$$

四、字典處理及變異補償

在以 *i*-vector 為參數的架構下，*i*-vector 的總變異矩陣是假設訓練資料標籤不同所訓練而成，因此，它存在與語者相關的變異，這是我們想要的，同時它存在一部分錄音通道及說話內容造成的變異，因此，以往的研究都會加入 Linear Discriminant Analysis(LDA)及 Within-Class Covariance Normalization (WCCN)去補償錄音通道的變異[33]，希望即使是在錄音通道不同的狀態下，找出類別間的變異最大化，類別內的變異最小化的空間，使變異排除，另外說話內容的變異也可以由 LDA 的處理解釋，因為它將語者的說話內容做變異最小的假設，消除說話內容變異造成的問題。

本節提出對 *i*-vector 字典的處理及補償辦法，包括以低秩矩陣還原以及核化稀疏表示分類器(Kernel SRC)分別對說話內容及錄音通道變異做補償，並增加字典的鑑別性。

4.1 低秩矩陣還原字典處理及變異補償

低秩矩陣還原[34]提供一種訊號拆解的方式，假設訊號可以被拆解成一個低秩(Low Rank)矩陣 **A** 及稀疏誤差(Sparse Error) **E** 的和，如下式：

$$\mathbf{D} = \mathbf{A} + \mathbf{E} \tag{15}$$

在 **A** 與 **E** 皆未知的情況下，我們希望讓 **A** 能以最少的 rank 還原原訊號，並且 **E** 能符合 Sparse 的特性，因此整理成以下的最佳化式：

$$\min_{\mathbf{A},\mathbf{E}} rank(\mathbf{A}) + \gamma\|\mathbf{E}\|_0 \tag{16}$$

進而，整理成一個凸最佳化的問題，並用 Augmented Lagrange Multiplier (ALM)求解。

透過低秩矩陣還原，我們將每個語者類別的字典分別作低秩矩陣還原分解，得到與原來字典大小相同的低秩矩陣 **A**，取代原來的字典，讓字典中每個語者的特徵更為凸顯。

4.2 核化稀疏表示分類器

藉由核化方法(Kernel Trick)，稀疏表示分類器可進一步非線性化，稱作核化稀疏表式分類器 [32]。輸入空間的資料經過非線性核化映射(Kernel Mapping)投射至高維參數空間，讓原本在輸入空間混淆的參數資料在高維空間變成可分離的。透過更進一步的核化降維方法，我們可得到測試資料的稀疏組合係數(Sparse Combination Coefficients)來進行分類的動作。

我們利用稀疏表示具鑑別力的特性，應用於語者識別問題上，利用 *i*-vector 作為特徵參數，以固定維度的向量表示語音訊號。假設有 c 個不同語者類別的訓練資料，每一筆訓練資料為一個 i-vector，我們需要建構一個跨類別的(Global)字典 D，作法是將所有語者類別的字典組在一起 $\{\mathbf{a}_i, y_i\}_{i=1}^{Q}$，其中 $\mathbf{a}_i \in \mathbb{R}^P$, $y_i \in \{1,2,\ldots,c\}$, 一筆測試資料 $\mathbf{a} \in \mathbb{R}^P$. 令 Φ 表示 $k(\cdot,\cdot)$ 的非線性映射，可將輸入空間 Input Space χ 的資料投射到高維空間 F：

$$\Phi : \mathbf{a} \in \chi \rightarrow \Phi(\mathbf{a}) \in F \tag{17}$$

與稀疏表示分類器相同，參數空間的測試資料可表示為訓練資料的線性組合：

$$\Phi(\mathbf{a}) = \sum_{i=1}^{Q} x_i \, \Phi(\mathbf{a}_i) = \mathbf{\Phi}_{\mathbf{A}} \mathbf{x} \tag{18}$$

其中 $\mathbf{\Phi}_{\mathbf{A}} = \left[\Phi(\mathbf{a}_1), \Phi(\mathbf{a}_2), \ldots, \Phi(\mathbf{a}_Q)\right]$，且 $\mathbf{x} = [x_1, x_2, \ldots, x_Q]^T$。

根據稀疏表示的概念，稀疏係數向量 $\mathbf{x}$ 可以從下式最佳化問題解出：

$$\hat{\mathbf{x}} = \arg\min_{\mathbf{x}} \|\mathbf{x}\|_1 \quad \text{subject to} \ \|\Phi(\mathbf{a}) - \mathbf{\Phi}_{\mathbf{A}}\mathbf{x}\|_2 \le \varepsilon \tag{19}$$

當核化空間的維度是未知且遠高於訓練資料的個數時，會導致式子(14)的解會不夠稀疏，因此會需要在參數空間進行降低維度的動作。令 P 表示投射矩陣 (Projection Matrix)。則(19)可改成下式：

$$\hat{\mathbf{x}} = \arg\min_{\mathbf{x}} \|\mathbf{x}\|_1 \quad \text{subject to} \ \|\mathbf{P}^T \Phi(\mathbf{a}) - \mathbf{P}^T \mathbf{\Phi}_{\mathbf{A}}\mathbf{x}\|_2 \le \varepsilon \tag{20}$$

具有最小重建誤差(Reconstruction Residual)的類別則為核化稀疏表示分類器的分類結果：

$$\hat{i} = \arg\min_{i} r_i(\mathbf{a}) = \|\mathbf{P}^T \Phi(\mathbf{a}) - \mathbf{P}^T \mathbf{\Phi}_{\mathbf{A}} \delta(\mathbf{x}_i)\| \tag{21}$$

其中 $\delta(\mathbf{x}_i)$ 是 $\hat{\mathbf{x}}$ 的第 i 個語者的非零稀疏系數。

Kernel SRC(KSRC)即結合 Kernel LDA 及 SRC 兩個方法，將原始特徵向量由 Kernel 投影至高維後，再由 LDA 降維，在先前的文獻有提到，i-vector 存在 Channel 的變異，因此，我們透過 Kernel LDA 補償，希望錄製方式不同產生的干擾能藉由最大化 Between-Class 變異及最小化 Within-Class 變異得到補償。

五、實驗結果

我們以 NIST2005 [30] 做為語者資料庫，NIST 每年都會錄製語者資料庫，許多產業界、學術界都會以此作為評估效能的標準，而 2005 年發布的資料庫以電話對話語音數據為主，同時收集一些輔助麥克風接收的數據，這些數據主要來自英語演講，並包括四種額外語言。我們挑選其中 Male 8con-1con 的 Condition 做為測試資料庫，其中 8con 為訓練資料，而 1con 是測試資料。

為了驗證巴雷特檢定是否能進一步改善辨識系統，我們定義另一套主軸個數選取方式:各個高斯成份在統一主軸個數下與透過檢定方式挑選適合主軸個數下的差別，最後

再經由轉換到 *i*-vector 上。藉由比較巴雷特檢定與我們定義的主軸選取方式來判斷巴雷特檢定的必要性。在我們的實驗中，如表一所示，固定每個高斯成份的主軸個數為 27 時來到最高 76.91%，不過隨著主軸個數的減少辨識率也降低。而加入巴雷特檢定後，我們設定巴雷特檢定的$\alpha = 0.05$。各個高斯成份降維的數目不固定，有效的提升辨識率到 77.01%。在接下來的實驗中，我們會以這個辨識率為 77.01%的系統作為後續實驗的基準(Baseline)，測試提出/採用的改進方法是否有效。

《表一》不同主軸個數與巴雷特檢定選取之辨識率比較。

方法			辨識率
PPCA-SV	30個主軸	+ *i*-vector + SRC	76.60%
	27個主軸		76.91%
	24個主軸		76.40%
	21個主軸		76.20%
	18個主軸		75.99%
	15個主軸		72.23%
PPCA-SV + Bartlett Test + *i*-vector + SRC			77.01%

在以下實驗中，我們比較了四種不同語者識別系統。Baseline 我們使用目前 state-of-the-art 辨識方法，*i*-vector based cosine distance，即以 *i*-vector 為參數下，將輸入特徵與每個 Class 字典的 8 筆 *i*-vector 做內積求平均，挑選內積最大的語者類別，表示相似度為最大，通常在參數後面會加上 LDA 與 WCCN 對錄音通道變異補償。其餘三個系統分別為基於稀疏表示器的系統、基於核化稀疏表示器作字典補償之識別系統以及基於低秩矩陣還原之識別系統。實驗數據如表二所示，透過低秩矩陣還原方法建構的字典具有最高的辨識率 80.57%，比 Baseline 以及沒有變異補償的系統分別多了 13.63%以及 3.56%的辨識率。與沒有變異補償的系統相比，Kernel LDA 達到變異性補償的效果，增加了字典的鑑別性，辨識率提升了 2.24%。

《表二》不同語者識別系統之辨識率比較。

方法	辨識率
GMM-SV + *i*-vector + LDA + WCCN + CD (Baseline)	66.94%
PPCA-SV + Bartlett Test + *i*-vector + SRC	77.01%
PPCA-SV + Bartlett Test + *i*-vector + Kernel SRC	79.25%
PPCA-SV + Bartlett Test + *i*-vector + SRC (Low-Rank Matrix Recovery Based Dictionary)	80.57%

六、結論

這篇論文提出一套基於稀疏表示分類器為基礎的辨識系統，在前端以 PPCA-Supervector 為參數，加入巴雷特檢定作為準則，決定每個高斯 Component 挑選主軸的辦法，使每個高斯 Component 的維度可以針對資料的不同，決定適當的維度，接著，訓練出總變異矩陣，將 Supervector 投映至總變異空間上，以 *i*-vector 作為辨識參數。在字典的建構上，我們提出以低秩矩陣還原以及 Kernel SRC 進行變異補償，去除說話內容以及通道變異造成的干擾。從實驗結果看來，PPCA-Supervector 在未做巴雷特檢定前就有比 GMM-Supervector 好的效果，而再加入巴雷特檢定後，效果更加提高，與傳統基於 *i*-vector 的識別系統相比，辨識率提升了 10.07%。此外，再加入兩種變異補償方法後，低秩矩陣還原以及 Kernel SRC 分別可以再提升系統的辨識率 3.56%以及 2.24%。

參考文獻

[1] D. A. Reynolds and R. C. Rose, "Robust text-independent speaker identification using Gaussian mixture models," *IEEE Trans. Speech Audio Process.*, vol. 3, no. 1, pp. 72–83, Jan. 1995.

[2] B. L. Pellom and J. H. L. Hansen, "An efficient scoring algorithm for Gaussian mixture model based speaker identification," *IEEE Signal Process. Lett.*, vol. 5, no. 11, pp. 281–284, Nov. 1998.

[3] W. M. Campbell, J. P. Campbell, D. A. Reynolds, E. Singer, and P. A. Torres-Carrasquillo, "Support vector machines for speaker and language recognition," *Comput. Speech Lang.*, vol. 20, pp. 210–229, 2006.

[4] J. L. Gauvain and C. H. Lee, "Maximum *a posteriori* estimation for multivariate Gaussian mixture observations of Markov chains," *IEEE Trans. Speech Audio Process.*, vol. 2, no. 2, pp. 291–298, 1994.

[5] M. R. Hasan, M. Jamil, M. G. Rabbani, and M. S. Rahman, "Speaker identification using Mel frequency cepstral coefficients," *3rd international Conference on Electrical & Computer Engineering ICECE 2004*, 28-30 December 2004, Dhaka, Bangladesh.

[6] H. Hermansky. "Perceptual Linear Predictive (PLP) Analysis of Speech," *Journal of the Acoust. Society ofAmer.,* 87: 1738- 1752, April, 1990.

[7] W. Campbell, D. Sturim, D. Reynolds, and A. Solomonoff, "SVM based speaker verification using a GMM supervector kernel and nap variability compensation," in *Proc. ICASSP*, Toulouse, France, 2006, pp. 97–100.

[8] W. Campbell, D. Sturim, and D. Reynolds, "Support vector machines using GMM supervectors for speaker verification," *IEEE Signal Process. Lett.*, vol. 13, no. 5, pp. 308–311, May 2006.

[9] T. Kinnunen and H. Li, "An overview of text-independent speaker recognition: From features to supervectors," *Speech Commun.*, vol. 52, no. 1, pp. 12–40, 2010.

[10] B. G. B. Fauve, D. Matrouf, N. Scheffer, J.-F. Bonastre, and J. S. D. Mason, "State-of-the-art performance in text-independent speaker verification through open-source software," *IEEE Trans. Audio, Speech, Lang. Process.*, vol. 15, no. 7, pp. 1960–1968, 2007.

[11] A. Solomonoff, W. M. Campbell, and C. Quillen, "Channel compensation for SVM speaker recognition," *in Proc. Odyssey04*, 2004, pp. 57–62.

[12] O. Glembek, L. Burget, N. Brummer, and P. Kenny, "Comparison of scoring methods used in speaker recognition with joint factor analysis," in *Proc. IEEE Int. Conf. Acoust., Speech, Signal Process.*, Taipei, Taiwan, Apr. 2009, pp. 4057–4060.

[13] P. Kenny, P. Ouellet, N. Dehak, V. Gupta, and P. Dumouchel, "A study of interspeaker variability in speaker verification," *IEEE Trans. Audio, Speech, Lang. Process.*, vol. 16, no. 5, pp. 980–988, Jul. 2008.

[14] A. Kanagasundaram, R. Vogt, D. Dean, S. Sridharan, and M. Mason, "i-vector based Speaker Recognition on Short Utterances," in *Interspeech*, 2011.

[15] P. Matejka, O. Glembek, F. Castaldo, O. Plchot, P. Kenny, L. Burget, and J. Cernocky, "Full-covariance ubm and heavy-tailed plda in i-vector speaker verification," *Proc. ICASSP '11*, pp. 4828–4831, 2011.

[16] J.M.K. Kua, J. Epps, E. Ambikairajah, "i-vector with sparse representation classification for speaker verification, " *Speech Commun*, 2013.

[17] K. Huang and S. Aviyente, "Sparse Representation for Signal Classification," *Neural Information Processing Systems*, 2006.

[18] J. M. K. Kua, E. Ambikairajah, J. Epps, and R. Togneri, "Speaker verification using sparse representation classification," in *Proc. ICASSP*, May 2011, pp. 4548–4551.

[19] R. Saeidi, A. Hurmalainen, T. Virtanen, and D. A. van Leeuwen, "Exemplar-based Sparse Representation and Sparse Discrimination for Noise Robust Speaker Identification," in *Odyssey speaker and language recognition workshop*, Singapore, 2012.

[20] T. Hasan and J. H. L. Hansen, "Factor analysis of acoustic features using a mixture of probabilistic principal component analyzers for robust speaker verification," *in Proc. Odyssey*, Singapore, Jun. 2012.

[21] M. Tipping and C. Bishop, "Mixtures of probabilistic principal component analyzers," *Neural Computation*, vol. 11, no. 2, pp. 443–482, 1999.

[22] M. Y. Lee, Perceptual Factor Analysis for Speech Enhancement, Master Thesis, Institute of Computer Science and Information Engineering, National Cheng Kung University (2004).

[23] M.S. Bartlett, "Tests of significance in factor analysis," *British Journal of Psychology*, Statistical Section 3, 77–85, 1950

[24] M. Aharon, M. Elad, and A. Bruckstein, "K-SVD: an algorithm for designing overcomplete dictionaries for Sparse Representation," *IEEE Trans. Signal Process.*, vol. 54, no. 11, pp. 4311–4322, Nov. 2006.

[25] A. Y. Yang, J. Wright, Y. Ma, and S. S. Sastry, "Feature selection in face recognition: A sparse representation perspective," EECS Dept., Univ. California, Berkeley, CA, Tech. Report UCB/EECS-2007-99, 2007.

[26] J. Wright, A. Y. Yang, A. Ganesh, S. S. Sastry, and Y. Ma, "Robust face recognition via sparse representation," *IEEE Transaction Pattern Analysis and Machine Intelligence*, vol. 31, no. 2, pp. 210–226, 2009.

[27] R. Duda, P. Hart, and D. Stork, *Pattern Classification*, 2nd edition New York: Wiley, 2000.

[28] S. Z. Li, "Face recognition based on nearest linear combinations," *IEEE Computer Society Conference on Computer Vision and Pattern Recognition*, pp. 839–844, 1998.

[29] K. C. Lee, J. Ho, and D. Kriegman, "Acquiring linear subspaces for face recognition under variable lighting," *IEEE Transaction Pattern Analysis and Machine Intelligence*, vol. 27, no. 5, pp. 684–698, 2005.

[30] NIST 2005 Speaker Recognition Evaluation plan, http://www.nist.gov/speech/tests/spk/2005/sre-05_evalplan-v6.pdf.

[31] T. Hasan and J. H. L. Hansen, "Acoustic factor analysis for robust speaker verification," *IEEE Trans. Audio, Speech, and Lang. Process.*, vol. 21, no.4, pp.842-853, Apr. 2013.

[32] L. Zhang, W. D. Zhou, P. C. Chang, J. Liu, Z. Yan, T. Wang, and F. Z. Li, "Kernel sparse representation-based classifier," *IEEE Trans. Signal Processing*, vol. 60, no. 4, pp. 1684–1695, Apr. 2012.

[33] A. Kanagasundaram, D. Dean, R. Vogt, M. McLaren, S. Sridharan, M. Mason, "Weighted LDA techniques for i-vector based speaker verification," *IEEE International Conference on Acoustics, Speech and Signal Processing*, pp. 4781–4784, 2012.

[34] J. Wright, A. Ganesh, S. Rao, and Y. Ma, "Robust Principal Component Analysis: Exact Recovery of Corrupted Low-Rank Matrices via Convex Optimization," Submitted to the Journal of the ACM, 2009.

利用核依賴估計來進行多軌自動混音

Automatic Multi-track Mixing by Kernel Dependency Estimation

吳宗庭　Tsung Ting Wu
國立中央大學資訊工程研究所
Department of Computer Science and Information Engineering
National Central University
101522015@cc.ncu.edu.tw

張嘉惠　Chia-Hui Chang
國立中央大學資訊工程研究所
Department of Computer Science and Information Engineering
National Central University
chia@csie.ncu.edu.tw

摘要

近年來由於數位音樂的蓬勃發展，錄音器材越來越普及。使得非混音專業人士也能利用錄音界面(Audio Interface)錄製出不錯的成品；但是一旦錄製了多軌(Multi-Track Recording)就會面臨到混音(Mixing)的問題，即需要把多軌的聲音混合在同一個軌中。混音牽扯到許多音響及聲學心理學的相關技術與知識，非專業人士要混出尚可的成品有一定的難度，所以我們提出了自動多軌混音系統(Automatic Multi-track Mixing System)，希望藉由監督式學習的方式學習各軌間混音參數的調配，產生每首的基礎混音(Basic mix-down)來幫助非混音專業人士也能混出不錯的成品(Mix-down)。由於混音參數取得不易，我們會先藉由分軌及混音好的關係估計出各個混音參數，接著利用其參數進行混音模型(Model)的建立。在參數學習(Parameter Learning)方面由於每軌的混音參數是有依賴關係的(Dependency)，我們採用了核依賴估計(Kernel Dependency Estimation)[1]的參數學習(Parameter Learning)方式來預測每軌的混音參數。

Abstract

Due to the revolution of digital music, people can create recordings in a home studio with cheaper gear. However multi-track recordings need to be mixed to combine them into one or more channels. The question is that mixing requires background knowledge in sound engineering and psychoacoustics. It is difficult to get good mixdown for non-specialist in sound engineer. In this paper, we use supervised learning method for automatically mixing multi-track recording into coherent and well-balanced piece. Due to lack of mixing parameters, first we estimate the weight of mixing parameters by using the relation between raw multi-track and mixdown. Given the mixing parameters for any music genre, we use kernel decency estimation method to create our mixing model. The experiment show KDE is able to make a more satisfactory estimation than treating each parameter independently.

關鍵詞：核依賴估計，音樂資訊檢索，音樂製作，混音

Keywords: Kernel Dependency Estimation, Music IR, Music Production, Mixing.

一、 緒論

在音樂的製作(Music Production)上大致分為三個階段，創作編曲(Pre-Production)、聲音錄製(Production)、後製(Post-Production)。其中後製又分為混音(Mixing)及母帶後製(Mastering)兩部分; 混音在音樂製作上是個非常重要的過程; 其主要的工作是要把先前錄製好的多軌(Multi-Track)的聲音，如人聲、吉他、爵士鼓等聲軌混合進同一個立體聲軌(stereo channel)或單聲軌(Mono Channel)中。

近年來由於數位音樂的蓬勃發展，錄音器材越來越普及。使得非混音專業人士也能利用錄音界面(Audio Interface)錄製出不錯的成品; 但是一旦錄製了多軌(Multi-Track Recording)就會面臨到混音(Mixing)的問題，即需要把多軌的聲音混合在同一個軌中; 混音牽扯到許多音響及聲學心理學的相關技術與知識，非專業人士要混出尚可的成品有一定的難度，混出來的結果往往會照成整首歌聆聽的清晰度降低、聲音不扎實、音量落差太大、空間感不夠、聲音雜亂等問題; 而且混音的處理方式基本上會隨著樂器、音樂類型而有所不同，不同的音樂類型會有不同的混音風格(Mixing Style)，這更加增加了一般非專業人士學習混音的難度。所以要如何藉由電腦來幫助混音便是本篇論文的目標。接下來將會詳細介紹混音的相關背景知識。

1.1 混音(Mixing)

混音在音樂製作上是非常重要的過程，不同的混音方式在最後的成品上會有截然不同的模樣。混音的好壞會影響整首歌的表現，好的混音可以掩蓋瑕疵、放大優點，提升整體的質感。在混音的過程中，混音師(Mixing Engineer)會依照各音軌/樂器間的頻率(Frequency) 、響度(loudness) 、音色、音場定位(Panoramic Position) 、空間感等聲音元素加以調配，以讓每個音軌(track)/樂器最佳化，讓每個音軌在最後混在一起時一樣能保持清晰，保有層次，使得音樂呈現更生動、更動聽。

在開始混音前，混音師會先作混音規劃(Mixing Design)，規劃整首歌的音像(Sound Image)，決定每個音軌在整首歌裡的定位以及其重要性。如下圖 1 為一首爵士樂的混音規劃示意圖，我們可以發現在這首歌中人聲(Vocal)設計在音像的正中間，吉他(Guitar)分別落在人聲的左右; 音量方面主吉他(Lead Guitar)略大於人聲等等，混音的過程中主要就是調配這些音量(Volume)、等化(Equalization)、擺位(Pan)來達成我們的混音規劃讓整體更加和諧，讓個樂器融入其中。

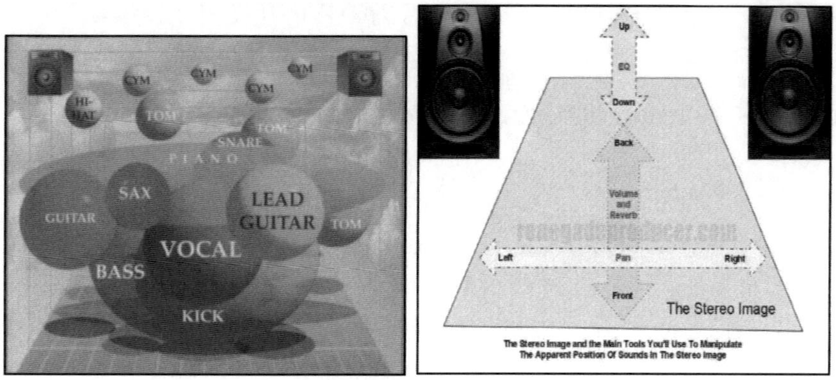

圖 1 混音設計示意圖：人聲(Vocal)居中 圖片來源：
The Art of Mixing – David Gibson

1.2 研究動機(Motivation)

在自動混音(Automatic Mixing)的研究中，大多都是利用聲音特徵間的關係估計以及預測其混音的參數，所使用的聲音長度大多為一首歌中 30 秒的片段，最後所混音出來的成品當然也會相似於這 30 秒的片段。但是混音實際上是會因為橋段的不同而有不同的混音方式的，例如在主歌(Verse)與副歌(Chorus)的混音方式會是不一樣的，後者其橋段通常為歌曲中激昂的部份，配器使用會前者多，在音量或頻率上比例會有所不同。

再者歌曲音樂類型也會影響混音的方式，同樣是爵士鼓在流行歌與爵士樂中音色與其占有的比例也會有所不同，同樣的樂器在不同的音樂類型中會有不同的音色以及角色，例如，在爵士樂中鼓手也可以是樂曲中的主角，在流行歌中主角往往是人聲或是電吉他。所以若利用 30 秒片段建立的模型來套用在整首歌曲的混音將會造成整首歌較平淡無味;在 Jeffrey Scott et al.[2]的訪問中也有提到，混音其實是個別的(Case By Case)，混音師基本上都會依照各音軌的聲響、音樂類型不同而有不同的處理方式，再者音樂感受是非常主觀的，不同的人會有不同的偏好，所以比較難去訂出一個通則(General Rule)來進行混音。

一個混音模型包括音量、頻率(Equalization)、樂器擺位(Panning)等多個參數，大多數的研究都是獨立的去預測各軌的混音參數，如多線性迴歸，利用各軌特徵間的關係去建立各軌的迴歸模型。但實際上每軌間的混音參數是有依賴關係的(Dependency)，舉例來說有一軌的音量上升勢必就會有一軌的音量下降，這樣整首歌的音量才不會忽大忽小，若是對各軌獨立去建立其模型的話，最後的成品將會喪失其依賴關係。所以在參數預測的方法選用上我們認為需要考慮到依賴性的問題。

由以上三點，本篇論文採用對不同的音樂類型不同的橋段，利用和依賴估計(Kernel Dependency Estimation)[1]的方法來建立最後的模型。首先我們會先需要使用者先提供一些該歌曲的訊息，例如音樂形態、橋段、分軌的樂器標籤等等，接著在對個別的橋段套用該音樂類型的核依賴模型預測出混音參數後即完成混音。(圖 2)

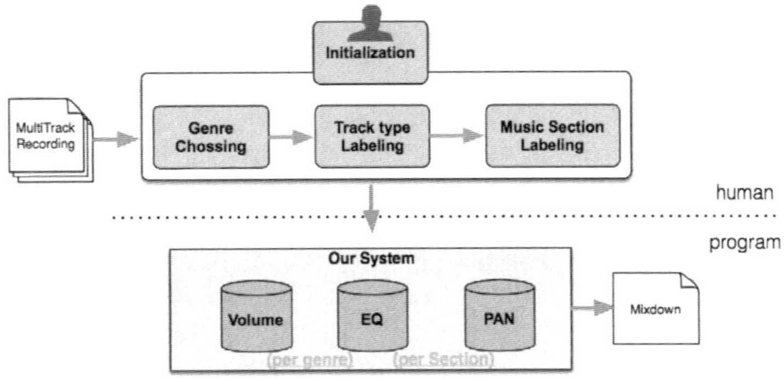

圖 2 系統使用概念圖

本篇論文的架構如下，第二章將會討論自動混音的相關研究，第三章則會介紹本篇論文的研究方法及所使用的資料集，第四章為實驗，我們會對我們的混音模型去做交叉驗(Cross validation) 來評估模型的正確性以及依賴性的功用，第五章為結論以及未來工作。

二、 相關研究

在介紹混音參數預測模型之前，我們必須設法取得一些歌曲的混音參數以作為訓練資料，不過混音參數在實際上是難以取得的，由於混音師使用的軟體不同，不同的器材/軟體會有不同的設定、基準及刻度，這讓得到混音參數這一類的資訊變得非常困難， 且混音師在混音時也鮮少會把參數記錄下來。所以在多軌混音(Multitrack Mixing)的相關 研究中大部份的研究著重於如何估計出混音參數，包括：音量(Volume)、頻率(Frequency)、 動態(Dynamic)等等。另一部份的研究著重在如何建立混音參數模型。

2.1. 混音基本元素(Basic Factor of Mixing)

在混音的過程中音量平衡是件很重要的事，混音師(Mixing Engineer)會調整每個音軌間彼此之間的音量(圖 1)，決定各軌在這首歌中的音量比例，即是決定各軌在音像(Image)的前後順序; 若其中一音軌的音量比其他音軌還要大很多的話，整首歌將會聽起來頭重腳輕。

在音色修正的過程中，混音師(Mixing Engineer)會用到等化器(Equalizer, EQ)的工具來去對每個音軌的頻率做修正調整。例如我們發現吉他的音色跟其他的樂器相比太亮太尖銳，以至於無法融入這首歌中，我們就可以用等化器去對吉他的高頻部分做衰減(cut)。頻率間的平衡在混音過程中也是重要的過程之一。

樂器擺位是將錄製好的聲音訊號放置於新的雙聲道或多聲道的聲場(Sound Field)。由於我們一般音響設備的環境基本上是以雙聲道為主(stereo)，雙聲道的混音可以在聆聽上增加平面的聽感，而不是只有一點;所以我們在混音的時候會決定各樂器的擺位，看是要擺在中間還是擺在靠近左聲道/左喇叭還是右聲道/右喇叭等等來增加整體的空間感，而非全部的樂器都擠在一起。在實作上即是分別調整左聲道與右聲道的音量，如下(1)式

$$Left\_output = cos(p)*input$$

$$Right\_output = sin(p)*input \quad (1)$$

其中 p 為偏離中央點的角度，*Left_output, Right_output* 分別為左聲道右聲道的輸出。

2.2. 混音參數估計(Mixing Parameter Estimation)

如前一節研究動機所提到，由於混音參數難以取得，我們需要利用原始分軌和混音成品(Mixdown)間的關係來估計出每首歌的混音參數。在 Jeffrey Scott et al. [2]的研究中，他們採用了訪問(interview)的方式，訪問了線上的混音師(Mixing Engineer)了解他們如何混音、如何處理聲音，利用訪問後得到的一些通則來當作他們最後混音模型建立的依據。在大部分自動混音(Automatic Mixing)的研究中[3, 4]，在混音參數估計上大多是假設其分軌和混音成品是聲音特徵(Sound Feature)的線性組合關係，如圖 3 所示 X_i 為第 i 聲軌的特徵向量，β_i 為第 i 軌之混音參數權重，y 為混音成品的特徵向量。利用最小平方法的方式(Least Square Method)最小化 y 至 col(X)平面的距離來做各音軌混音參數權重估計。

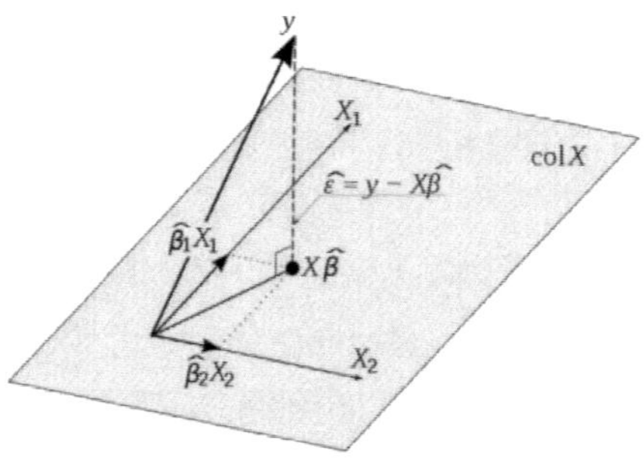

圖 3 最小平方法

由於採用線性組合的假設，每軌間彼此要是線性獨立(Linearly independent)的，這會影響最後聲音特徵的選用以及音軌的選擇，選擇含有較多串音的音軌(例如錄製 overhead 時會連大鼓小鼓等其他鼓組的聲音一併錄進)，在實務上因為包含多個樂器的聲音，使得音軌間彼此並非獨立會造成其估計結果會有誤差。

2.3. 混音參數預測

參數預測大多是採用機器學習(Machine Learning)上參數預測(Parameter Prediction)的方法，如[3] [5]採用了多線性迴歸(Multiple Linear Regression)方法，利用大量的 sample 建立最後的回歸模型，利用最佳化的方法去最小化分軌及成品間的尤拉距離(Euclidean Distance); 在[3]中同時利用了 Linear Dynamic System 的方法，將混音參數視為一個潛藏的狀態(Latent State)，利用聲音特徵當作動態系統的輸出。另外在[6]採用了不一樣的方式，利用_例子混音_(Mixing by Example)。其概念類似理髮師的概念，混音前提供例子供使用者選擇，最後藉由複製該例子的混音設計(Copy Mixing Design)的方式來達成混音。

三、　研究方法

本系統主要流程如下圖 4 所示，我們會先把原始的分軌錄音檔依照使用者提供該音樂的資訊做前處理，接下來做聲音特徵的擷取(Feature Extraction)以便之後模型(Model)的訓練及測試。由於不同的類型、不同橋段的音樂會有不同的混音方式，在模型建立時我們會特別依照不同的音樂類型建立個別的混音參數模型，在依不同的橋段去建立模型，如圖 5 我們會對 ROCK 的的音樂類型建立 Intro、Verse、Chorus，POP 音樂類型也建立其三個橋段的模型，以此類推。訓練(Training)的部分有兩大步驟; 第一步驟是混音參數估計(Parameter Estimation)，由於混音參數難以取得，原始訓練資料中也無此資訊，我們會先利用原始分軌錄音和混音成品(Mixdown)做最小平方法估計(Least Square Estimation)，藉此來估計出訓練資料中每首歌的混音參數的權重(Weight of Mixing Parameter)　。

第二步驟是核依賴估計(Kernel Dependency Estimation)的模型建立，我們會利用每首歌的混音參數權重及特徵向量來當作訓練核依賴估計(Kernel Dependency Estimation)的依據，訓練好的模型將會用來預測各個混音參數的權重。最後依照模型預測出的權重進行混音。

在接下來的章節我們會詳細介紹各步驟的做法，在章節 3.1 會先對我們所使用的資料集(Data Set)做介紹以及前處理的部分。章節 3.2 會介紹我們如何利用最小平方法來估計各個混音參數及為何需要做混音參數估計。章節 3.3 我們會介紹核依賴估計(下面簡稱 KDE)的核心概念以及在本篇論文的問題中該如何設計。

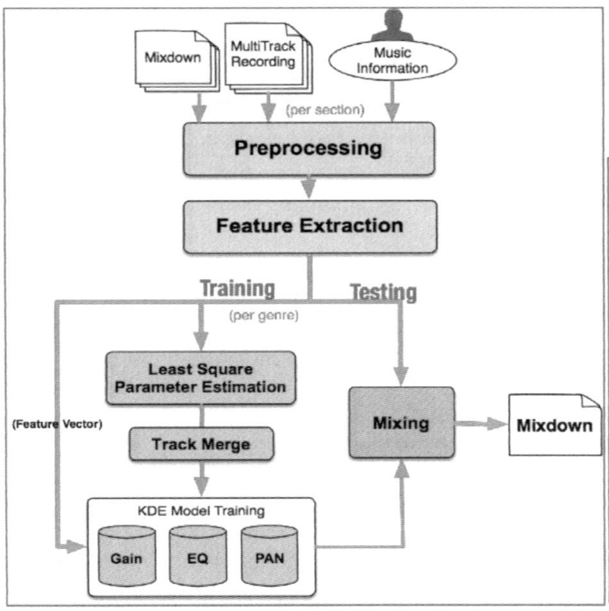

圖 4 系統架構圖

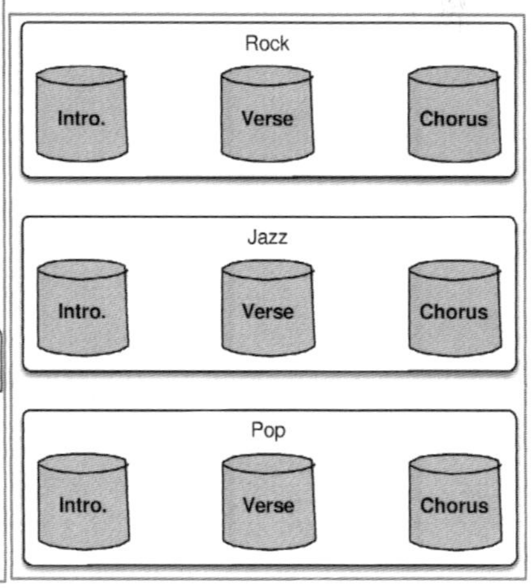

圖 5 混音參數模型

3.1 資料集 (DATASET)

我們使用的資料集(Data Set)是來自國外一本關於混音的專門書籍_Mixing Secrets for Small Studio_[7]，此書有提供多首原始分軌檔案給讀者用於混音練習用，其含括的音樂類型搖滾、爵士、鄉村等多種音樂類型，如下表 1 所示，此書將相似的音樂類型分成四大類。此資料集較特別的點在於提供的聲音檔案長度是整首歌(Full Multitrack)，一般以往音樂資訊探勘(Music Information Retrieval)研究所使用的資料集大多是 20~30 sec 的長度，鮮少有提供整首歌的資料集。此特點有利於幫助我們對於不同的音樂橋段(Music Section)去建立不同的模型，來讓最後的模型能更適用於實際的情況，此資料集所提供的混音成品(Mixdown) 一樣也是整首歌的長度。 檔案格式為無損 WAV 檔(uncompressed WAV files, 24bit and 44.1 kHz sample rate)。

表 1 音樂類型統計表

Genre	# of Song
Alt Rock / Blues / Country Rock / Indie / Funk / Reggae	7
Rock / Punk / Metal	17
Pop / Singer-Songwriter	10
Acoustic / Jazz / Country / Orchestral	8
Total	42

資料集前處理的部分，由於此資料集涵蓋的音樂類型包括 Alt Rock/Blues、Rock/Punk、Pop/Singer-Songwriter、Acoustic/Jazz/Country 等，每個音樂類型所使用的配器會略有不同，例如在爵士樂中管樂器的使用比例會比搖滾樂來的高。這樣會造成之後無法將此資料集套用至我們的模型中。所以為了解決此問題我們統計了各音樂類型所使用的配器，決定出每個類型基本音軌(Basic Track)如表 2，我們定義了 12 種音軌的形態。前處理的部分會先對分軌做音樂格式上的轉換，待每首歌的混音參數權重估計出來後會做基本軌的合併(Track Merge)，將同一類型的音軌依照其權重先合併成該類型基本音軌，將同一類型的檔案先合併成一個;例如在某一首歌中吉他錄了兩把，我們會先將這兩把的錄音合併成一個，以方便之後訓練及測試該類型的音樂。

表 2 基本軌表

12 Basic Track Type					
(1)Kick	(2)Snare	(3)Hihat	(4)TOM	(5)DrumRoom	(6)OVERHEAD
(7)PERCUSSION	(8)BASS	(9)Electric Guitar	(10)Acoustic Guitar	(11)LeadVox.	(12)BackVox

3.2 混音參數估計 (PARAMETER ESTIMATION)

我們的系統最終的目的是要希望藉由訓練資料(Training Data)來對每一種混音參數 建立一個模型，藉由每一軌的特徵來預測其參數的值。所以訓練的過程中勢必需要原始的分軌檔案及最後各混音的參數來進行監督式學習(Supervised Learning)。但是實際上混音參數的資訊是非常難取得的。由於混音師使用的軟體不同，不同的器材/軟體會有不同的設定、基準及刻度，而且混音師在混音時也鮮少會把參數記錄下來，這讓得到混音參數這一類的資訊的取得變得非常困難。為了之後的監督式學習，我們必須先估計出資料集中每首歌的混音參數， 利用原始分軌檔案(Raw Multi-track) 及最後混音成品(Mixdown)來估計出每首歌的混音參數，針對每一首歌求得其混音參數當作之後監督式學習(Supervised Learning)的依據。

為了從原始分軌檔案估計出其混音參數，我們假設原始分軌與最後混音的成品(Final Mix)的關係是一個線性的組合(Linear Combination)，如下(2)式為一首歌的線性組合關係。

$$\alpha_1 U_1+\alpha_2 U_2+\ldots\ldots+\alpha_k U_k=V \quad (2)$$

α_i 為第 i 軌的混音參數權重，$U_i = [u_{1i}, u_{2i}, \ldots, u_{Ni}]^T$ 為第 i 軌特徵向量， V為最後混音結果的特徵向量(Feature Vector)，每一軌抽取 N 個 frames 做為其代表。其中在不同的混音參數會用不同的聲音特徵，例如在音量參數方面會採用聲音的方均根來當作衡量的依據，頻率參數方面會採用聲音的頻譜(Spectrum)等等。利用此線性組合的關係，我們可以利用最小平方法(Least Square Method)來估計出混音參數 的數值，最小平方法(Least Square Method) 是以觀測值 U 與預測值 α 之差的平方和作為最佳化的目標函數(Objective Function)。以音量參數為例，令 u_{Nk} 為第 k 軌第 n 個音框(Frame)的方均根值(RMS)，每個音框長度約為 20 毫秒，則(1)即可表示為

$$\begin{bmatrix} u_{11} & u_{12} & u_{13} & \cdots & u_{1k} \\ u_{21} & u_{22} & \cdots & \cdots & u_{2k} \\ \vdots & \vdots & & & \vdots \\ \vdots & \vdots & & & \vdots \\ u_{N1} & \cdots & \cdots & \cdots & u_{Nk} \end{bmatrix} \begin{bmatrix} \alpha_1 \\ \alpha_2 \\ \vdots \\ \vdots \\ \alpha_k \end{bmatrix} \approx \begin{bmatrix} v_1 \\ v_2 \\ \vdots \\ \vdots \\ v_N \end{bmatrix} \quad (3)$$

在混音時由於混音的參數眾多，本篇論文只討論了其中三個最重要參數：Volume、Frequency、Pan，在估計不同的參數時我們會使用不同的聲音特徵。接下來會對各參數所用的特徵來做介紹

音量 (VOLUME)

音量參數也被稱作增益(Gain)，主要在控制每個音軌間的音量使得整體音量達成平衡。本篇論文使用了方均根(Root Mean Square)的方式去測量同一個音框(Frame)中各音軌的聲壓(Sound Pressure Level)，以此作為音量參數的特徵向量，寫成矩陣形式如(4)式。G_k 為第 k 軌的權重，N 為音框的長度。

$$\begin{bmatrix} RMS_{11} & RMS_{12} & RMS_{13} & \cdots & RMS_{1k} \\ RMS_{21} & RMS_{22} & \cdots & \cdots & RMS_{2k} \\ \vdots & \vdots & & & \vdots \\ \vdots & \vdots & & & \vdots \\ RMS_{N1} & \cdots & \cdots & \cdots & RMS_{Nk} \end{bmatrix} \begin{bmatrix} g_1 \\ g_2 \\ \vdots \\ \vdots \\ g_k \end{bmatrix} \approx \begin{bmatrix} V_{RMS_1} \\ V_{RMS_2} \\ \vdots \\ \vdots \\ V_{RMS_N} \end{bmatrix} \quad (4)$$

頻率(Frequency)

頻率參數即是控制整首歌中各音軌在頻率上的平衡。在混音過程中為了修正音軌的音色或頻率時會用到等化器來幫助我們對聲音的頻率作調整，也就是說頻率參數即是等化器(Equalizer)參數。在設計等化器時會先將整個頻譜切成多段(Multi-band)，如切成三塊的話即是高頻、中頻、低頻。接著選出各頻段的中心頻率(Center Frequency)及頻寬(bandwidth)後即完成設計。本篇論文在頻率參數方面一樣採用多頻段等化方式(Multi-band Equalization)來模擬實際等化器的操作，即是把頻率參數估計的問題切成了多個聲音參數的子問題。如下圖 6 所示。

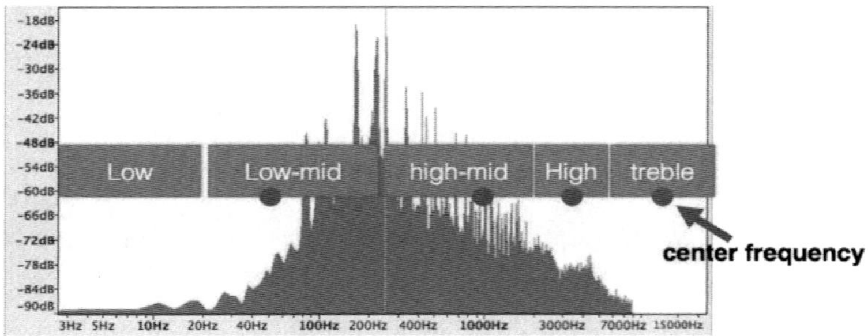

圖 6 多頻段頻譜

在進行頻率參數估計時，我們會先用快速傅立葉轉換(Fast Fourier Transform)先得到各音軌的頻譜(Spectrum)，接著把各音軌的頻譜依照我們預先分段的頻率分別去解迴歸問題(Regression Problem)，以估計出各頻段在各軌間的平衡參數。如下(5)式

$$\begin{aligned}
&\alpha_{Treble_1}U_{Treble_1}+\alpha_{Treble_2}U_{Treble_2}+\cdots+\alpha_{Treble_k}U_{Treble_k}=V_{Treble}\\
&\alpha_{High_1}U_{High_1}+\alpha_{High_2}U_{High_2}+\cdots+\alpha_{High_k}U_{High_k}=V_{High}\\
&\alpha_{H\text{-}mid_1}U_{H\text{-}mid_1}+\alpha_{H\text{-}mid_2}U_{H\text{-}mid_2}+\cdots+\alpha_{H\text{-}mid_k}U_{H\text{-}mid_k}=V_{H\text{-}mid}\\
&\alpha_{L\text{-}mid_1}U_{L\text{-}mid_1}+\alpha_{L\text{-}mid_2}U_{L\text{-}mid_2}+\cdots+\alpha_{L\text{-}mid_k}U_{L\text{-}mid_k}=V_{L\text{-}mid}\\
&\alpha_{Low_1}U_{Low_1}+\alpha_{Low_2}U_{Low_2}+\cdots+\alpha_{Low_k}U_{Low_k}=V_{Low}
\end{aligned} \tag{5}$$

樂器擺位(PANNING)

樂器擺位即是決定該音軌在左聲道及右聲道之音量比例，如式(1)。在本篇論文我們將擺位參數的問題轉化成前一章節音量參數估計的問題，即左聲道做一次音量參數估計，右聲道做一次音量參數估計，這樣即可決定該音軌在左右聲道之比例，如下式(6)、(7)所示。

$$\alpha_1 u_{L1}+\alpha_2 u_{L2}+\ldots\ldots+\alpha_k u_{Lk}=V \tag{6}$$

$$\alpha_1 u_{R1}+\alpha_2 u_{R2}+\ldots\ldots+\alpha_k u_{RK}=V \tag{7}$$

3.3 核依賴估計模型建立(Kernel Dependency Estimation Model)

估計完資料集中每首歌的三種混音參數(Volume、EQ、Panning)後，我們有了每首歌的特徵向量(X)，及每首歌的混音參數(Y)，即可藉由學習出 X, Y 間的關係建立我們最後的混音模型。在模型建立的部分我們會依照不同的音樂類型，不同的音樂橋段建立一組模型，其中一組模型包括了音量模型兩個(左聲道、右聲道)，頻率模型五個(5

sub-band)。利用此模型建立的方法讓最後的成品更能應用在實際的歌曲中，訓練模型的樣本數我們自各訓練歌曲中隨機抽取 3000 個樣本來當作我們的訓練資料。如圖 7，u_{nk} 為該模型的第 n 個樣本的第 k 軌的聲音特徵值， $_{nk}$ 為第 n 個樣本之第 K 軌的混音參數權重值;K 為分軌的個數，在本篇論文為 12。

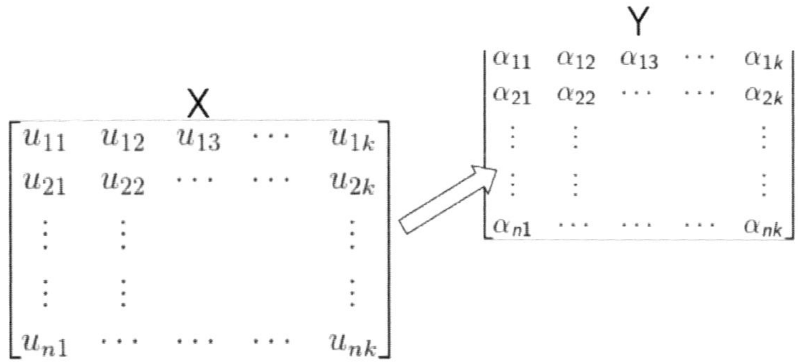

圖 7 混音參數預測示意圖

這個問題基本上是可以利用常見的參數預測(Parameter Prediction)的方法分別去求解，例如多線性迴歸(Multiple Linear Regression)、動態線性系統(Linear Dynamic System);但是由於在混音時每一軌間的參數間是有互相影響的，其中一軌的音量變大後勢必其他軌會變小聲些，彼此是依賴關係的(dependent)。若用各別訓練模型來預測我們的混音參數的話，我們將會得到 k 個獨立的迴歸模型，這對於混音結果可能會產生較不和諧的影響。所以本篇論文採用了核依賴估計的方式來解決上述的問題，用核依賴估計訓練出我們最後的模型。接下來將會先介紹核依賴估計的基本精神。

3.3.1 核依賴估計(Kernel Dependency Estimation)

核依賴估計(以下簡稱 KDE)是一種用於尋找輸入 X 與輸出 Y 間依賴關係的學習架構，KDE 的流程如下圖 8 所示，步驟主要分為三個步驟：

1. 投影(Projection)：對輸出 Y 做主成份分析(Principal Component Analysis)，將輸出 Y 也就是參數向量 $y_i \in R^k$ 投影至 m 個主成份(Principal Component)所形成的空間上，即對輸出 Y 做降維的動作，投影至較低的維度下形成 Y ˘。

2. 學習(Learning The Map)：對每個基礎原件(Principal Component)j，1HjHm ，我們會 學習一個對應函數(Mapping Function)r_j(X)，對應函數 r 會將會把 X 對應至 Y ˘第 j 個基礎原件，即是在較低的空間上去解 m 個迴歸問題。

3. 預測(Prediction)：對於一個新的輸入 x˘，我們可以利用先前學習好的對應函數求出 y˘˘ = [r_1(x˘) r_2(x˘)ǔ ..r_m(x˘)]，y˘˘ ∈R^m。最後再將 Y ˘˘投影回原本的空間上，即求出 X ˘所對應的Y值。

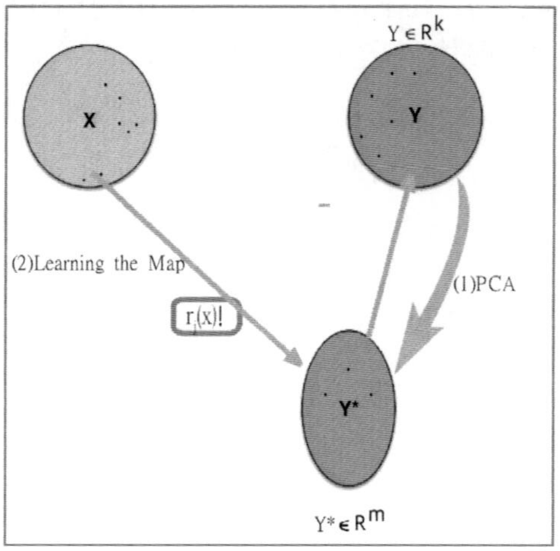

圖 8 KDE 示意圖

用於本篇論文的主題來說，我們的X就是我們每首分軌的聲音特徵向量，Y 就是我們原先估計出來的混音參數 $Y \in R^k$，在 KDE 的過程中我們會先將 Y 降維至 m 維的 PCA 空間上，接著在 m 維的空間上我們去學習 m 個基礎原件的對應函數。在對應函數方面我們使用了 ridge regression 的方法來解決 m 個迴歸問題。在做預測時，新的一首歌分軌特徵向量 x˘，會先利用先前學習的 m 個對應函數 r_j 求出 y˘˘， $y˘˘ \in R^m$，接著再將 y˘˘ 投影回原本的 k 維空間上即求出各軌混音參數權重。

四、 實驗

實驗分為三個部分作討論，第一部分的實驗是評估由核依賴估計所建立的模型的正確性; 第二部分是評估 KDE 依賴性(Dependency)的效果，比較不同的 m 值對模型正確性的影響程度; 第三部分是評估不同的音樂類型混音方式的差異性。實驗評估的方式是利用一次挑一個交叉驗證對同一音樂類型的歌做均方誤差(Mean Square Error)評估。均方誤差的計算方式如下：

$$MSE = \frac{1}{n}\sum_{i=1}^{n}(\widehat{\alpha}_i - \alpha_i)^2 \qquad (8)$$

$\widehat{\alpha}$代表由 KDE 模型所預測的混音參數權重， 是由參數估計得出實際的混音參數權重值。

4.1一次一個交叉測試(Leave-one-out Cross Validation)

表 3 為每個音樂類型副歌音量參數的一次一個交叉驗證(Leave-one-out Cross Validation)的結果，其值為 KDE 模型所預測的值與實際混音參數權重的均方誤差值(Mean Square Error)，測試時會先對測試歌曲做隨機抽樣 3000 個樣本來做測試，m 值皆為 8。由表可知由 KDE 所訓練出的模型均方誤差平均大約落在 0.129 左右的數值，預測出的權重有著還不錯的準確度，但由於是採用隨機抽樣的方式，若抽到的聲音樣本為較

安靜的樣本(即是說在該樣本的當時有較多軌音量是趨近於 0)時會導致均方誤差值飆高，形成 Outlier，如搖滾類中的第 17 首的結果。

表 3 副歌音量模型交叉驗證結果

	Rock/Metal	POP	Jazz/Country	Alt Rock/Funk
song1	0.137	0.043	0.145	0.027
song2	0.148	0.224	0.005	0.087
song3	0.192	0.057	0.018	0.040
song4	0.172	0.030	0.018	0.053
song5	0.205	0.056	0.138	0.038
song6	0.035	0.070	0.037	0.426
song7	0.166	0.067	0.017	0.018
song8	0.135	0.055		
song9	0.052			
song10	0.120			
song11	0.199			
song12	0.040			
song13	0.092			
song14	0.048			
song15	0.269			
song16	0.748			
song17	**2.175**			
Mean	0.290	0.075	0.054	0.099

圖 9 是其中一種音樂類型中副歌(Chorus)交叉驗證的詳細圖表，X 軸代表其隨機抽樣測試的聲音樣本(Sound Sample)， Y 軸為其所對應均方誤差，圖表中同樣顏色的線條代表同一首歌的聲音樣本。可以發現 KDE 所訓練出的模型在對同一首歌的聲音樣本時會有一致效果。

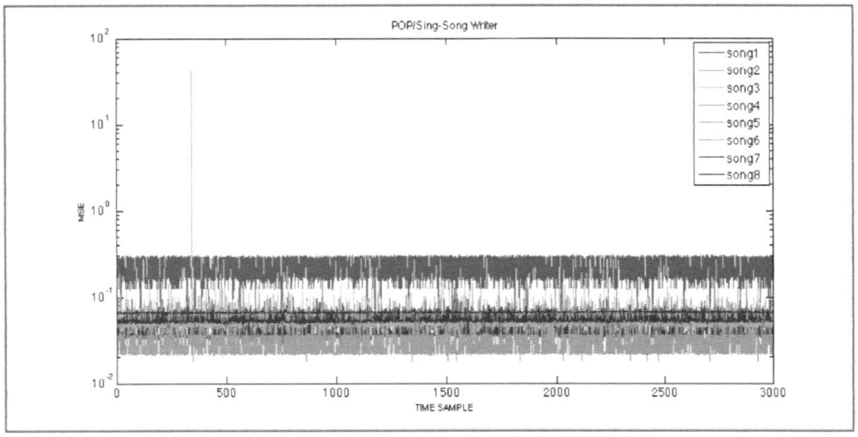

圖 9 POP/Sing-Song writer

在另一方面由音軌的觀點來看，如圖 10，我們可以發現在 Kick、DrumRoom、Overhead 等音軌上各類型會有較大的誤差出現，其原因要歸咎於在實際上多軌同步錄音(Multi-track Recording)時，單一軌也會參雜著其他軌的聲音(串音)，如 Overhead、DrumRoom 等軌會包含 kick、snare 等其他鼓組的樂器。此原因違反了當初研究方法一開始的假設: 我們假設分軌即混音成品間是個線性組合的關係，分軌間必須要是線性獨立; 但由於串音的因素會導致估計及預測有效果不佳的情形。

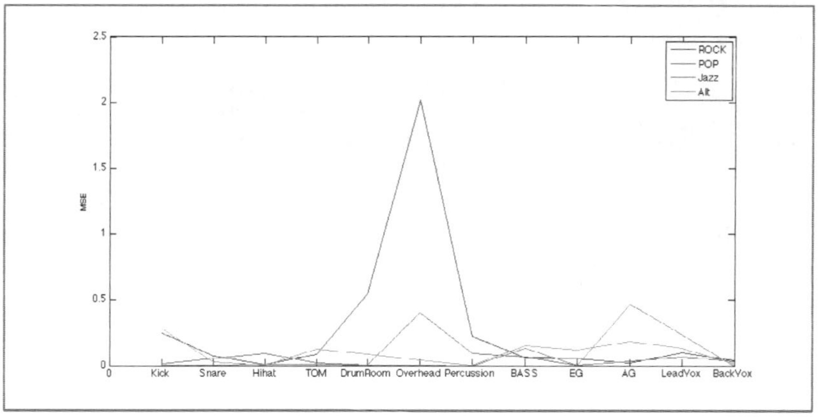

圖 10 音軌比較圖

在頻率(Equalization)模型方面我們同樣也作了交叉驗證，由表中可知大致上各分軌的準確率約為 0.015，顯示在頻率參數預測上有著較好的表現。

表 4 頻率模型交叉驗證

	Rock/Metal	POP	Jazz/Country	Alt Rock/Funk
Kick	0.011	0.019	0.003	0.008
Snare	0.043	0.015	0.011	0.018
Hihat	0.003	0.001	0.020	0.021
TOM	0.008	0.017	0.013	0.007
DRUMROOM	0.013	0.004	0.036	0.001
OVERHEAD	0.017	0.028	0.003	0.046
PERCUSSION	0.008	0.006	0.025	0.005
BASS	0.011	0.007	0.004	0.017
EG	0.006	0.019	0.024	0.005
AG	0.000	0.004	0.015	0.006
LEADVOX	0.021	0.013	0.005	0.025
BACKVOX	0.002	0.003	0.032	0.017
Mean	**0.012**	**0.011**	**0.016**	**0.015**

4.2 KDE 方法的效果(Effect of KDE Method)

第二部分的實驗是要來評估 KDE 即其依賴性的成效，首先我們討論了不同的 m 值所帶來的影響，結果如下圖 11，為 ROCK 在副歌時不同 m 值的均方差，X 軸為不同的 m 值，Y 為所對應其混音。我們可以發現當 m 值越低 KDE 模型會有較好的結果，較低的 m 值也可加速 KDE 的計算(eg.PCA space 從 R^{12} 降低為 R^{8})。這結果也顯示了依賴性對於混音參數預測的幫助。

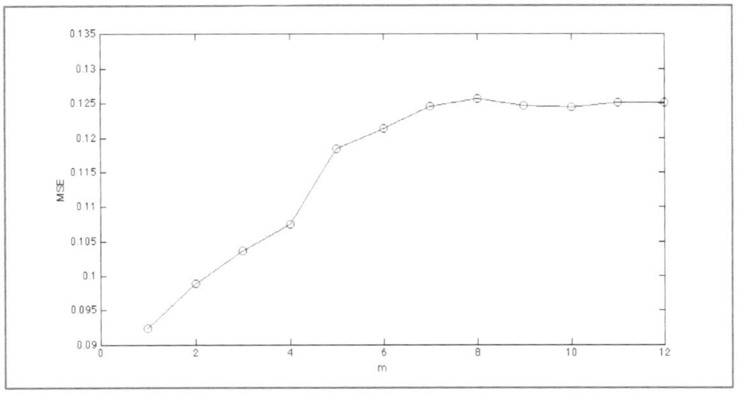

圖 11 不同 m 值比較

接著我們實作了相關研究中[3]所使用的多線性迴歸(無考慮依賴性)與本篇論文的 KDE(考慮依賴性)的方法做比較，結果如下圖 12，可發現在大多數的軌上 KDE 比多線性迴歸有較好的表現。顯示其依賴性估計方式較能考量各軌之間的平衡。

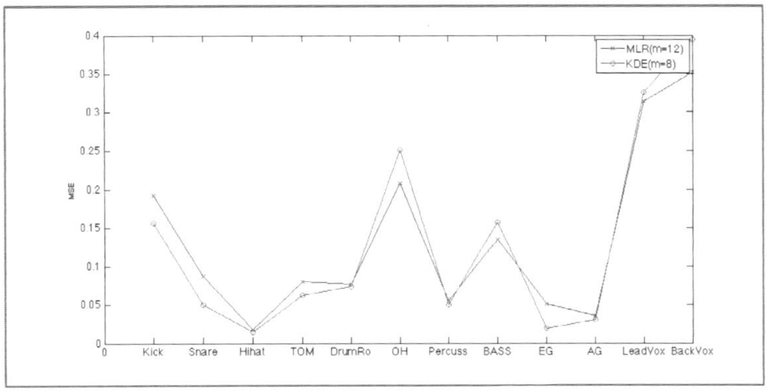

圖 12 KDE 與 MLR 比較圖

4.3 跨類型測試(Cross Genre Testing)

在第一部分的實驗模型的建立以及測試都侷限在同一個音樂類型中，在第三部分的實驗，我們想要評估不同的音樂風格的音樂是否有其混音特色，我們將會套用由不同類型所訓練出的模型來看看其效果是否有差別。結果如下圖 13，X 軸分別是先前定義的基本軌，Y 軸是其對應的均方誤差值，當中測試資料為 ROCK 這一類的歌，一共有 17 首，圖中的線條為分別用 POP、jazz、Alt Rock 所訓練出的模型套用至 ROCK 類別的測試結果。我們可以發現將別的類別的模型套用在不同類型的歌時會導致模型的正確度下降、誤差增大，如圖中的 POP 與 JAZZ 的結果，兩類別的模型套用在 ROCK 音樂上其結果顯示不太適合。我們也發現音樂類型相似的歌其混音方式會較相近如圖中 ROCK 與 Alt ROCK 的均方誤差值較為接近。經由此實驗我們可以得知不同的音樂類型有其不同的混音方式，所訓練出來的模型有其獨特性。

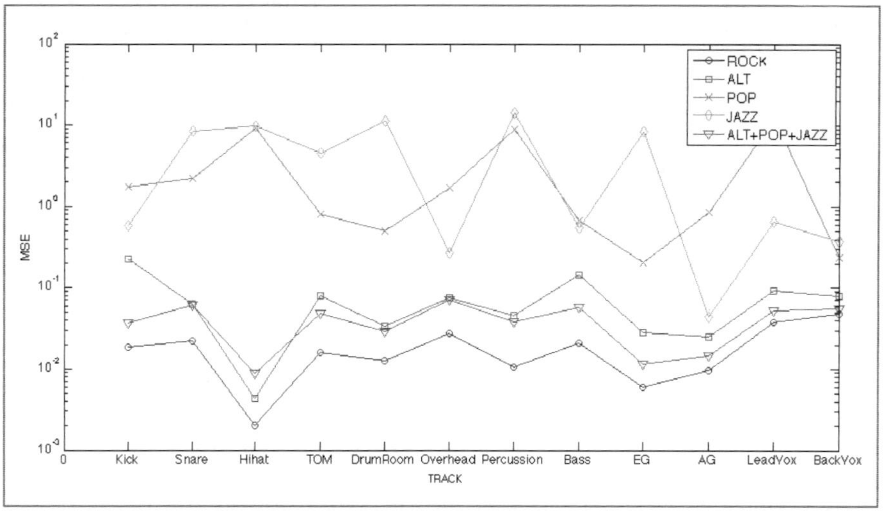

圖 13 類別交叉驗證

五、 結論與未來工作

在音樂製作上混音是非常重要的一個過程，音樂成品品質好壞，取決於混音是否混得好而且混音牽涉到許多音響及聲學心理學的相關技術與知識，非專業人士要混出尚可的成品有一定的難度，所以本篇論文提出一個利用監督式學習來進行自動多軌混音的系統。與其他篇相關研究不同的是其主要的核心方法是核依賴估計(Kernel Dependency Estimation)，利用混音參數間的依賴性(dependency)，來做混音參數的預測; 另一個與其他相關論文不同的是訓練的單位不同，由於混音其實是非常個別的(Case By Case)，混音師基本上都會依照各音軌的的聲響、音樂類型不同而有不同的處理方式; 所以在本篇論文的模型建立的過程我們會依照不同的音樂類型以及橋段建立不同的模型，以方便最後實際上的利用。由實驗結果得可知，不同的音樂類型其混音方式是有其獨特性的。

未來工作方面，由於本篇論文有分成四大音樂類型去做模型建立，導致各類別訓練資料有偏少的傾向，未來希望合併其他資料集以補足其數量;再者由於混音參數是非常難取得的，本篇論文是採用估計的方式估計其資料集中的混音參數權重，未來可以改用相關研究的估計方式或是實際收集混音參數以讓最後的混音模型能更貼近實際上的情況，例如建構一個線上混音系統的方式讓使用者實際混音記錄其混音參數。另外在 KDE 方法的部分由於本篇未套用其核函數(Kernel function)的部分，未來可以在做投影前先套用核函數來提升混音模型的效果。實驗部分評估的對象也可以新增跟資料集的混音成品做比較試著看看目前的混音模型與實際上的差距如何。

參考文獻

[1] J. Weston, O. Chapelle, A. Elisseeff, B. Scholkopf, and V. Vapnik, "Kernel Dependency Estimation," *Neural Information Processing Systems,* 2002.

[2] J. Scott and Y. E. Kim, "Instrument Identification Informed Multi-track Mixing,"

International Society for Music Information Retrieval, 2013.
[3] J. Scott and Y. E. Kim, "Analysis of Acoustic Features of Automated Multi-Track Mixing," *International Society for Music Information Retrieval,* 2011.
[4] D. BARCHIESI and J. REISS, "Reverse Engineering of a Mix," *Audio Engineering Society,* 2009.
[5] D. Barchiesi and J. Reiss, "Automatic Target Mixing Using Least-squares Optimization of Gains And Equalization Settings," *Digital Audio Effects(DAFx-09),* 2009.
[6] H. Katayose, A. Yatsui, and M. Goto, "A Mix-Down Assistant Interface with Reuse of Examples," *Automated Production of Cross Media Content for Multi-Channel Distribution,* 2005.
[7] Mike.Senior, "Mixing Secrets for the Small Studio," 2011.
[8] D. Ward, J. D. Reiss, and C. Athwal, "Multi-track mixing using a model of loudness and partial loudness," 2012.
[9] Kolasinski and Bennett, "A Framework for Automatic Mixing Using Timbral Similarity Measures and Genetic Optimizatio," *Audio Engineering Society,* 2008.
[10] S. H. Nielsen and E. Skovenborg, "Evaluation of Different Loudness Models with Music and Speech Material," *Audio Engineering Society,* 2004.
[11] B. C. J. Moore, B. R. Glasberg, and M. A. Stone, "Why Are Commercials so Loud? ' Perception and Modeling of the Loudness of Amplitude-Compressed Speech," *J. Audio Eng. Soc,* 2003.
[12] Balster and Alex, "Audio Control Facilities in Modern Recording Studios," *Audio Engineering Society,* 1972.
[13] N. Montecchio and A. Cont, "Accelerating The Mixing Phase In Studio Recording productions By Automatic Audio Alignment," *International Society for Music Information Retrieval,* 2011.
[14] E. R. R. 128, "Algorithms To Measure Audio Programme Loudness And True-peak Audio Level," *EBU,* 2010.

中文轉客文文轉音系統中的客語斷詞處理之研究

Research on Hakka Word Segmentation Processes in Chinese-to-Hakka Text-to-Speech System

黃豐隆 [1]、余明興 [2]、林昕緯 [2]、林義証 [3]

[1] 國立聯合大學 資訊工程所，flhuang@nuu.edu.tw

[2] 國立中興大學 資訊科學與工程所，msyu@dragon.nchu.edu.tw; lin@sinwei.tw

[3] 建國科技大學 資訊管理學系，yclin@ctu.edu.tw

摘要

語言(Language)是文化傳承與推廣的首要工具，尤其是少數族群的語言，如：台灣的客語 或原住民語言。臺灣的客家族群約佔總人口七分之一，為閩南語語系外之第二大族群。根據近 年來相關臺灣客語使用狀況調查報告指出，阻礙客語傳承之主因是：不太會講。由於台灣學習 環境使然，導致連客籍家庭的學童亦少能以客語說話、交談，具有聽、說客語能力者逐年下 降， 能說客語的人口大量減少，台灣出現客語失聲、客家文化失傳之危機。

我們為了建置線上客語的數位學習系統，已開發出以大量合成單元為基礎的客語四縣腔及海陸腔的中文轉客文的文轉音系統(Hakka Text-to-Speech, HTTS)，以及相關的應用系統，如：線上國客雙語有聲詞典 [13]、國客雙語有聲地圖社群系統 [14] 等。

我們的系統，主要是提供不太會講客語或不會講客語的使用者來使用、學習客語。因此系統的輸入為「中文文句」，輸出為「客語語音」。這樣的操作設計，學習者或使用者能不需額外再學習客語輸入法、客語拼音，只需使用最熟悉的中文，即可透過本系統來學習客語。

為了更進一步改善與提升文轉音的效果，本論著重在改善系統中的客語文句分析模組的客語斷詞處理。在系統中，使用者輸入中文文句後，透過我們提出的客語斷詞方法，能將「中文文句」轉換為「客語文句及斷詞和詞性標記結果」。透過這個提升後的斷詞與詞性標記結果，來得到更佳的文句分析結果、提升文轉音中的文意正確性，如：韻律階層的求取、停頓類型的求取及讀音的求取。

本論文提出混合型的 N-Gram 序列分數算法，搭配中文斷詞模組及動態規劃演算法的客語斷詞方法。在嚴重資料稀疏的客語語料下，對中文轉客語斷詞結果的精確率有 80.78%。相較於傳統中文詞直翻客語詞的方法，已提升不少。

Abstract

Language is a major tool for cultural inheritance especially for the minority nationality, for example Hakka and aborigine language in Taiwan. As second ethnic besides Minnan dialect, the population of Hakka in Taiwan is one seventh. According to the recently reports of Hakka usage survey in Taiwan, the difficulties to inherit the culture of Hakka is missed in spoken Hakka language, the reason is the environments for learning and has led to the results of descending population for communicating by Hakka. It will become crucial for the cultural inheritance of Hakka.

Therefore, we has developed the Text-to-Speech method and system for Hakka language, and our goal is building environments for leaning the Hakka language, our some applied system such as:

"Web Hakka Phonetic Dictionary" [13] and "Blogging System of Bilingual Language by Integrating Mobile Cells and Google Map" [14] ,etc.

Our system is provided for users who interested in Hakka language, who can input the Chinese texts and system will output the speech of Hakka, users need not to learn the typing and phonetic writing of Hakka, and can take the advantage to learning Hakka with familiar language.

For the advanced improvements of Hakka Text-to-Speech, this article will emphasis on the word segmentation processing of Hakka text. In our system, when user enter the Chinese text, our proposed methods can convert the Chinese text to Hakka text and assign the part-of-speech for each Hakka text segments. By the better performance of text segments and part-of-speech in Hakka, We can improvements the Hakka text analysis module.

We proposed an hybrid N-gram sequence score, and Chinese word segmentation module developed by the dynamic programming algorithm, in the data-sparseness of Hakka corpus, the accuracy of Chinese to Hakka word segmentation is 80.78%.

Keywords: Hakka Text-to-Speech, Hakka Word Segmentation, Dynamic Programming, Hakka Text Analysis.

1. 緒論

一個斷詞系統的效果，通常跟語料的大小有關。但目前客語語料的收集非常困難，現有的電子資料，如：客委會初級、中高級的認證教材、教育部編著的國小客語教材 等，對於自然語言處理來說，資料規模仍然屬極小量語料。因此，想要建置出更多的客語語料，幾乎都需要從客語書籍、文章中，透過人工輸入、建置成電子檔的方式來取得。但有了這些文本資料只是第一步，後續仍有許多的處理工作，如：斷詞、詞性標記的處理，擷取出這些語言特徵後，才能做更進一步的分析與應用。

客語詞的判定是一件嚴謹的事情，理論上我們必須遵照詞的定義 [1] 來標記，但有極少數的情況下，我們仍會將詞組標記成一個客語詞，如：滑溜溜，在中文斷詞被斷為：滑/溜溜，我們視它是一個詞。而對於非客語語言專家的標記人員來說，其最有效率的方法，是透過具有平行資訊 [2] 的語料，先將中文語料輸入至中文的文句處理系統，取得中文的斷詞、詞性標記的特徵後，再對其對應的客語文章，以人工方式去判斷客語詞的邊界與詞性的標記。這個方法普遍被使用 於同類型 [3] 的平行語料標工作記上，如 Tsai 的碩士論文 [1]也是用此方法。因為中文文句處理系 統中，在文句斷詞資訊標記的技術方面已經相當成熟，而客語與中文的文法結構也相近，實際 上中文的斷詞、詞性特徵，幾乎都能直接對應於客語詞。

目前客語語料的收集與建置，在學界有許多學者專家已積極的在做努力，建置出客語研究的相關基礎資料庫。如屏東教育大學的「學術研究基礎建置暨客家文化研究計畫 [2]」，他們歷時了至少三年的時間，在收集、建置客語語料及詞頻庫。這項創舉能有助於客語文句處理的發展，如：客語斷詞系統、客語文句分析系統、客語文句剖析系統、客語語音合成系統、智慧型的客語輸入法　等，都非常需要足夠的客語語料來支持其發展。

[1] 詞(Word)，是指最小、有完整明確意義且可以自由使用的中文語言單位。

[2] 具有中文文句和客文文句 1 對 1 對應的平行資訊的語料。

[3] 客語與中文都屬於漢語，文法結構幾乎相同，僅有少數俚語、特殊的客語構詞不同。

本研究旨在提出一個中文轉客文斷詞資訊的方法，針對嚴重資料稀疏的情況下，提出搭配中文斷詞模組與客語語言模型的混合式 N-Gram 序列分數的算法。透過兩階段方式，將中文文句以中文斷詞模組得到第一階段的斷詞及詞性標記結果後，再以國客語對照辭典找出所有可能被轉換的客語詞序列，以少量客語 Bi-gram、Uni-gram 語言模型為基底，搭配混合式 N-gram 序列分數的算法，找出分數最高的客語詞轉換序列，來得到第二階段轉換後的結果。

因礙於人力有限、語料收集的困難，仍有許多無法突破之處，如：語料的規模、人工標記資料的正確性。但使用本論文方法的客語斷詞法，以內部測試結果可知，若在訓練語料充足的情況下，能得到一個不錯的斷詞效能，其內部測試的精確度達 94.46%。相信在未來持續增加客語語料的規模後，本論文所提出的方法，效能會有更顯著的提升。

2. 文獻探討

2.1 中文斷詞

中文斷詞法每年都有新的研究與技術，甚至每年都會有舉辦斷詞比賽，知名的比賽如：SIGHAN 所舉辦的國際中文分詞競賽。第一屆競賽起始於 2003 年在日本札幌舉行。而之後每年都有相當多高手共襄盛舉。

在這麼多琳瑯滿目的斷詞技術中，常見的中文斷詞技術可分為三大類：(一)統計式斷詞 法、(二)法則式斷詞法和、(三)混合式斷詞法。

(A)統計式斷詞法

統計式斷詞法藉由收集詞彙資料，如詞彙長度和詞彙出現的頻率或次數等統計上的資訊。然後系統運用此訓練資料經由演算法分析來取得斷詞序列。常見的演算法如 Xue 使用的 Maximum Entropy [15]，最後實驗得到最好的 F 分數是 94.98%，或是 Lo 使用的 Conditional Random Field [4]，最後實驗得到最好的 F 分數是 96.40%。這些演算法都是利用字元之間的資訊當作特徵。然後把斷詞問題轉換成為字元之間的分類問題。

而過去常被使用的演算法是 Hidden Markov Model。如 Fu 和 Luck [5]從訓練語料中統計詞頻、字元在詞中出現位置的次數等資訊，組合過後做實驗。得到 F 分數最好可達 93.7%。而 Lin 和 Chang [4]使用兩階段特製化的方式，藉著擴充觀測符號及狀態符號來改善隱藏式馬可夫模型的斷詞效果。得到 F 分數最好可達 96.3%。

(B)法則式斷詞法

法則式斷詞法主要是根據一些經驗法則做為斷詞的標準，藉以達到較好的斷詞序列。常見的法則如「長詞優於短詞」、「與左邊詞的結合優於與右邊詞的結合」。而這類型的斷詞法常被參考的是 Chen 和 Liu [17]，他們在該篇論文中提出了六條法則(heuristic rules)，並且根據這些法則解決了歧義性的問題及剔除一些較不可能的詞彙組合，以完成中文斷詞的工作。在實驗上效果相當不錯。

不過，此種斷詞法容易受到詞典的好壞而影響效能。若是句子中出現未知的新詞彙時，則正確率就可能下滑。

(C)混合式斷詞法

每種方式的斷詞法都有好壞、優缺點，因此後來學者們才會嘗試去混合兩種斷詞方式。早期的 Nie 等人[18]提出結合詞典、經驗法則及統計資訊來對中文斷詞。而令人印象深刻的是 Wu 和 Jiang [19]提出結合剖析器和斷詞器的方法，在斷詞時先使用查詞典來產生所有可能的斷詞組合，再使用經驗法則剔除不可能的詞彙組合，然後再利用剖析器解決剩下的歧義問題，最後得到斷詞序列。在實驗上 F 分數高達 99%。

而比較不同的做法是 Gao 等人 [20]提出的專有名詞法則，這些法則幫助系統抓取未知的專有名詞如:人名、地名、組織名、外來語音譯人名。在最後實驗上 F 分數約為 96%左右。

2.2 客語斷詞

因客語語料稀疏的緣故，目前針對中文轉客文的相關研究非常少，客語斷詞系統的實做，先以(一)輸入為客語、(二)輸入為中文，分為兩大種類。第一類是直接針對客語文句做斷詞，第二類是針對中文文句翻譯成客語斷詞結果。

而目前仍沒有任何一篇是針對客語斷詞做深入研究的論文，其中對客語斷詞有做效能評估的論文，也僅有 Tsai 的碩士論文 [1]—基於隱藏式馬可夫模型之客語文句轉語音系統。顯見目前客語斷詞的研究，不管是語料的建置，還是斷詞的方法，仍非常多待探討與解決的問題。

(A) 輸入為客語

這一類的系統，適合具備客語輸入能力及熟悉客語的使用者，對於一般不熟悉客語的使用者而言，較不方便。這類系統常見的做法，是直接使用中文斷詞系統，對客文做斷詞。當然，這樣會有一些客語造字或客語用詞無法辨別的問題，針對這部份，是使用國客語對照辭典，來解決客語未知詞(Out of Vocabulary, OOV)問題。

如 Tsai 的論文 [1]，他們透過 Conditional Random Field 方法實做中文斷詞系統，並加入國客語對照外部辭典，配合客語構詞規則，實做出客語斷詞模組。最後的實驗效能，客語斷詞的 F 分數為 82.87%，客語詞性標記的 F 分數為 77.14%。

(B) 輸入為中文

這一類的系統，使用者不需使用客語輸入法，也不需熟悉客語，很適合客語初學者使用。這類系統常見的做法，是使用中文斷詞系統，先將輸入的中文文句斷詞，找出詞與詞性後，再將詞透過國客語的平行對照辭典，翻譯成客語詞。如本實驗室的線上客語語音合成系統，Wu [5]、Lo [6]的斷詞方法皆相同，都是使用 Jiang [7]所提出的中文斷詞系統，將中文文句斷詞後，再透過國客語對照辭典，將中文詞翻譯成客語詞。經測試後，其不含詞性標記的客語斷詞效能的 F 分數分別為 69.82%及 66.72%。

另一種是僅透過國客語對照辭典，將中文文句直翻成客語。如 Lee [8]，他們建置出一套國客語對照辭典，將輸入的中文文句字串切割成 1 到 4 字詞，並查找對照辭典、翻譯成客語詞。而他們沒有針對中文翻客語詞做效能評估，因此無法得知效果如何。

3. 準備工具及語料

3.1 中文斷詞工具

本論文的中文斷詞系統，是使用 Lai 於 2011 提出的「應用多詞及多詞性語言模型的中文斷詞及詞性標記方法 [9]」。此斷詞方法採用兩階斷式，第一階斷是斷詞，第二階斷是詞性標記。其斷詞的 F 分數有 96.69%，詞性標記的 F 分數 92.04%。

3.2 國客語對照辭典

我們所建置的國客語對照辭典，主要來源有：(一)客委會初級、中級暨中高級認證語料 [10, 11]、(二)台北市客委會-現代客語詞彙彙編。對於斷詞系統而言，辭典是決定正確率的重要因 素， 理論上辭典越大，斷詞效能也就越好。因此除了現有的辭典來源外，我們也利用標記客語文句斷詞答案的同時，找出一些尚未被收錄在辭典中的國客語對照之詞目。最後，也針對每個詞目，進行人工校正工作，去除重複或不合理的詞目以及標記拼音。

表一、國客語對照辭典資料樣貌

欄位	內容	說明
ID	13267	資料庫中 ID
Chinese	年輕人	中文詞用詞
Hakka	後生人	客語詞用詞
Pinyin	heu1 sang2 ngin3	客語拼音
Pos	Na	客語詞性
Pos_pattern	Na	中文詞性組
Hakka_pos_feq	25	客語含詞性詞頻
Hakka_nonpos_feq	25	客語不含詞性詞頻
Chinese_pos_feq	21138	中文含詞性詞頻
Chinese_nonpos_feq	21138	中文不含詞性詞頻

表二、2014 版，興大國客語對照辭典分佈統計及比較

字詞	2014 興大客語辭典	Wu[5]	Lo[6]	交大客語辭典[1]
一字詞	3457	780	838	6747
二字詞	20800	16362	16540	18078
三字詞	7309	5654	5826	5095
四字詞	4093	3769	3861	4217
五字詞	312	273	283	250
六字詞	84	80	84	80
七字詞	65	63	68	60
八字詞	9	12	14	14
總計	**36129**	**26993**	**27514**	**34541**

3.3 客語四縣腔語言模型的建置

語言模型是斷詞系統中，用來選擇斷詞結果的重要元件。而語料經過統計詞頻後，就能得到該份語料的機率分佈模型，即是語言模型。因此，語料越大，能得到的統計資訊越多，語言模型能包含的情況越多，效能也會越好。

但是，現今電腦上的客語語料仍非常匱乏，能用來建置語言模型的語料非常有限。因此，我們開發了一個半自動式的客語語料建置工具來建置客語語料，透過這個工具，可以將具平行資訊[4]的客語語料，標記出客語斷詞資訊，再透過該語料統計出客語 Uni-gram 及 Bi-gram 語言模 型。

[4] 具有中文文句和客文文句 1 對 1 對應的平行資訊的語料。

3.3.1 語料來源

我們用來建置客語語言模型的客語語料，主要來源是客委會四縣腔初級、中高級客語認證教材 [10, 11]。這份語料，句子數分別有初級 1678 句、中高級 4962 句，共 6640 句，每一句都有中文、客語的詞目、拼音及例句，如表：

表三、客委會語料的資料樣貌

客語詞	光線
中文詞	光線
客語拼音	gong ˋ sien ˇ
中文例句	這個房間的光線不好，不適合做書房。
客語例句	這隻房間个光線毋好，毋適合做書房。

3.3.2 客語斷詞標記工具及人工標記原則

客語與中文的文法結構相近，因此中文斷詞和詞性的標記，大部分都能與客語完全對應，僅有少部分的客語俚語或特殊用詞例外。而中文語料的處理，因目前中文斷詞系統的發展已相當成熟，因為中文語料的龐大，以規則法配合機率模型的混合式斷詞法所發展出來的中文斷詞系統，斷詞效能及詞性標記的 F 分數已達到 96.69%及 92.04%。因此都能直接以中文斷詞系統來得到可靠的斷詞及詞性特徵標記的結果。但客語文章的處理，因目前市面上及學界的客語斷詞系統仍處於發展中的階段，還沒辦法依賴任何客語斷詞系統來自動處理。因此我們開發出一套工具，以半自動的方法，快速的針對客語句子，做客語斷詞的標記。

3.3.2.1 客語斷詞標記工具介紹與操作

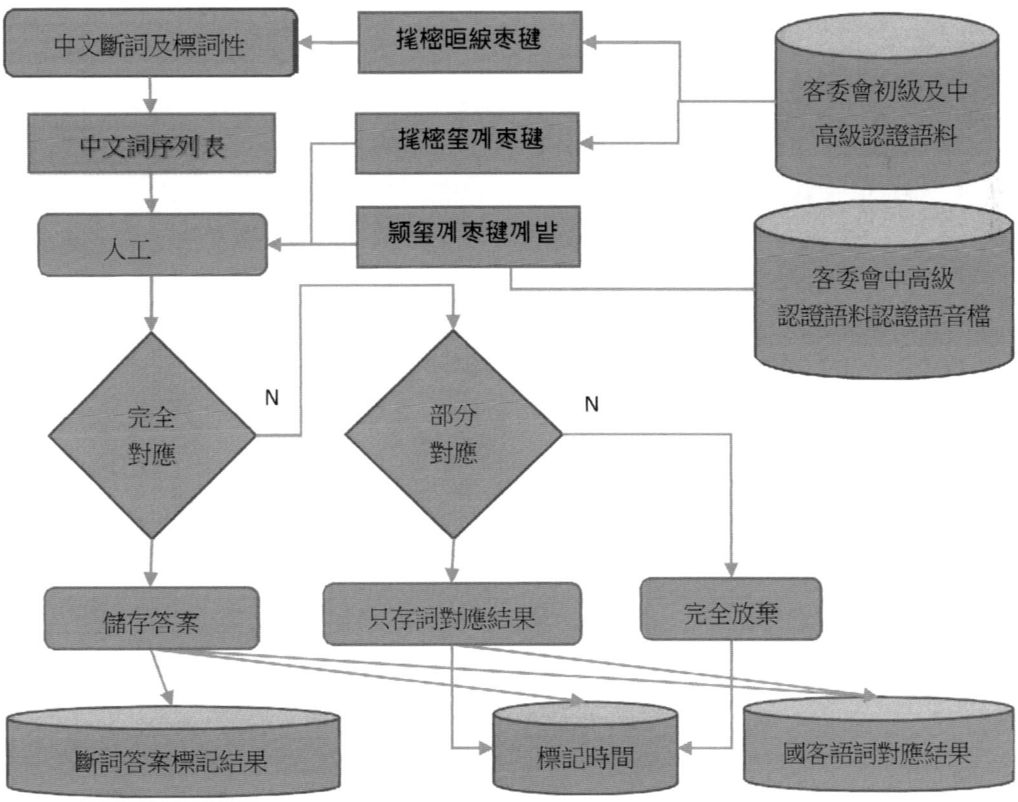

圖一、客語斷詞答案標記工具架構圖

我們將客委會四縣腔認證教材的客語語料 6640 句句子，依照句子的編號順序，由小到大分為語料 A 及語料 B，語料 A 有 4196 句，語料 B 有 2444 句，並再將 B 語料依編號順位分為 4 份，B1-B4，每份 611 句。

將 A、B 語料，分別找(標記者 1)一位碩士生、(標記者 2~5)四位大學在學生，使用本論文開發的客語斷詞答案標記工具，以半自動人工判斷方式，標記出客語斷詞的答案。其中每人的標記速度如表四：

表四、客語斷詞標記工具的標記時間統計，時間單位：秒。

標記者	1	2	3	4	5	總平均
語料編號	A	B1	B2	B3	B4	
處理句數[5]	4500	615	622	611	646	
儲存句數	4018	346	451	504	419	
總時間[6]	91798	28698	25297	18864	17219	
平均每句	20.39	46.66	40.67	30.87	26.65	33.04

表中可看出，標記速度平均 33.04 秒能完成一句。而標記完成的資料，會儲存其 1.中文句子、2.中文斷詞及詞性標記結果、3.客語句子、4.客語斷詞及詞性標記結果、5.客委會語料中的句子編號，等五個欄位資料，儲存結果如下表：

表六、客語斷詞標記結果的資料樣貌

中文句子	這個房間的光線不好，不適合做書房。
中文斷詞結果	這(Nep) 個(Nf) 房間(Nc) 的(DE) 光線(Na) 不(D) 好(VH) ，(COMMACATEGORY) 不(D) 適合(VH) 做(VC) 書房(Nc) 。(PERIODCATEGORY)
客語句子	這隻房間个光線毋好，毋適合做書房。
客語斷詞結果	這(Nep) 隻(Nf) 房間(Nc) 个(DE) 光線(Na) 毋(D) 好(VH) ，(COMMACATEGORY) 毋(D) 適合(VH) 做(VC) 書房(Nc) 。(PERIODCATEGORY)
句子編號	01-001

將這些標記完成的資料再經過一次經人工篩選後，最後確認有效句數為：A 語料 4018 句，B1-B4 語料共 1282 句，我們使用語料的分佈如表所示：

表七、客語語料的使用分佈

	訓練	測試
句數	4018	1282
詞數	45304	17646
字數	65572	25478

[5] 處理句數的統計，包含重新處理曾經放棄的句子，因此實際處理可能會比分配到的筆數多。
[6] 時間單位為秒。

圖二、標記工具操作畫面

3.3.2.2標記原則

因為這份客語認證教材語料，專家們編審的主要目的是為了客語教學用，並不是為了要建立「國語/客語斷詞對應」的語料，所以在撰寫例句時並不會特別求強或注意到國客語的完全對應。

因此，我們在進行人工標記時也發現，其實大部分出現無法對應的情況，都可以以人工修改中文句子或用詞的方式，做適當的修飾與調整，來達到不影響文意、又能與客語句子對應完全的目的。但某些句子仍無法確認如何標記時，標記者也可選擇放棄該句的標記，或只存能對應到的詞，而不將這些未完成對應的句子視為斷詞答案。以下為標記時的 6 大標記原則：

原則 1：標記時，都以不修改客語句子為原則，但可跳過不影響文意的字串。

表八、標記原則 1 範例

中文	這泉水的水質很甜很清澈。
客語	這**窟**泉水个水質當甜當清。
中文改	這泉水的水質很甜很清澈。
客語改	這泉水个水質當甜當清。

此例子中，窟這個字只是指一窟井或一窟水池的意思，省略後也不至於影響整句文意。

表九、範例 1 標記後樣貌

中文改	這(Nep) 泉水(Na) 的(DE) 水質(Na) 很(Dfa) 甜(VH) 很(Dfa) 清澈(VH) 。(P)
客語改	這(Nep) 泉水(Na) 个(DE) 水質(Na) 當(Dfa) 甜(VH) 當(Dfa) 清(VH) 。(P)

原則 2：如果有很明顯且離譜的斷詞錯誤，要人工介入修正。

表十、標記原則 2 範例

原斷詞	這(Nep) 群(Nf) 小孩子(Na) ，(COMMACATEGORY) 每(Nes) **天都(Na)** 在(P) 沙洲(Na) 上(Nes) 玩(VC) 摔跤(VA) 。(P)
人工修正	這(Nep) 群(Nf) 小孩子(Na) ，(COMMACATEGORY) 每(Nes) **天(Nf) 都(Da)** 在(P) 沙洲(Na) 上(Nes) 玩(VC) 摔跤(VA) 。(P)

此例子中，「天都」一詞，被誤斷成一個普通名詞，這跟「天、都」意思不同，「天都」指的是地方名，而其正確斷詞應該斷成「天(Nf) 都(Da)」。

原則 3：可微調中文句子用詞及詞的順序以求對應到客語，但修改後的文意不能改變。

表十一、標記原則 3 範例 1

中文	今天的天氣很好，太陽下山以後就**可以看得到**滿天的星星。
客語	今晡日个天時當好，日頭落山以後就**看得著**滿天个星仔。
中文改	今天的天氣很好，太陽下山以後就**看得到**滿天的星星。
客語改	今晡日个天時當好，日頭落山以後就**看得著**滿天个星仔。

此例子中，若直接省略「可以」這個詞，也不會影響到原句的文意。

表十二、標記原則 3 範例 2

中文	古時候的人會觀察**天上的星宿變化**，來判斷人間的吉凶。
客語	上早个人會觀察**天頂星宿个變化**，來判斷人間个吉凶。
中文改	古時候的人會觀察**天上星宿的變化**，來判斷人間的吉凶。
客語改	上早个人會觀察**天頂星宿个變化**，來判斷人間个吉凶。

此例子中，客語「天頂星宿个變化」與中文「天上的星宿變化」雖然詞的詞順序不同，但中文句子中的「的」調換後，也不影響文意。而修改句子的動作，我們只建議修改中文，客文 若非必要儘量保持原句。原因是較能保持客語句子原來的特性、結構、用語　等資訊。

原則 4：以客語句子為主體，發現中文詞和客語詞的對應有爭議時或太過模糊時，要找過一個最佳選擇的詞替換。

表十三、標記原則 4 範例

中文	古早的人若是看到流星雨，會想到**一些**壞兆頭。
客語	上早个人係看著星仔瀉屎，會想著**麼个**壞兆頭。
中文改	古早的人若是看到流星雨，會想到**什麼**壞兆頭。
客語改	上早个人係看著星仔瀉屎，會想著**麼个**壞兆頭。

在此例子中，客語的「麼个」翻成中文「一些」，依客語文意來看過於模糊。因此，可透標記工具中的詞典查詢功能，找到客語詞「麼个」能翻成的國語詞有哪些，發現到「什麼」這個中文詞最貼近文意。因此，手動將中文句子的「一些」改為「什麼」，重新與「麼个」配對。

原則 5：若沒辦法標記完一整句，但部分詞能對應，則選擇「放棄，儲存詞配對結果」。

表十四、標記原則 5 範例

中文	一身乾鷩簡單粗陋的衣服都沒有能力買。
客語	一身腊食皮無才調買。

此例子中，我們發現這句除了「一/一、身/身、無/沒有、才調/能力、買/買」這些詞能對應外，其他詞皆無法非對應。因此此次的不納入正確答案範本內，但有部分詞能對應，也將這些詞的國客語對應結果儲存起來，待後續的工作中，仍可應用。

原則 6：配對時以「詞」為單位，不要以片語為單位。 通常，非成語的片語，用法可能只是偶然出現，因此儲存這類資料沒意義。

表十五、標記原則 6 範例

中文	現在外面既颳風又下雨，要怎麼樣回家？
客語	這下外背風合雨，愛仰般形轉屋下？

此例子中，發現到「既颳風又下雨」和「風合雨」看似能對應，但實際上可能只有在這句曾出現這種情況。因此，這種非成語的片語，也許只是偶然出現，我們不儲存此類的答案和詞配對。但依照原則 5，我們發現「要怎麼樣回家/愛仰般形轉屋下」可配對，成「要/愛、怎麼樣/仰般形、回家/轉屋下」。因此這句可儲存其「詞配對」成功的部份，但放棄儲存為斷詞答案。

4. 研究方法

本系統實驗有包括兩大種基底，(一)中文斷詞邊界優先、(二)客語詞邊界優先，經實驗發現第一種方法的外部測試正確率較高。但這可能跟標記語料時採用的：先中文斷詞、再人工對應客語詞的方法有關。但文章篇幅有限，本篇論文寫的實驗數據都以第一種方法為基底。

所謂(一)中文斷詞邊界優先，是先將輸入中文文句做斷詞，得到確定的詞邊界後，再以這些中文詞去查找國客語對照辭典，找出可能的客語詞轉換候選。而(二)客語詞優先，是先從國客語對照辭典中，找出所有可能被轉換的客語詞，最後再與中文斷詞邊界的詞一起做為候選詞。

兩種方法的不同之處：方法(一)的詞邊界已被固定，相對能找出的候選客語詞也較少、較侷 限，方法(二)的詞邊界是自由的，可從國客語對照辭典及原中文斷詞斷的中文詞中，找出一條 最佳的斷詞路徑。兩種方法其實各有好處，第一種方法在外部測試有較佳的正確率，第二種方 法在內部測試有較佳的正確率。其意義是：如果在訓練語料充足的情況下，第二種方法會更 好。 而第一種方法適合用在訓練語料稀疏的情況。

4.1系統架構

在本論文的客語斷詞系統中，輸入是「中文文句」，輸出是「客語文句」的斷詞及詞性標記結果。簡而言之，以中文文句輸入後，經此客語斷詞模組處理，產生具有斷詞與詞性的客語文句的輸出。標記斷詞及詞性兩種特徵後的結果，可再使用文法剖析器分析、得到文法結構樹，做更進一步的文句分析處理。如：用於 Hakka Text to Speech (HTTS)中的停頓預估模型中，預測出句子中的 no break、minor break 及 major break 三種停頓類型，讓合出的語音可辨度更高、讓使用者能更輕易的聽懂句子內容。

因此，一個良好的客語斷詞系統是客語語言處理所不可或缺的，應是提升客語語音合成效果的重要因素。本系統中客語斷詞的架構，參見圖三。

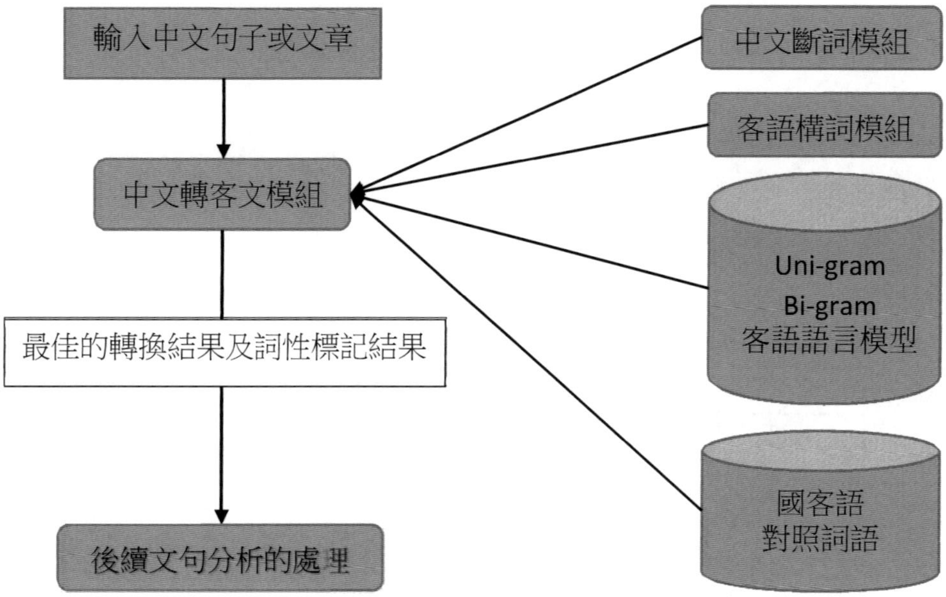

圖三、客語斷詞模組架構圖

4.2 修改中文斷詞辭典

前文有提到，本論文採用第一種方法「中文斷詞邊界優先」為基底，因此為了讓一些客語用詞有機會成為被轉換的候選詞，我們將國客語對照辭典中，所有中文詞欄位的詞資料，都加入到中文斷詞辭典裡。如此做法能提高原本完全不會被找到的客語詞，有機會成為被轉換的候選詞。以下是一個例子：

表十六、中文斷詞邊界限制，範例 1

中文句子	泥鰍滑溜溜，
中文斷詞	泥鰍/滑/溜溜/，
中文翻客語	鰗鰍仔/滑/溜溜/，
正確答案	鰗鰍仔/滑溜溜仔/，

透過中文斷詞得到「泥鰍/滑/溜溜/，」的斷詞邊界，再透過以上方法找出最佳詞頻的客語詞並轉換為「鰗鰍仔/滑/溜溜/，」。但其實我們的國客語對照詞典中，有收錄「滑溜溜/滑溜溜

仔」這筆個國客語對照資料，但礙於中文斷詞邊界之限制，只能由一個詞「滑溜溜仔」轉成「滑/溜溜」兩個詞。此情況會直接的影響到轉換的正確率。

表十七、中文斷詞邊界限制，範例 2

中文句子	大家來去客家庄走一走。
中文斷詞	大家/來去/客家庄/走/一/走/。
中文翻客語	大家/來去/客家庄/行/一/行/。
正確答案	大家/來去/客家庄/遶遶啊/。

上面的例子「走一走」被斷成「走/一/走」，但實際上我們詞典有收錄「走一走/遶遶啊」 這個對照詞組，但礙於中文斷詞邊界，我們沒辦法選到該詞組。

基於以上的原因，我們決定將國客語對照辭典中的中文詞欄位，加入到中文斷詞辭典。而這些新加入的中文詞，要決定出它們的詞頻大小，因為這兩個語料規模相差非常龐大，我們的 中文斷詞辭典總詞頻數高達 462729801 個詞，而客語訓練語料僅有 47079 個詞。因此我們將中 文斷詞辭典的平均詞頻取 Log 以 2 為底乘上 15(經實驗得到，15 有最佳的正確率)，再與國客語 對照辭典的詞頻相乘，得到該詞新的詞頻。步驟如下：

1. 統計出中文斷詞辭典原始的分佈，我們得到其平均詞頻為 464 次。

表十八、中文斷詞辭典資料分佈

總詞數	995642
總詞頻	462729801
平均詞頻	464

2. 我們以下列公式，計算出每個要加入中文斷詞辭典中的中文詞，其新詞頻 $C(W_i)^*$，其中 $W_i \in (Woyd\ Length > 1)$：

$$C(W_i)^* = log_2(464) * 15 * 〔C(W_i) + 1〕 \quad (1)$$

一個國客對照詞「植物/植物」，其詞頻轉換的例子：

表十九、國客語對照辭典的中文詞詞頻換算

中文	植物
客語	植物
未含詞性特徵的詞頻	3
新詞頻 $C(W_i)^*$	$Ceil(log_2(464) * 15 * 〔3+1〕) = 532$

依照上述方法，產生以下新增候選列表：

表二十、客語詞新詞頻候選表

中文詞	詞頻
植物	532
雕刻	266
信仰	443
八仙	355
筵席	178

3. 將步驟 2 產生的新增候選列表的結果，加入中文斷詞辭典，若有相同的中文詞，則其詞頻相加。

最後我們評估修改前與修改後的中文斷詞系統，其正確率的差異。測試為外部測試，使用「中研院中文平衡語料庫 3.0」。如表二十一：

表二十一、中文斷詞辭典修改前後比較

	Precision	Recall	F-Measure
修改前	97.16%	96.21%	96.69%
修改後	97.15%	96.16%	96.65%

可看到 F-Measure 略低 0.04%，但改善了以下問題：

表二十二、加入客語詞後的中文斷詞辭典的改善

中文句子	泥鰍滑溜溜，
原中文斷詞	泥鰍/滑/溜溜/，
改善後中文斷詞	泥鰍/滑溜溜/，
原中文翻客語	鰗鰍仔/滑/溜溜/，
改善後中文翻客語	鰗鰍仔/滑溜溜仔/，
正確答案	鰗鰍仔/滑溜溜仔/，

原本的斷詞系統無法將「滑溜溜」判斷出來，修正辭典後已能正確斷出，並轉為客語詞「滑溜溜仔」。

4.3 客語斷詞方法

4.3.1 中文斷詞搭配國客語對照辭典的直翻法

本方法的流程：

1. 透過中文斷詞系統得到中文斷詞及標詞性結果。
2. 查找國客語對照辭典，找出對應的客語詞，並選擇資料 ID 排序第一位者，並將中文詞轉換成該詞。
3. 若步驟 2 時查不到對應的客語詞，則沿用中文斷詞的結果。

圖四為此斷詞法的流程：

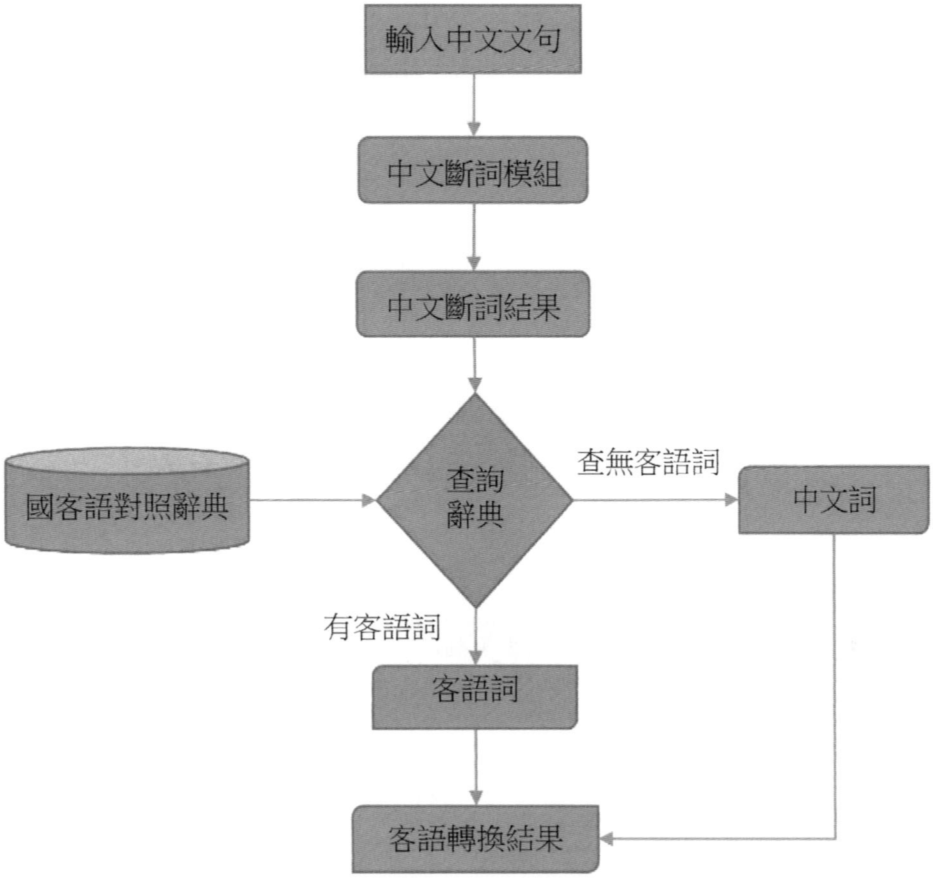

圖四、中文斷詞搭配國客語對照辭典的直翻法流程圖

4.3.2 中文斷詞搭配客語詞頻的直接翻譯法

以下是本方法的程式流程：

1. 透過中文斷詞系統得到斷詞及標詞性的結果。
2. 查找國客語對照詞典，找出對應的客語詞。
3. 挑選詞性與詞性標記結果相同者且詞頻最高、字長最短者為結果，若都找不到則以中文詞為結果。

圖五為本方法流程：

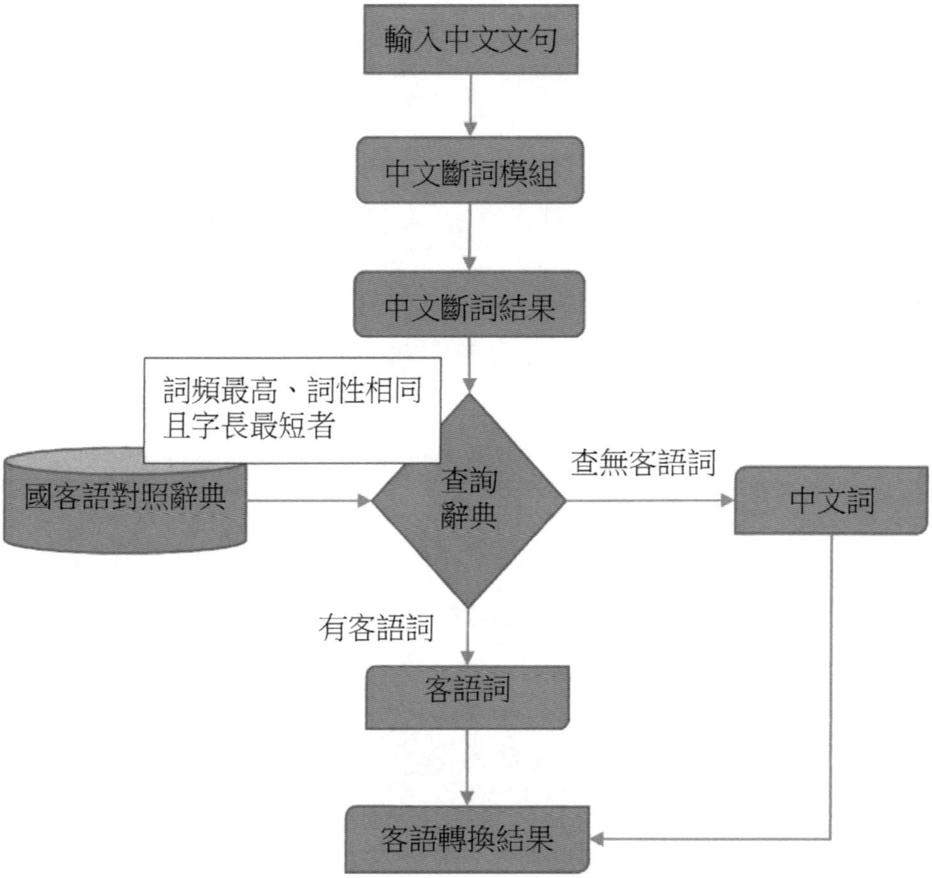

圖五、搭配客語詞頻的直接翻譯斷詞法

4.3.3 中文斷詞搭配客語 **Uni-gram** 及 **Bi-gram** 語言模型的混合式分數算法

本斷詞法，是先將輸入的中文句子，以中文斷詞模組做斷詞，得到一個確定的中文詞邊界後，再將這些中文詞查詢客語辭典，找出所有的可能候選詞。若找不到客語詞，則以僅有的中文詞當候選詞。最後將這些候選詞建立成一個所有斷詞路徑的有向圖，再以最短路徑演算法配合 Uni-gram 及 Bi-gram 混合式的分數算法，找出一條分數最佳的斷詞序列。

分數的計算方法：

本斷詞方法的分數計算方式，是混合式 Mix-gram(Uni-gram+Bi-gram)分數算法，如下列式子：

$$Seoye(<S>, W_1, W_2, W_3, \ldots, W_n) =$$

$$\alpha\gamma gmin 一 \{log_e(P(W_1|<S>) * P(W_1)) + \sum^{n}_{i=2} Log_e(P(W_i|W_{i-1}) * P(W_i))\} \quad (2)$$

其中 $P(W_i|W_{i-1})$可利用 maximum likelihood estimation(MLE)來計算：

$$P(W_i|W_{i-1}) \text{ 起 } \frac{C(W_{i-1},W_i)}{C(W_{i-1})} \quad (3)$$

若遇到訓練資料 $C(W_{i-1}, W_i) = 0$ 時，我們將Bi-gram機率以為 α 值代替，轉換如下：

$$P(W_i|W_{i-1}) = \begin{cases} \frac{C(W_{i-1},W_i)}{\sum_{W \in v} C(W_{i-1},W)}, & if\ C(W_{i-1}, W_i) > 0 \\ \alpha, & if\ C(W_{i-1}, W_i) = 0 \end{cases} \quad (4)$$

其中 $P(W_i)$：

$$P(W_i) = \frac{1+C(W_i)}{v+[\sum^{v}_{j=1} C(W_j)]} \quad (5)$$

$\sum^{v}_{j=1} C(W_j) = 47079$，為客語Uni-gram語言模型中的總詞頻數。

$V = 8931$，為Uni-gram語言模型的總type數(詞數)。

$\alpha = 10^{-3}$，為代替當 $C(W_{i-1}, W_i) = 0$ 時，用以替代 $\frac{C(W_{i-1},W_i)}{\sum_{W \in v} C(W_{i-1},W)}$ 的值，這是經由實驗得到，我們測試了 $10^{-1}, 10^{-2}, 10^{-3}, \ldots, 10^{-8}$ 等值。

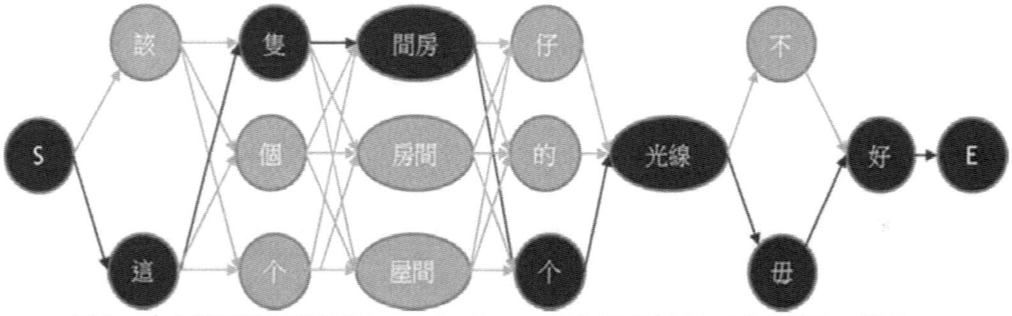

圖六、中文斷詞搭配客語 Uni-gram 及 Bi-gram 語言模型的混合式分數算法，範例。

以上圖為例，如要計算上條斷詞序列 *Seoye*（*S, 這, 隻, 間房, 个, 光線, 毋, 好*），其Mix-gram的分數計算公式如下：

Seoye（*S,這,隻,間房,个,光線,毋,好*）=

[P（這|S）*P（這）]*[P（隻|這）*P（隻）]*[P（間房|隻）*P（間房）]* [P（个|間房）*P（个）]*[P（光線|个）*P（光線）]*[P（毋|光線）*P（毋）]* [P（好|毋）*P（好）]

5. 系統效果評估

5.1評估方法

本測試所輸出的句子，是中文未斷詞的句子，輸出客語斷詞及標詞性的結果。目前只測試單純客語分詞的效能。效能評估的計算方法，我們使用精確率(Precision)、召回率(Recall)、以及F-分數(F-score)來評估系統的效能，這三種方法的定義如下所示：

$$\text{精確率} = \frac{\text{系統正確斷出的詞數}}{\text{系統斷出的總詞數}} \quad (6)$$

$$\text{召回率} = \frac{\text{系統正確斷出的詞數}}{\text{標準答案的總詞數}} \quad (7)$$

$$\text{F 分數} = \frac{2 * \text{精確率} * \text{召回率}}{\text{精確率} + \text{召回率}} \quad (8)$$

基於下列原因，除了上述的評估方法外，我們進一步運用編輯距離演算法(Levenshtein Distance)，評估轉換後的客語句子相似度(Similarity)。

原因 1：

中文翻客文的處理，是一個中文詞對多種可能客語字詞的問題，且客語常有一意多詞的問題，如：中文「收到」客語可翻成「收」或「收着」，若正確答案標記為「收着」，但系統輸出為「收」，在斷詞評估角度看，兩者詞不同，正確率為 0，但以相似度來看，兩者僅差一個字，相似度仍有 50%。

因此，除了斷詞邊界的評估標準外，其字串轉換後的相似度也可以是一個評估效能的方法。且客語文句的文法結構與中文幾近相同，沒有翻譯後文法結構對齊的問題，因此可用此方法計算其相似度。

原因 2：

本論文的斷詞系統，是用於客語語音合成系統中，因此，翻譯後的字串，距離標準答案的相似度越高，能將字念對的可能性也越高。

此演算法計算兩個字串 A、B 間，由字串 A 轉換成字串 B 的最小編輯距離(Insertions, Deletions 或 Substitutions)，計算方式如下：

$$D(i,j) = \min \begin{cases} D(i-1,j) + InseytCost(tayget_i) \\ D(i-1,j-1) + Su\text{必}stituteCost(souyee_j, tayget_i) \\ D(i,j-1) + DeleteCost(souyee_j) \end{cases} \quad (9)$$

其中：

$$Su\text{必}stituteCost = \begin{cases} 0, & if\ tayget(i) = souyee(j) \\ 1 & otheywise \end{cases}$$

$$InseytCost = 1$$

$$DeleteCost = 1$$

並由以下公式，將距離轉換成 0 到 1 之間的值，即為 A、B 字串間的相似度：

$$Similayity(A,\text{的}) = 1 - \frac{D(A,B)}{Max\ Length(A,B)} \quad (10)$$

5.2 測試語料

本實驗所使用的客語斷詞訓練與測試語料，是採用客委會四縣腔初級及中高級語料中的例句，共 6640 句句子。我們將這份語料，分為語料 A 及語料 B，語料 A 有 4196 句，語料 B 有 2444 句，並再將 B 語料依編號順位分為 4 份，B1-B4，每份 611 句。

而這些標記完成的資料，再經過一次經人工篩選後，確認有效句數為：訓練語料 4018

句，測試(B1-B4)語料共 1282 句，我們使用語料的分佈如表所示：

表二十三、客語語料的使用分佈

	訓練	**測試**
句數	4018	1282
詞數	45304	17646
字數	65572	25478

5.3評估結果與討論

5.3.1　中文斷詞搭配國客語對照辭典的直翻法

實驗 A：使用 Lo[6]的國客語對照辭典。 **實**
驗 B：使用 Wu[5]的國客語對照辭典。

實驗 C：使用本論文所建置的國客語對照詞典。

表二十四、直接翻譯斷詞法效能評估-內部測試

	Precision	Recall	F- Measure	字串相似度
實驗 A	68.41%	69.12%	68.76%	73.29%
實驗 B	72.66%	73.42%	73.04%	75.68%
實驗 C	75.02%	75.80%	75.41%	78.36%

由此實驗可得知，詞典的校正與詞目的增加，能顯著的改善客語斷詞系統的效能。

5.3.2　中文斷詞搭配客語詞頻的直接翻譯法

實驗 A：輸入中文文句，評估其中文轉客語的斷詞效能。 **實**
驗 B：輸入中文文句，評估其中文轉客語及詞性標記效能。

表二十五、中文斷詞搭配客語詞頻的直接翻譯法-斷詞及詞性標記內外部測試結果

		Precision	Recall	F- Measure	字串相似度
實驗 A	**訓練**	88.16%	87.48%	87.82%	91.08%
	測試	80.32%	79.08%	79.69%	83.68%
實驗 B	**訓練**	87.46%	86.78%	87.12%	-
	測試	79.90%	78.66%	79.27%	-

以實驗結果來看，顯示客語詞頻的應用能顯著的提升選詞的正確率。但外部測試的正確率仍偏低，已接近未使用詞頻特徵的結果。此情況的原因，是因為用來統計客語詞頻的語料仍不足，因此造成統計資料稀疏的問題。但從實驗結果的特性觀察到，若能持續的增加客語語料、建置出更多的客語詞頻，能提升中文轉客文系統的效能。

而就目前的窘況而言，提升正確率的方法，僅能靠規則法(Rules-base)，如找出客語的構詞規則和文法規則，來提升客語斷詞的正確率。客語構詞部份，是下一階段即將進行的工作。

5.3.3　中文斷詞搭配客語 Uni-gram 及 Bi-gram 語言模型的混合式分數算法

實驗 A：輸入中文文句，評估其中文轉客語詞的斷詞效能。

實驗 B：輸入中文文句，評估其斷詞及詞性標記效能。

表二十六、中文斷詞搭配客語 Uni-gram 及 Bi-gram 語言模型的混合式分數算法

		Precision	Recall	F- Measure	字串相似度
實驗 A	**訓練**	94.46%	93.73%	94.10%	96.17%

	測試	80.78%	79.53%	80.15%	84.04%
實驗 B	**訓練**	93.96%	93.24%	93.60%	-
	測試	80.37%	79.11%	79.74%	-

加入 Bi-gram 後，內部測試的效能有顯著的提升，但外部測試僅略升 0.46%。原因是因為客語語言模型資料稀疏的關係，許多 Bi-gram pattern 未出現在客語 Bi-gram 語言模型中，或就算出現在 Bi-gram 語言模型中，也不符合句子實際的狀況，這是資料稀疏的問題。

而在下一階段的工作中，我們將要增加客語構詞規則以及持續增加客語語料，客語構詞包括了：重複、附加、附合、合併 等構詞規則。

6. 結論及未來工作

本論文針對中文轉客文文轉音系統(Hakka Text-to-Speech System, HTTS)中的客語斷詞處理，已提出一個基礎的研究架構。但因為目前客語電子語料有嚴重不足的問題，對於本論文所探討的主題而言，是一項非常艱困的挑戰。研究之初，我們並沒有客語斷詞語料可使用，僅有少量一句句未處理的國客語對照文句。因此，我們投入了大量時間在客語語料的標記、建置及辭典的校正、標音。我們也持續的從國小客語教材、客語朗讀比賽文章 等電子文本中，人工建置出更多的客語斷詞語料及客語新詞。而目前用來測試的語料，皆是我們自行建置的，所以我們也非常需要更多不同來源的客語斷詞語料，做更公證客觀的效能評估、比較。

本論文在客語斷詞方法方面，不同於過去的架構，我們提出了使用客語 Uni-gram 及 Bi-gram 語言模型的混合式斷詞序列分數算法，可看見在內部測試的評估上，顯示在語料充足的情況 下， 將會有不錯的斷詞表現。但詞性標記的正確率僅能做為參考，因為我們自己標記產生的標 準答 案，其詞性大部份都是依照中文斷詞系統給出的詞性為主，除離譜的錯誤外，很少當下進 行修 正。因此，語料的斷詞、詞性標記資訊，仍需要經專家再一次做更嚴謹的校正。

本論文提出混合型的 N-Gram 序列分數算法，搭配中文斷詞模組及動態規劃演算法的客語斷詞方法。在嚴重資料稀疏的客語語料下，對中文轉客文的外部測試精確率有 80.78%，內部測試有 94.46%。相較於傳統中文詞直翻客語詞的方法，已獲得提升。相信未來持續增加客語語料的規模後，使用本論文所提出的方法，效能會有更顯著的提升。

客語斷詞的應用層面極廣，不僅止使用於我們中文轉客文文轉音系統中的文句分析模組，還可獨立用於客語的數位學習、客語文句處理、客語語音辨識 等領域。本論文提出的研究方法，應能提供未來客語斷詞相關研究做為基礎與參考。

我們接下來要進行的工作有：

1. 持續擴充國客語對照辭典。
2. 加入客語構詞規則。
3. 最佳化語言模型平滑化問題，如：Good-Turing Katz、Kneser-Ney。
4. 持續標記、建置客語語料。

致謝

客家委員會提供給本論文實驗用之客語認證語料以及獎助部份經費，特此致謝。

参考文獻

[1] 蔡依玲，基於隱藏式馬可夫模型之客語文句轉語音系統，國立交通大學電信程所碩士論 文，2009。

[2] 鍾屏蘭、江俊龍，學術研究基礎建置暨客家文化研究計畫，屏東教育大學客家文化所計畫成果報告書，2009。

[3] 羅永聖，結合多類型字典與條件隨機域之中文斷詞與詞性標記系統研究，國立台灣大學資訊工程所碩士論文，2008。

[4] 林千翔，*Chinese Word Segmentation using Specialized HMM*，國立中央大學資訊工程所碩士 論文，2005。

[5] 吳俊毅，線上客語語音合成系統中產生韻律訊息之研究，國立中興大學資訊科學與工程所碩士論文，2010。

[6] 羅丞邑，以資料探勘之技術解決線上客語語音合成系統中多音字發音歧義之研究，國立中興大學資訊科學與工程所碩士論文，2011。

[7] 江昶毅，應用多種特徵的中文斷詞及詞性標記方法，國立中興大學資訊科學與工程所碩士論文，2010。

[8] 李雪貞，客語語音合成之初步研究"，國立臺灣科技大學資訊工程所碩士論文，2002。

[9] 賴亦傑，"應用多詞及多詞性語言模型的中文斷詞及詞性標記方法"，國立中興大學資訊科學與工程所碩士論文，2011。

[10] 客委會出版，客語能力認證基本詞彙-中級、中高級暨語料選粹四縣版上冊。

[11] 客委會出版，客語能力認證基本詞彙-中級、中高級暨語料選粹四縣版下冊。

[12] 林東毅，客語文句翻語音系統之實作，國立交通大學電信工程所碩士論文，2007。

[13] 黃豐隆，線上國客雙語有聲詞典建置之研究，全國計算機會議(NCS-2009)，台灣，2009。

[14] 黃豐隆，國客雙語有聲地圖社群系統，聯合大學資工所客委會計畫成果報告書，2013。

[15] Nianwen Xue, *Chinese Word Segmentation as Character Tagging*, Computational Linguistics 2003 February, Vol. 8, No. 1, pp.29-48.

[16] Guhong Fu and K.K. Luke., *A Two-Stage Statistical Word Segmentation System for Chinese*, Proceeding of The Second SIGHAN Workshop on Chinese Language Processing 2003, Vol. 17, pp.156-159.

[17] Keh-Jiann Chen and Shing-Huan Liu, *Word Identification For Mandarin Chinese Sentences*, Proceedings of COLING 1992, pp.101-107.

[18] Jian-Yun Nie, Marie-Louise Hannan, and Wanying Jin, *Unknown Word Detection and Segmentation of Chinese Using Statistical and Heuristic Knowledge*, Communications of COLIPS 1995, Vol. 5, pp.47-57.

[19] Andi Wu, Zixin Jiang, *Word Segmentation In Sentence Analysis*, International Conference on Chinese Information Processing in Beijing China 1998, pp.169-180.

[20] Jian-feng Gao, Mu Li, and Chang-Ning Huang, *Improved Source-Channel Models for Chinese Word Segmentation*, the 41st Annual Meeting on Association for Computational Linguistics 2003, Vol. 1, pp.272-279.

The 2014 Conference on Computational Linguistics and Speech Processing
ROCLING 2014, pp. 78-88

基於發音知識以建構頻譜 HMM 之國語語音合成方法

A Mandarin Speech Synthesis Method Using Articulation-knowledge Based Spectral HMM Structure

古鴻炎*、賴名彥*、洪尉翔*、陳彥樺*

Hung-Yan Gu, Ming-Yen Lai, Wei-Siang Hong, and Yan-Hua Chen

摘要

在有限語料的情況下，本論文提出一種 HMM 的結構設計，來掌握各個語音單元之文脈相依的頻譜特性，以便改進合成語音的流暢度。此外，在決策樹之文脈分群方法之外，我們依據音素的發音知識，來作文脈分群而大幅降低文脈組合數量。為了評估所提出的 HMM 結構，我們使用三種不同的 HMM 結構方式去建造對應的國語語音合成系統，以作相互的比較。在這些系統裡，使用的韻律參數值是一樣的，都是使用之前研究的 ANN 模組來產生；但是頻譜係數則是使用各自的 HMM 模型來產生；至於信號波形的合成，則都是使用之前研究的基於諧波加雜音模型(HNM)的信號合成模組。聽測實驗的結果顯示，使用本論文提出的 HMM 結構所合成出的語音，比用其它 HMM 結構所合成的明顯地更為流暢；此外，依據錄音語句與合成語句之間的平均頻譜距離的量測結果，也顯示本論文的 HMM 結構，比其它 HMM 結構更能夠降低頻譜距離。

關鍵詞: 語音合成、HMM 結構、發音知識、頻譜流暢度、離散倒頻譜係數

Abstract

In this paper, a new HMM structure is proposed to work with a limited training corpus in order to obtain improved synthetic-speech fluency. Spectral fluency is improved because this HMM structure can model the context-dependent spectral characteristics of a speech unit. In addition, instead of using a decision tree to cluster contexts, the knowledge of phoneme articulation is based to cluster contexts and reduce the enormous quantity of context combinations. To evaluate the proposed HMM structure, we construct three Mandarin speech synthesis systems each uses one different HMM structure for comparisons. In these systems, the prosodic parameters are all generated with same ANN modules studied previously

*國立臺灣科技大學資訊工程系 Department of Computer Science and Information Engineering, National Taiwan University of Science and Technology
E-mail: {guhy, M9615074, M10115035, M10215005}@mail.ntust.edu.tw

but the spectral coefficients are generated with different HMM adopted by its corresponding system. As to the synthesis of signal waveform, the signal model, harmonic plus noise model (HNM), studied previously is commonly adopted in the three systems. According to the results of listening tests, the speech synthesized by the system using the proposed HMM structure is indeed more fluent than the speeches synthesized by the other two systems. In addition, average spectral distances are measured between recorded sentences and synthetic sentences. The results show that the HMM structure proposed here also obtains smaller average spectral distance than the other two HMM structures.

Keywords: Speech Synthesis, HMM Structure, Articulation Knowledge, Spectral Fluency, Discrete Cepstral Coefficients.

1. 緒論

近年來許多研究者早已利用隱藏式馬可夫模型(hidden Markov model, HMM)，來建造語音單元(如音素、音節等)之頻譜演進(spectrum progression)模型(Yoshimura *et al.*, 1999; Zen *et al.*, 2007; Yan *et al.*, 2009; Gu *et al.*, 2010)，之後在合成一個語句時，就會使用訓練得到的 HMM 模型來產生一序列的頻譜特徵向量，然後使用所產生的頻譜特徵向量序列去合成出語音信號。使用 HMM 來作語音信號的合成，通常能夠獲得增進的可理解性(intelligibility)與流暢性(fluency)。更好的是，Tokuda 等人基於 HTK (HMM tool kits)所發展的 HTS 語音合成軟體(Zen *et al.*, 2007)，提供公開的程式原始碼、並且可供下載，所以研究語音合成時，使用 HTS 能夠減少許多時間與氣力。不過，當未使用全域變異數(global variance, GV)匹配時，HTS 軟體所產生的頻譜包絡會發生過於平滑的現象，使得合成出的語音變得悶悶的(muffled) (Toda & Tokuda, 2005)。

在本論文中，我們並不打算沿用、修改 HTS 的程式碼，因此必須自行發展 HMM 模型訓練的程式、及頻譜特徵向量序列之產生程式，這樣的決定是因為，我們想要研發一個具有彈性(flexibility)的語音合成系統，能夠容易地擴增額外的功能。例如音色轉換(timbre transformation)之功能，能夠把合成語音的音色從成年女性轉變成男孩(Gu & Tsai, 2013)；另一項預計擴增的功能則是，同步地播放合成出的語音信號及其對應的拼音符號，此功能可應用於人形機器人上，讓語音發聲和嘴型同步。除了擴增額外功能的原因之外，我們與其他研究者使用 HTS 的經驗(Hsia *et al.*, 2010)，發現 HTS 所產生的國語語音的基週軌跡(pitch contours)聽覺上並不令人滿意，因此本論文建造的國語語音合成系統，就決定使用不同的方法來產生各個音節的基週軌跡。

在先前的一次研究中(Gu *et al.*, 2010)，我們曾嘗試去建立音節單位的 HMM 模型，以掌握音節內的頻譜演進(spectrum progression)方式，但是此 HMM 模型所合成出的語音信號並不夠流暢，在音節邊界處的頻譜不連續(spectral discontinuities)情形經常會被聽出來，我們認為發生頻譜不連續的原因是，設定的語音單位_音節_太大，使得一個音節 X 和前後音節所組合出的不同文脈數量非常龐大，以至於無法為該音節 X 建立良好的文脈相依 HMM 模型。因此，本論文決定使用較小的語音單位，即聲母和韻母，接著根據標記檔裡記載的拼音符號序列，去建構文脈相依的 HMM 模型，並且依據發音知識來對 HMM 模型作分組訓練。HMM 結構的設計方式將會在第二節詳細說明。

我們建造的國語語音合成系統，其合成階段之處理流程如圖 1 所畫，區塊(a)進行輸入文句之分析；區塊(b)使用類神經網路(Artificial Neural Network, ANN)模組來產生各個音節的基週軌跡參數和時長(duration)值，詳細作法可參考(Gu & Wu, 2009)；區塊(c)依據第二節介紹的挑選方法來為各個聲韻母選出對應的 HMM 模型；區塊(d)採用 Tokuda 等人提出的方法(Yoshimura *et al.*, 1999)，去計算 HMM 各狀態分配到的時長音框數；區塊(e)採用先前研究提出的加權線性內插法(Gu *et al.*, 2010)，去產生各音框的頻譜係數；區塊(f)依據基週軌跡參數去計算出各個有聲音框的音高頻率(pitch frequency)值；最後，區塊(g)使用諧波加雜音模型(Harmonic plus noise model, HNM)，去合成出信號波形，詳細作法可參考(Gu & Tsai, 2013)。

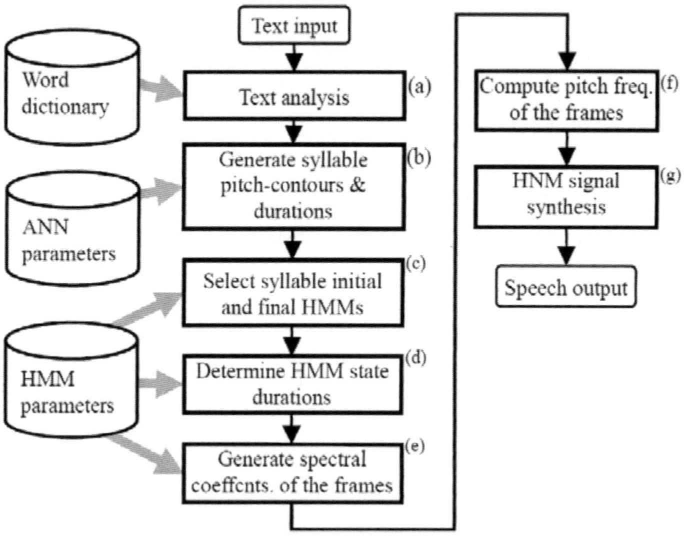

圖 1. 合成階段之主要處理流程

2. 聲韻母分類及文脈組合

在語音辨識領域，基本的 HMM 結構就如圖 2 所示之左至右(left to right)結構，然而此結構並未處理左右兩邊界的文脈相依關係，因此其效能(辨識率)會顯現衰退的情形。

在傳統上，一個國語音節被分割成聲母(開頭子音)和韻母(結尾母音群)兩個部分，若採取聲、韻母作為語音單位，則一個語音單位的左右文脈之組合量可以比音節單位時的文脈組合量大幅減少。但是採用聲、韻母作為語音單位時，可能組合出的文脈量仍是非常龐大，如韻母的前後文脈組合量約有十二萬四千個，詳細數目是(21+37) B 37 B (21+37)

= 124,468，其中 21 表示 21 種聲母，37 表示 37 種韻母，因此有需要再對聲、韻母作進 一步的分類。

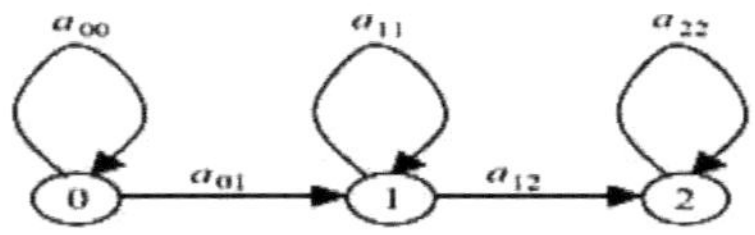

圖2. 左至右HMM 結構

在一個聲母的左邊，可能遇到前一音節的韻母或靜音，在此我們把韻母尾端之可能發音口形分類成 11 類，詳細分類方式如表 1 所列(含靜音 _sil _)。相對地，在一個聲母的右邊只會遇見韻母，在此我們把韻母開頭之可能發音口形分類成 8 類，詳細分類方式如表 2 所列。當把聲母前後可能遇到的韻母發音口形作了分類之後，再考慮國語共有 21 個聲母，由此可推算出聲母可能組合出的文脈數量是(11+1)B21B8=2,016 個。

表 1. 韻母結尾之發音口形分類

Index	0	1	2	3	4	5	6	7	8	9	10	11
Gesture class	a	o	ə	e	i	u	yu	ii	er	n	ng	sil

表 2. 韻母開頭之發音口形分類

Index	0	1	2	3	4	5	6	7
Gesture Classes	a	o	ə	e	i	u	yu	ii

類似於前一段的敘述，如果目前音節沒有聲母時，則在此音節韻母的左邊，將會遇到前一音節的韻母或靜音，在此也把前一音節韻母尾端之可能發音口形分成 11 類，如表 1 所示。另一種情況，當韻母左邊遇到的是本音節的聲母時，在此我們根據聲母的發音位置把可能遇到的聲母分成 6 類，詳細分類方式如表 3 所列。舉例來說，/b/, /p/, /m/, /f/ 的發音位置皆在嘴唇，所以它們都被分類至 _b_類別；同樣道理，/d/, /t/, /n/, /l/的發音位置皆在齒槽，所以把它們都分類至 _d_類別。

表 3. 聲母依發音位置之分類

Index	0	1	2	3	4	5
Consonant Classes	b ㄅ	d ㄉ	z ㄗ	zh ㄓ	j ㄐ	g ㄍ

考慮目前音節韻母的右邊可能遇到的語音單元，第一種情況是，後接的音節沒有聲母，在此我們把後接音節的韻母開頭之可能發音口形分成 9 類，詳細分類方式如表 1 中的 9 個類別，但不包含/n/和/ng/；第二種情況是，後接的音節具有聲母，在此我們把後

接音節聲母的可能發音口形分成 6 類，詳細分類方式如表 3 所列；第三種情況是，後接音節不存在(即目前音節是語句的最後音節)，相當於後面銜接的是靜音。當把韻母前後可能遇到的聲、韻母發音口形作了分類之後，再考慮國語共有 37 個韻母，由此可推算出國語韻母可能組合出的文脈數量是(11+6+1) B 37 B (9+6+1)=10,656 個。 如果我們依據前述

的文脈組合方式去建造 HMM 模型，則需要訓練的 HMM 模型會

有 2,016 + 10,656 個，這意味著在準備訓練語料時，必須錄製數倍於 10,656 個音節數量的音節發音。然而準備大量的訓練語料需要付出昂貴的費用，這暗示使用前述之文脈相依 HMM 模型是不切實際的。對於此問題的解決辦法，先前研究者提出使用決策樹(decision tree)來對 HMM 模型作分群，再對各群分別去訓練一個共用的 HMM，如此就可大幅降低所需的訓練語料數量，如 HTS 軟體就是採取此種作法。不過，本論文採取另外一種研究方向(approach)，就是先依據發音知識來對聲、韻母作分類(這相當於對 HMM 作分群)，再研究新的 HMM 結構之設計，以便解決前述的需求大量訓練語料的問題。

3. 建構新的 HMM 結構

如圖 3 所畫的是擁有 6 個狀態之韻母 HMM 的原本結構，此結構表示該韻母 HMM 是左右文脈相依的，符號 FY_XY 表示此 HMM 是韻母 Y 的模型(F 表示左右文脈相依)，並且 CX 表示韻母 Y 前接的文脈樣式(context type)，CZ 則表示 Y 後接的文脈樣式。根據表 1 和表 3 得知文脈樣式 CX 共有 12+6=18 種；相對地，從表 1(除了/n/與/ng/之外)及表 3 得知文脈樣式 CZ 共有 10+6=16 種。此外，國語有 37 種韻母 Y，所以國語韻母的文脈相依之 HMM 模型總計多達 10,656 個。

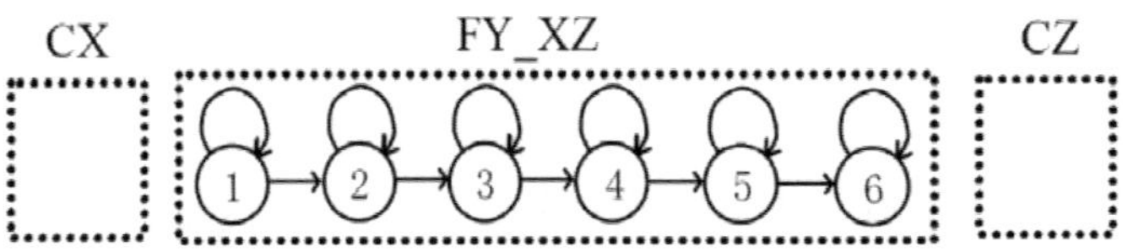

圖3. 左右文脈相依之HMM 模型結構

為了減少實作上需要投入的費用與人力(例如準備大量的訓練語料)，因此我們嘗試對圖 3 的 HMM 模型 FY_XZ 去重作結構安排。我們的解決方法是，假設圖 3 中前面半數的狀態(即狀態 1、2、3)會相依於前接文脈 CX，但是和後接文脈 CZ 不相關；類似地，我們也假設圖 3 中後面半數之狀態(即狀態 4、5、6)只相依於後接文脈 CZ，但是和前接文脈 CX 不相關。根據前述的兩項假設，圖 3 裡左右文脈依之 HMM 模型 FY_XZ，就可以被分解成圖 4 與圖 5 之半段式 HMM 模型 GY_X 和 HY_Z，亦即我們要以半段式 HMM 模型 GY_X 和 HY_Z 之串接來取代 HMM 模型 FY_XZ。

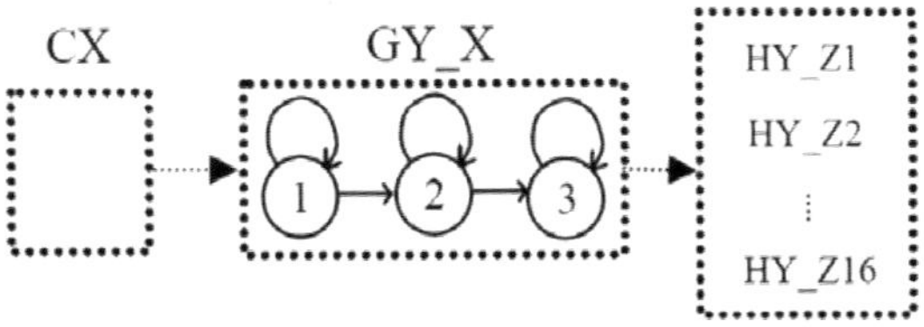

圖4. 韻母Y 前半段之左文脈相依HMM 結構

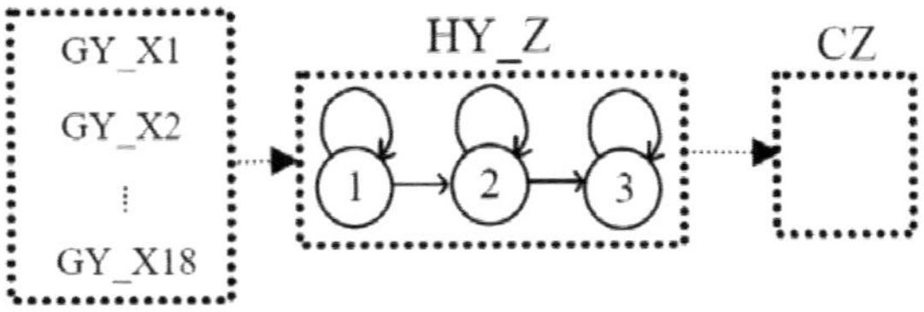

圖5. 韻母Y 後半段之右文脈相依HMM 結構

由於一個韻母前接的文脈被分類成 18 種文脈樣式，所以我們需要建立 18 個半段式 HMM 模型 GY _X 1, GY _X 2, ǔ , GY _X 18 (如圖 5 裡列出)，來掌握韻母 Y 的前半段部分，符號 GY 之 G 表示半段式 HMM 之前半段。類似地，一個韻母後接的文脈被分類成 16 種文脈樣式，所以我們需要建立 16 個半段式 HMM 模型 HY _Z1, HY _Z2, ǔ , HY _Z16 (如圖 4 裡列出)，來掌握韻母 Y 的後半段部分，符號 HY 之 H 表示半段式 HMM 之後半段。如此，一個韻母需要建立的半段式 HMM 模型數量是 18+16=34 個，而國語有 37 種韻母，所以總共需要建立的半段式 HMM 的數量是，34 B 37 = 1,258 個，1,258 比起 10,656 個左右文脈相依之韻母 HMM 少了許多。

關於國語 21 個聲母的 HMM 模型的建立，我們把前述之韻母 HMM 模型的假設套用進來。由於一個聲母前接的文脈被分類成 12 種文脈樣式，所以我們需要為一個聲母建立 12 個半段式 HMM 模型，來掌握該聲母的前半段部分；此外，一個聲母後接的文脈被分類成 8 種文脈樣式，所以我們需要為一個聲母建立 8 個半段式 HMM 模型，來掌握該聲母的後半段部分。如此，一個聲母需要建立的半段式 HMM 模型數量是 12+8=20 個，而國語有 21 種聲母，所以總共需要建立的半段式 HMM 的數量是，20 B 21 = 420 個，420 比起 2,016 個左右文脈相依之聲母 HMM 少了許多。

4. 實驗評估

4.1 訓練階段

我們邀請了一位成年男性至隔音錄音室錄製 1,208 個語句的發音，這些語句的腳本(script)是隨機地從無關的文章中挑選出，總計有 10,173 個音節，而錄音的取樣率為 22,050 Hz。為了標記這些語句中各音節的拼音符號，我們首先使用 HTK 套件來作 forced alignment 處理，而得到初步的音節邊界之標記，然後以人工操作 WaveSurfer 軟體去更正錯誤的音節邊界標記。

我們將各個音節的音檔切割成一序列的音框，音框長度設為 512 個樣本點，而音框位移設為 128 個樣本點。每個音框經分析計算後擷取出 39 個頻譜參數 c_0, c_1, ǔ , c_{38}，實際上是離散倒頻譜係數(discrete cepstral coefficients, DCC) (Capp¶ & Moulines, 1996)，DCC 係數的擷取方法，請參考我們先前的研究論文(Gu & Tsai, 2009)。此外，一個音框的週期性資訊也會被記錄在另一個維度中，即存入 c_{39}，如果一個音框被偵測出是週期性的，則設定 c_{39}的值為 1，反之則設定 c_{39}的值為 0。一個 HMM 經過訓練之後，我們就可以依據平均向量的 c_{39}的值，來判斷各個 HMM 狀態是否為有聲(voiced)或無聲(unvoiced)之狀態，然後就可為有聲的 HMM 狀態去產生基週軌跡。另外，頻譜參數的差分值也是有用的，所以我們把頻譜特徵向量增加 40 維，以儲存 DCC 係數的一階差分值。在訓練完一個 HMM 之後，除了記錄 HMM 的模型參數之外，也要記錄各個 HMM 狀態被駐留的音框個數之平均值與變異數。

在本論文中，一個韻母的前半與後半部分之半段式 HMM 模型皆是由 3 個狀態建造而成，並且狀態移轉方式都是由左至右，就如圖 4 和圖 5 所示。不過，對於一個聲母的半段式 HMM 模型，我們僅使用 2 個狀態去建造。關於高斯混合組件(Gaussian mixture component)的數量，在每一個 HMM 狀態上，我們只設置一個高斯混合。對於半段式 HMM 之訓練，我們依據分段式 K 中心(segmental K-means)演算法(Rabiner & Juang, 1993)，去發展了訓練程式。

4.2 語音合成處理

本論文製作的國語語音合成系統，其合成階段之處理流程如圖 1 所示，區塊(a)作 文句分析(text analysis)，每次會從輸入的檔案讀取一個文句進來，然後以查詞典及檢查數個構詞規則的方式去作剖析，把讀入的文句切割成一序列的詞語(words)，並且每一個詞語經由查詞典也可得知它的拼音符號。接著，在區塊(b)產生各音節之音高軌跡(pitch contour)及時長(duration)值，對於每一個音節，先準備好它的文脈資料項，再將文脈資料輸入至兩個類神經網路(ANN)，以分別預測出音高軌跡參數和時長參數的值，關於 ANN 的輸出/輸入資料項、及結構的細節，請參考我們先前的研究論文(Gu & Wu, 2009)。

在區塊(c)挑選聲母、韻母之 HMM 模型，首先依據各個音節的拼音符號去查詢出對應的聲母和韻母之拼音符號與編號，並且決定聲、韻母在表 1、表 2、與表 3 的分類編號，然後依據各個單元(聲母或韻母)的編號和其前後文脈的分類編號，從訓練出的半段式 HMM 模型中，找出一個單元(聲母或韻母)對應的前、後兩個半段式 HMM，接著把聲、韻母的四個半段式 HMM 依序串接成一個音節的完整 HMM 模型。在區塊(d)決定各個

HMM 狀態的駐留音框數，我們採用 Tokuda 等人提出的方法(Tokuda *et al.*, 2004)，依據 ANN 產生的音節時長值，去計算一個音節 HMM 之各個狀態所應分配到的時長音框數。接著，在區塊(e)產生各音框之頻譜係數(即 DCC 係數)，一個常被使用的方法是最大似然估計法(Maximum likelihood Estimate, MLE) (Tokuda *et al.*, 2004)，不過，本論文使用的是先前我們提出的加權式線性內插法(weighted linear interpolation, WLI) (Gu *et al.*, 2010)，來計算各個音框的 DCC 係數。

在區塊(f)計算各個音框的音高值，一個有聲單元(例如聲母/m/和韻母/a/)的各個音框都必須被指派一個音高頻率值(單位 Hz)，在此我們拿 ANN 產生的基週軌跡參數去作拉格蘭日內插(Lagrange interpolation)，以求得各個音框的音高頻率值。接著，在區塊(g)採用 HNM 信號模型作語音信號合成，我們把一個單元各音框的 DCC 係數與音高頻率值，按照音框次序逐個音框送給 HNM 語音信號合成模組，去合成出語音信號，關於 HNM 信號合成之細部處理方法，可參考我們先前的研究論文(Gu & Tsai, 2013; Gu & Tsai, 2009)。

4.3 頻譜距離量測

在此以代號 SYC 與 SYD 表示本研究所建造的兩個國語語音合成系統，SYC 表示完整的系統，對於一個音節的前接與後接文脈都納入考慮，這意味聲母的前半段 HMM 的左文脈有作區分(例如圖 4 之 GY_X)，並且韻母的後半段 HMM 的右文脈也有作區分(如圖 5 之 HY_Z)，所以對於各個不同的文脈樣式分類(如 CX)，就需要去建造一個對應的半段式 HMM (如 GY_X)。相反地，在簡化的系統 SYD 裡，對於一個音節的前接與後接文脈就不去作區分了，亦即聲母的前半段 HMM 不去區分它的左文脈，如此一個聲母就僅需訓練出一個前半段之 HMM，然而聲母後半段之 HMM，則仍然需訓練出數個半段式 HMM，以區分右文脈；類似道理，韻母的後半段 HMM 就不去區分它的右文脈，如此一個韻母就只需訓練出一個後半段之 HMM，然而韻母前半段之 HMM，則仍然需訓練出數個半段式 HMM，以區分左文脈。此外，以 SYP 表示先前研究裡所建造的國語語音合成系統(Gu *et al.*, 2010)，在 SYP 系統裡，我們對於每一種國語音節都建造了一個或數個音節寬度的 HMM，至於一種音節所建造的 HMM 個數，則和該音節在訓練語句中的發音次數有關。在本研裡，我們使用相同的訓練語句，來訓練這三個系統: SYC、SYD 和 SYP。

藉由這三個系統，我們就可以把錄音語句與合成語句相對應的音框拿去作頻譜距離的計算。詳細情形是，把 50 句測試語句的標記檔逐一輸入給 SYC、SYD 和 SYP 系統去處理，以取得三個系統對應於各句測試語句的的合成音檔，然後分別拿各句的錄音語句去和合成語句去作 DCC 分析，以計算出兩個 DCC 頻譜特徵向量的序列。接著，偵測兩 DCC 序列中各組對應音框是否都為有聲，若對應的音框都偵測為有聲，就拿該組音框去計算音框之間的 DCC 向量幾何距離，然後我們拿 50 句測試語句的所有有聲音框算出的幾何距離，計算出一個跨語句的平均距離。

表 4 所列出的數值，就是這三個系統的平均頻譜距離，從表 4 可知 SYC 系統所產生的音框 DCC 向量，最靠近於錄音語句分析出來的 DCC 向量，而 SYP 系統所產生的音

框 DCC 向量，最遠離錄音語句分析出來的 DCC 向量。此外，只要一個音節中的聲母和韻母之間的文脈相依性有被掌握(modeled)，即 SYD 系統的情況，則量測出的 DCC 頻譜距離，就會比 SYP 系統的好很多，這表示圖 4 和圖 5 所列出的半段式 HMM 結構，的確可幫忙掌握兩個相鄰語音單元之間的文脈相依之頻譜特性。

表4. 平均DCC 頻譜距離

System	SYC	SYD	SYP
Avg. dist.	**0.633**	**0.640**	**0.732**

4.4 主觀聽測實驗

聽測實驗使用一篇訓練語句沒有用到的短文，該短文包括 70 個音節，我們將它分別輸入到三個系統去合成出語音音檔，在此分別以 WC、WD 和 WP 來表示 SYC、SYD 和 SYP 這三個系統所合成的音檔，這些音檔可到如下的網址去下載與試聽：http://guhy.csie.ntust.edu.tw/hmmhalf/。

透過 WC、WD 和 WP 三個音檔，我們進行流暢度比較的聽測實驗，一共邀請了 12 位受測者，在第一次聽測實驗裡，受測者以隨機次序聆聽 WC 和 WD 音檔；在第二次聽測實驗裡，受測者以隨機次序聆聽 WC 和 WP 音檔；在第三次聽測實驗裡，受測者則以隨機次序聆聽 WD 和 WP 音檔。在各次聽測實驗中，當一位受測者聽完兩個音檔後，我們要求他給一個分數來顯示流暢度的聽測結果，評分的範圍為-2 到 2 分，2(-2)分表示後者(前者)比前者(後者)流暢很多，1(-1) 分表示後者(前者)比前者(後者)稍微流暢，0 分表示分辨不出來。

三次聽測實驗之後，我們依音檔播放次序來調整分數的正負號，然後計算出各次實驗的平均分數和標準差，結果得到如表 5 所示的數值。從表 5 可知第一次和第二次實驗的平均分數為-0.833 和-0.417，負的分數表示音檔 WC 比 WD 和 WP 較為流暢，如果全部受測者都具有語音合成研究的背景，我們認為兩負分的絕對值應會更大，所以半段式 HMM 結構的確可以有效的提升合成語音的流暢度。至於第三次實驗的平均分數 0.250，該分數的絕對值最小，我們覺得這表示 WD 和 WP 音檔的流暢度應無明顯的差異。

表5. 聽測實驗之平均評分

	WC vs. WD	WC vs. WP	WD vs. WP
AVG	**-0.833**	**-0.417**	**0.250**
STD	**0.718**	**0.900**	**0.866**

5. 結語

在本論文中，我們應用音素的發音知識於取代決策樹，來對一個語音單元(聲母或韻母)的左右文脈作分類，以降低文脈組合之數量；此外，更進一步研究提出文脈相依之半段式 HMM 結構，以便在有限語料的情況下，掌握一個語音單元的文脈相依頻譜特性。如此結合兩者，用以改進合成語音的流暢度。

為了評估本論文所提出的半段式 HMM 結構，我們進行了兩種實驗，即頻譜距離量測和流暢度聽測，量測出的平均頻譜距離顯示，使用半段式 HMM 結構所合成出的語句，和原始錄音語句之間的頻譜距離，可從 0.732 減少到 0.633；此外，聽測實驗的結果顯示，使用半段式 HMM 所合成出的語音，比使用另外兩種 HMM 結構的較為流暢，所以在訓練語句不充足的情況下，半段式 HMM 結構確實可改進合成語音的流暢度。

未來我們可在相同訓練語料的情況下，比較我們系統的合成語音與 HTS 軟體的合成語音，觀察兩者在客觀頻譜距離和主觀聽測上的差異。另外，本論文著重於改進語音單元之間頻譜銜接上的流暢度，未來可再考慮去改進韻律方面的流暢度，以更為提升系統整體的流暢度。

致謝

感謝國科會計畫之經費支援，國科會計畫編號: NSC 102-2221-E-011-129。

参考文獻

Capp¶, O., & E. Moulines (1996). Regularization techniques for discrete cepstrum estimation. *IEEE Signal Processing Letters*, 3(4), 100-102.

Gu, H. Y., & S. F. Tsai (2009). A discrete-cepstrum based spectrum envelope estimation scheme and its example application of voice transformation. *International Journal of Computational Linguistics and Chinese Language Processing*, 14(4), 363-382.

Gu, H. Y., & C. Y. Wu (2009). Model spectrum-progression with DTW and ANN for speech synthesis. In *Proc. ECTI-CON*, Pattaya, Thailand, 1010-1013.

Gu, H. Y., M. Y. Lai, & S. F. Tsai (2010). Combining HMM spectrum models and ANN prosody models for speech synthesis of syllable prominent languages. In *Proc. ISCSLP*, Tainan, Taiwan, Special Session 1.

Gu, H. Y., & C. L. Tsai (2013). Integrating speaker-nonspecific timbre transformation to an HNM based speech synthesis scheme. *Journal of the Chinese Institute of Engineers*, 36(3), 371-381.

Hsia, C. C., C. H. Wu, & J. Y. Wu (2010). Exploiting prosody hierarchy and dynamic features for pitch modeling and generation in HMM-based speech synthesis. *IEEE trans. Audio, Speech, and Language Processing*, 18(8), 1994-2003.

Rabiner, L. & B. H. Juang (1993). *Fundamentals of Speech Recognition*, Prentice Hall.

Toda, T., & K. Tokuda (2005). Speech parameter generation algorithm considering global variance for HMM-based speech synthesis. In *Proc. Eurospeech*, Lisbon, Portugal, 2801-2804.

Tokuda, K., H. Zen, & A. W. Black (2004). An HMM-based approach to multilingual speech synthesis. In *Text to Speech Synthesis: New Paradigms and Advances*, Editors: S. Narayanan and A. Alwan, Prentice Hall, 135-153.

Yan, Z. J., Y. Qian, & F. K. Soong (2009). Rich context modeling for high quality HMM-based TTS. In *Proc. INTERSPEECH*, Brighton, UK, 1755-1758.

Yoshimura, T., K. Tokuda, T. Masuko, T. Kobayashi, & T. Kitamura (1999). Simultaneous modeling of spectrum, pitch and duration in HMM based speech synthesis. In *Proc. Eurospeech*, Budapest, Hungary, 2347-2350.

Zen, H., T. Nose, J. Yamagishi, S. Sako, T. Masuko, A. W. Black, & K. Tokuda (2007). The HMM-based speech synthesis system (HTS) version 2.0. In *Proc. 6th ISCA Workshop on Speech Synthesis*, Bonn, Germany, 294-299.

Some Prosodic Characteristics of Taiwan English Accent

Chao-yu Su* , Chiu-yu Tseng* and Jyh-Shing Roger Jang**

Abstract

Recently the studies concentrating on computer assistant language learning (CALL) has been growing in numbers as they offer many advantagesthat couldn't otherwise be provided by a traditional classroom setting. In addtion to popular computer-assisted pronunciation teaching (CAPT) systems, computer-assisted prosody training system is another branch of CALL (Computer assistant language learning) system. The focus of pronunciation teaching system differs from the prosody training system as the former concentrates on segmental errors while the later on suprasegmental errors. In recent years studies focusing on suprasegmentals have shown that in addition to segmental information, prosodic information is indispensable for language learning. Moreover, reported studies that adopted prosodic training for second-language (L2) learners have demonstrated that computer-assisted prosody training systems could further improve the overall comprehensibility of L2 speech.

In order to better understand L2 English by native Taiwan Mandarin speakers (TW) and to apply the knowleage onto computer-assisted prosody training system, the present study examines prosodic characteristics of Taiwan L2 English in relation to native (L1) English, as TW speakers˘mother tongue, Mandarin.

The English speech data used in the present study is taken from the AESOP-ILAS (Asian English Speech cOrpus Project collected by the Institute of Linguistics, Academia Sinica). Representing accent of Taiwan L2 English, which is part of AESOP project that was designed and constructed to represent various kinds of L2 English spoken in Asia when linguistic knowledge was incorporated in the corpus design. The built-in linguistic knowledge aims to elicit production of English segmental and suprasegmental features including (1) word-level features by target words in carrier sentence; (2) phrase boundary phenomena by target words at phrase boundaries; (3) phrasal and sentential prominence (broad and narrow focus) by target words; (4) function words in stressed and unstressed positions, and (5) prosodic disambiguation of syntactic structures. As for the speech material of L1 Mandarin, the data is from the intonation balanced speech corpus in SINICA COSPRO, which aims to examine the role of intonation with respect to prosodic grouping in Mandarin speech. In totoal, English speech by 9 L1 (4M&5F)/9 L2 (5M&4F) speakers and Mandarin speech by 2 L1 (1M&1F) speakers are used for present analysis.

Our previous studies of L2 English have shown some distinct L2 suprasegmental features. These features include lack of pitch and loudness contrasts in prosodic realizations at both word and sentence levels. In another previous study we further showed native (L1) speakers may realize word stresses through a binary stress/no-stress contrast anchored by

* Institute of Linguistics, Academia Sinica, Taipei, Taiwan

** CS Dept., National Taiwan University, Taiwan

the position of primary stress. Post-primary syllables tend to be reduced to near-tertiary stress while pre-primary syllables could be elevated to near-primary magnitude in F0. Thus the 3-way primary/secondary/tertiary contrast is merged into a binary stress/no-stress contrast with robust prosodic contrasts between the primary stress and its following syllable(s). As results, the position-related merge of the secondary word stress turns out to be difficult for TW L2 speakers to carry out and it might be one of sources of L2 English accent. We also compared TW L2 English accent and TW Mandarin, the target L2 speakers˘ mother tongue, in order to uncover in what ways TW L2 accent could be attributed from their L1 Mandarin features. Following this line of research, the present study incorporates prosodic features found to contribute to TW L2 accent in previous studies to investegate: 1) how TW second-language (L2) English is different from L1 Englsish by intergrated prosodic feautres, 2) if any transfer effect from L2s˘ mother tongue contributes to L2 accent, and 3) what are the similarities/differences between L1 and L2 by prosodic templetes of target words/sentences.

To test how TW L2 English is different from L1 Englsish by intergrated prsodic feautres, L1 English, TW L2 English and TW L1 Mandarin are identified from each other by 2 classifiers, SVM and KNNC. Results show the prosody of TW L2 English is distinct from L1 English; however, TW L2 English and TW Mandarin share common prosodic characteristics which could be differentiated from L1 English. Further analyses by individual prosodic feature show distinct L2 features of TW English which might attribute to prosodic transfer from Mandarin. Another feature is the less tempo contrast in sentence that contributes to different rhythm; while narrower loudness range of word stress is yet another featurethat contributes to less strong/weak distinction in TW L2 English.

Prosodic templates of target word/sentnece are further compared between any two of L1/L2 speakers. We assume between-speaker similarity would be greater when the speaker-pair selected belongs to the same speaker group (L1/L2) than when the speaker-pair is from different speaker groups (L1/L2). The between-speaker similarity is defined as average cosine measure between two speakers by prosodic feature vectors. Theresult does show L1 and L2 speakers produce prosodic templates with greater within-group consistency respectively but their within-group patterns are distinct from their counterpart group. One distint pattern we found is loudness of sentence and another pattern the timing/pitch patterns of word. The above prosodic transfer effect and distict TW L2 patterns of prosody are found in relation to syntax-induced narrow focus and lexicon-defined word stress which echo our previous findings with regard to prosodic realizations TW L2 English.

We believe the above analyses with incorporated linguistic knowledge not only shed light on better understanding of TW L2 English, but can also be implemented in further refinments of the current CALL and CAPT systems .

網頁商家名稱擷取與地址配對之研究

Store Name Extraction and Name-Address Matching on the Web

林育暘 Lin Yu-Yang, 張嘉惠 Chang Chia-Hui
國立中央大學資訊工程學系
Department of Computer Science and Information Engineering
National Central University
101522052@cc.ncu.edu.tw, chia@csie.ncu.edu.tw

摘要

行動裝置的普及造就大量地域性查詢的需求，其中最常見的一種查詢，就是尋找附近的餐廳或加油站。然而當使用者在電子地圖上搜尋這些地點名稱 (POI，Point of Interest)時，經常無法找到，因為電子地圖上雖有地點名稱標註，但是相關資訊不足，而這些資訊其實大多可以在網頁中找到。因此使用者大多必須開啟瀏覽器搜尋商家名稱找出地址，並把地址輸入至電子地圖查詢路線。但行動裝置螢幕小，且輸入文字不便利，如果要反覆查詢將是一件耗時耗力的工作。如果這時候有一個商家地理資訊系統能事先將網路上的商家資訊進行整合，最後提供一個 APP 直接讓使用者查詢，將可以大幅度減少使用者與裝置間的互動次數，有效的提供便利性。

為建構商家地理資料庫，Chuang 等人[9]對於包含地址網頁提出三種抓取程式，並利用 Chang 等人[2]的地址擷取程式，取得大量中文地址。Li 與 Chang[1]並定義地址相關資訊擷取問題，希望藉此豐富每個 POI 的相關資訊，提高地理資訊檢索(Geographical Information Retrieval, GIR)的召回率。然而不論是 Li 與 Chang[1]或 Chang 等人[2]或 Chuang 等人[9]的相關資訊擷取方法都僅能從多筆地址網頁擷取資訊，所得資訊有限，對於單筆地址網頁的相關資訊擷取仍尚無研究。

本研究從地址的角度出發，利用已抓取大量包含地址的網頁，先找出網頁中的地址，再藉由地址找出對應的商家名稱進行配對。換言之，給定一個已知地址，我們希望能透過網路資料擷取出該地點的名稱（如：商家名稱、政府單位…等）。舉例而言：當我們已有地址「新北市板橋區中山路二段 88 號 3F」，我們希望能知道這個地址對應的名稱「大鈞醫學美容診所」，如此即可進一步藉由地址、名稱並利用搜尋引擎收集更多額外商家資訊。這些額外資訊不僅可以有效提昇 GIS 檢索系統的召回率，也可提昇商家分類的準確率[10]。

在辨識商家名稱的部分， 本篇論文使用了條件隨機域 (Conditional Random Field)[3]當作學習演算法。目前有許多關於中文組織名稱辨認的研究 [4] [5] [6] [7]，可以從新聞或一些較正式的文章中萃取出組織名稱，但是並沒有嘗試以一個 CRF-Model 直接對各種網站中的整個網頁內容進行中文組織名稱辨認。這兩者之間不同處在於新聞類文章屬於較正式的文章體裁，因此容易出現行政機關與正式的組織名稱，例如：行政院和維德食品有限公司，但是整個網路上商家組織名稱的命名方式傾向則不同，例如：吼牛排、努哇克咖啡、阿嬤祖傳菜包肉粽仙草…等，都是商家組織名稱。另外，一個完整的網頁內容有結構與非結構化的資訊交錯呈現，雖然結構化資訊會造成自然語言文字內容的破碎，但這些結構也隱含有可利用的資訊。

為了使商家辨識能以最少人力進行自動化學習，本研究使用自動標記方式建立訓練資料，我們先針對部份的黃頁網站撰寫 Parser 取得大量商家名稱與地址的組合，並以這些已經取得的商家名稱對網頁語料進行自動標記，再利用自動標記後的語料訓練 CRF 序列標記模型。然而一個地址可能出現在多個網頁之中，僅只仰賴其中一個網頁也有失之偏頗之慮，因此我們也收集了 Google Snippets 當作訓練資料進行比較。本篇論文的第二個主題則是商家地址的配對，由於一個網頁可能包含多個商家名稱，我們對網頁以簡單的規則進行分類後，使用了啟發式（heuristic）的配對規則，利用各類型的網站所具有的表達特性，對地址與商家名稱進行配對。

本研究承續 [8] [9]之研究，經由爬取網頁上包含地址的大量網頁（包括 Yellow Page 與 Surface Web）進行商家名稱擷取。其中 Yellow Page 提供了大量商家名稱以及地址與商家的配對資料，而 Surface Web 則利用 [2]之地址擷取模型擷取出了可能含有台灣地址的網頁與地址清單。本篇論文以已知可能含有台灣地址的中文網頁、每筆網頁的地址清單、大量商家名稱清單以及已知的地址與商家名稱配對資料為基礎，提出了一個商家名稱擷取系統，方法分為四大步驟：地址網頁的前處理、商家名稱命名實體辨認、及地址－商家名稱匹配。本研究在三個模型聯合標記商家名稱的方式下，地址與商家名稱的平均配對正確率為 0.57。

關鍵詞：商家地理資訊檢索、商家名稱擷取、商家名稱與地址配對、序列標記、條件隨機域

Keywords: POI, store name extraction, name-address matching, sequence labeling, conditional random field

参考文獻

[1] S.-Y. Li, Application and Extraction of Postal Addresses and Related Information, National Central University, 2009.

[2] C.-H. Chang, C.-Y. Huang and Y.-S. Su, "Chinese Postal Address and Associated Information Extraction," The 26th Annual Conference of the Japanese Society for Artificial Intelligence, 2012.

[3] L. D. John, M. Andrew and N. C. Fernando, "Conditional Random Fields: Probabilistic Models for Segmenting and Labeling Sequence Data," ICML Proceedings of the Eighteenth International Conference on Machine Learning, pp. 282-289, 2001.

[4] Z. Suxiang, Z. Suxian and W. Xiaojie, "Automatic Recognition of Chinese Organization Name Based on Conditional Random Fields," Natural Language Processing and Knowledge Engineering, pp. 229-233, 2007.

[5] Y. Xiying, "A Method of Chinese Organization Named Entities Recognition Based On Statistical Word Frequency, Part Of Speech And Length," Broadband Network and Multimedia Technology (IC-BNMT), pp. 637-641, 2011.

[6] L. Yajuan, Y. Jing and H. Liang, "Chinese Organization Name Recognition Based on Multiple Features," Pacific Asia conference on Intelligence and Security Informatics, pp. 136-144, 2012.

[7] C.-W. Wu, R. T.-H. Tsai and W.-L. Hsu, "Semi-joint labeling for chinese named entity recognition," Proceedings of the 4th Asia information retrieval conference, pp. 107-116, 2008.

[8] Y.-S. Su, Associated Information Extraction for Enabling Entity Search on Electronic Map, National Central University, 2012.

[9] H.-M. Chuang, C.-H. Chang and T.-Y. Kao, "Effective Web Crawling for Chinese Addresses and Associated Information," in EC-Web, Munich, Germany, 2014.

Public Opinion Toward CSSTA: A Text Mining Approach

Yi-An Wu[*], Shu-Kai Hsieh[*]

Abstract

Recently, the public of Taiwan has had a heated debate on the issue of Cross-Strait Service Trade Agreement (CSSTA). After months of simmering tensions between ruling party and opposition party strongly backed by the student-led Sunflower Movement, the debate has finally reached a breaking point on March 18, 2014, at which students occupied the Legislative Yuan. During this period, novel communication such as Facebook sharing, instant messaging, and discussions on PTT have reshaped the social movement since they are easily accessible and instantly responded. The social media has become the dominant source in opinion shaping and the accompanying sentiment spread.

The extraction and tracking of uprising political opinions and events such as CSSTA has become one of the most important topics that receive much attention. With the huge amounts of texts, it is not possible to analyze and interpreting the social and political texts manually. Instead, we propose to use the text mining approach, which automatically extract opinion and information profiles from the texts. Moreover, this approach also strengthens the objectivity, for the norms are set *a priori*, and thus human biases are reduced.

As a pioneering work in the context of Taiwan society, this research aims to trace the public opinion toward CSSTA from the perspective of text mining. The approach involves the manually extracting of political stance related keywords and phrases, supervised machining learning, and a statistical model of the trend. We focus on the individual posts on PTT rather than news since they are more representative. The potential political or commercial applications are valuable. One can discover the public opinion and response in a short time.

The materials we used in this research includes a list of manually created seed words and phrases representing the pro-and-con political polarity, respectively. These words are tested by the texts of the website `服貿東西軍_[è], which classifies the supporting and opposing texts. Another resource we used in this work is the PTT corpus, which is a popular online bulletin board favored by many of the youth.

[*] Graduate Institute of Linguistics, National Taiwan University

[è] http://ecfa.speaking.tw/imho.php

Our procedures follow the common text mining techniques: features extractions, Chinese word segmentation with custom dictionary, establish the model for the SVM classifier, and using the N-fold cross validation for evaluations. We choose the keywords as the first step since many terms can potentially reveal one˘s attitude. For instance, the supporter for CSSTA would call students `霸佔_, *occupy*, the parliament, while the opponent would use `留守_, *stay*, in the parliament. Then we use these keywords as features to train the SVM classifier. The gold standards of the texts are chosen from the `服貿東西軍_ website. The results are shown as follows:

Accuracy	Precision	Recall	F-score	Std. Dev.
0.850	0.850	0.859	0.855	0.040

We further extended our results to do the trend analysis. First, we apply the information gain calculated from the previous classifier, and then we sum keywords of each post, and sum over the posts of the same day. In other words, the score of each date is calculated as the following equation:

$$\text{Score} = \sum_i \sum_w IG(w) * C(w),\ i = \text{post index}, w = \text{word}$$

The figure demonstrates the popularity of this topic of each day. Second, we calculate the supporting information gain over the total information gain, and also sum over the posts in one day. This figure shows the ratio of supporting CSSTA from the analysis of posts.

Mining and tracking political opinions from texts in the social media is a young yet important research area with both scientific significance and social impact. The goal of this paper is to move one step forward in this area in Chinese context. We started from the manually created keywords and key phrases of CSSTA, used them to build a classifier and calculated their information gain, and then did the trend analysis of the PTT corpus. This approach involves interdisciplinary fields including information retrieval, data mining, statistics, machine learning, and computational linguistics. We hope that this text mining approach could discover the public opinion toward CSSTA, and further reveal political stances. Future works include more sophisticated language processing techniques applied to more broad domain of political topics, as well as developing dynamic tracking system gearing up for year-end election 2014.

The 2014 Conference on Computational Linguistics and Speech Processing
ROCLING 2014, pp. 96-109

Towards automatic enrichment of standardized electronic dictionaries by semantic classes

Elleuch Imen*, Gargouri Bilel* and Ben Hamadou Abdelmajid[1]

Abstract

In this paper we propose an approach for the automatic enrichment of standardized electronic dictionaries by the semantic classes. This approach consists of three phases. The first phase treat the semantic classification process founded on the studies of Gaston Gross. The second phase profites from the existed subject fields in the dictionary's lexical entries in order to attribute the suitable semantic classes. The final phase realizes syntactic analyses of the textual content of meanings's lexical entries. This phase, aims to refine the subject field based enrichment and also treats the non enriched meanings in the second phase. In addition, it attributes the same semantic classes for the synonym meanings. We used an available standardized Arabic dictionary to tested the performance of the proposed approach.

Keywords: Automatic enrichment, standardized electronic dictionnaries, semantic classes, Arabic language.

1. Introduction

Semantic knowledge, especially semantic classes which aim to characterize meanings of lexical units in dictionaries, have attracted considerable interest in both linguistic (Stede, 1998), (Dorr, 1997) and computational linguistics (Kipper et al 2000). Such semantic class can be definite as a semantic linguistic propriety classifying meanings and can therefore be used as a valuable means of comprehending the specific meaning of polysimous lexical units. Thus the need of dictionaries with semantic classes has become a necessity for Natural Language Processing (NLP) applications.

For various languages, various semantic classifications are now available. We can list the verbs classification (Pinker, 1989; Jackendoff, 1990; Levin, 1993, Dubois and Dubois-Charlier, 1997) that regroups together verbs that share both a common semantics and a set of syntactic alternations. Also, we notice WordNet (Fellbaum, 1998) that provides semantic ontological classification and FrameNet (Fillmore, 1985) that hierarchically classify lexical units using various relationship as synonymy, antonym and is-a relations. However, the referential classification is based on semantic features like [+/- human], [+/- concrete], etc. characterizing semantically each lexical unit outside of the meaning's contexts. Object classes (Gross, 1994) defines a semantic classification based on surface realization of predicate argument structure. A semantic class groups together predicates as arguments having the same syntactic constrictions. Rely on a semantic classification; two methods of enrichment lexical resources by semantic classes exist. The first one is manual. It is characterized by the large number of lexical units to be classified FrameNet

* FSEGS, B.P. 1088, 3018 Sfax, Tunisia
E-mail: { imen.elleuch, bilel.gargouri}@fsegs.rnu.tn

** ISIMS, B.P. 242, 3021 Sakiet-Ezzit Sfax, Tunisia
E-mail: abdelmajid.benhamadou@isimsf.rnu.tn

(Fillmore, 1985) this is why it is a costly and time-consuming method. The second method is automatic. It can use corpora (Fuchs & Habert, 2004), (Condamines, 2005) or in some cases, texts of the treated lexical resources (Rastier, 2001) and (Valette et al, 2006). The automatic method does not necessitate the intervention of the human expert during the enrichment process (Wilson et al., 2004). Both manual and automatic method of enrichment lexical resources with semantic classes requires the institution of the semantic classification. In addition, the ability of the structure's dictionary to receive semantic classes is important. In fact, some models of lexical resources do not supply the affectation of the semantic classes to lexical units.

In order to provide a unified framework for modeling lexical resources, in general, and to facilitate the exchange and integration into NLP applications, the LMF (Lexical Markup Framework) standard (Francopoulo & George, 2008) ISO 24613 is published. This standard allows the modelization of all linguistics levels such as the morphological, the syntactic, the semantic and the syntactico-semantic ones.

Considering the importance of the semantic classes to characterize the meaning of lexical units, and profiting from the fine model of LMF lexical resources to receive semantic classes, we propose in this paper an automatic approach for the enrichment of standardized LMF electronic dictionaries by semantic classes. In fact, the LMF standard offers particular fields (i.e., SubjectField) that can assist the identification of the relevant semantic class and provides synonymy relationships that can be used to improve the enrichment process. Also, in an LMF dictionary, the meaning of lexical entries is accompanied with a rich textual content. The proposed approach is founded on a semantic classification initiated by the Gaston Gross studies. An experimentation of this approach is carried out on an available standardized LMF Arabic dictionary.

The next part of this paper is organized as follows: We will start with a presentation of some related works related to semantic classification and enrichment methods. Then, we will present the LMF standard. Thereafter, we will detail the proposed approach for the enrichment of LMF standardized dictionaries with the semantic classes. After that, we will describe the experiment carried out on a standardized LMF Arabic dictionary and discuss some of the obtained results. Finally, in the conclusion, we will announce some future works.

2. Related works

This section is devoted to the representation of some related works of available semantic classifications and the semantic enrichment methods of lexical resources.

2.1. Semantic classification

Several semantic classifications exist in literature. We can mention the verbs classification (Pinker, 1989; Jackendoff, 1990; Levin, 1993, Dubois & Dubois-Charlier, 1997). It based on both a common semantics and a set of syntactic alternations to grouped lexical units into semantic classes. This type of classification is restricted to certain class types and treats only verbs. So no comprehensive classification is available limits the usefulness of the class for practical NLP tasks.

Moreover, we can note the ontological classification like WordNet (Miller, 1990) that intended to classify philosophical things as they exist in the world. It is particularly appropriate for object modeling, including their relationships and properties. Therefore, content of ontology does not interact directly but rather with relationships (i,e synonymy, antonym, part of, is-A,...). This semantic classification does not consider the use's context of lexical units, further it groups word into classes as presented in the real world without referring to the linguistics features.

Also, we can cite the referential classification (Gross, 1975) (Dichy, 2000) that used semantic features like [+/- concrete], [+/- human]. Those features are attached to lexical units to describe their appurtenance to the semantic classes. This semantic classification assigned semantic features to lexical entries without taking into account the uses of the lexical units.

Another kind of semantic classification is proposed by Gaston Gross (Gross, 1994). It classifies lexical units into semantic classes based on predicate-argument structure. Thus, a semantic class groups together predicates as arguments sharing syntactic and semantic behaviors. Therefore, this classification insures the taking into account the multiple meanings of senses lexical entries depending on a specific use context.

Finally, we can conclude that the ontological and the referential classification do not guarantee the polysemy of lexical entries because they do not take into account meanings in the classification process. Or the verbs classifications classify only verbs and neglect the other part of speech whereas, the Gaston Gross semantic classification defines a syntactico-semantic classification based on predicate-argument structure. Thus, the variety meaning of senses lexical entries related to an applicable context was ensuring.

2.2. Semantic enrichment

Firstly, the semantic enrichment was done manually. Doing so, this enrichment necessitates high linguist capacities in order to affect the pertinent semantic class to meaning. The LADL tables (Gross, 1975) is one of studies that is based on a manually affectation of semantic features to lexical units meanings.

It is clearly that this manual enrichment is the most relevant one, but it requires a costly time because the vast number of lexical units to be classified and it necessitate the availability of the linguist who attribute the adequate semantic classes to meanings.

With the progress characterizing the computational linguistic domain, the enrichment methods become automatic. This automatic enrichment uses both linguistics features and mathematics techniques to classifying lexical units. This enrichment is marked by three ways. The first uses the linguistic tools for preparing the corpus before classifying lexical units by means of clustering tools (Wilson et al., 2004). In fact, the construction of the corpus requires the annotation steps that represent a heavy and time consuming task. Several clustering algorithms can be used as Ripper (Cohen, 1996). The second way uses techniques of automatic clustering (Hatzivassiloglou & McKeown, 1997). In this case, it is necessary to add syntactic and semantic features in order to achieve the automatic enrichment. The third way consists of using linguistic and statistical approaches. The purpose of this way is to build several types of classifiers and combine their results, either by voting systems or by clustering algorithms (Dziczkowski & Wegrzyn-Wolska, 2008). This kind of enrichment needs heavier treatments than the other manners listed above.

3. LMF standardized model

LMF is a standard ISO 24613 for modeling lexical knowledge of the majority of natural languages (Francopoulo & George, 2008). It provides a common model for the representation of electronic lexical resources with guarantees the exchange of data between and among these resources. The LMF model is composed of a core package and a range of extensions referring to the various levels of linguistic analysis (i.e., morphological, syntactic, semantic and syntactico-semantic). The LMF core package describes the basic hierarchy of lexical entry information, including information on the form. The LMF extensions are added to the LMF core components in conjunction with the additional components required for the specific resource modeling. Indeed, to obtain lexical resources according to the LMF standard, it is sufficient to have the core package, then, optionally select packages of extensions necessary to the representation of the modeled dictionary. It is also, essential to select from each extension the corresponding LMF classes required to the treated language. For example, the core package provides the *Sense* and the *Definition* classes to describe the meaning of a lexical entry. The MRD (Machine Readable Dictionary) extension reserves the *Subject Field* class to represent the domain of use of a *Sense* and the *Context* class to describe the authentic context for the use of the word form managed by the lexical entry. The LMF semantic extension designates the *Sense Relation* class to describe the possible relationship between *Senses* instances such as synonymy and autonomy. Then, the resulting model will be decorated with the Data Categories Registry (DCR)[2] required for the modelization of the dealt language.

4. Proposed approach

In this section, we detail the proposed approach for the automatic enrichment of LMF standardized electronic dictionaries by the semantic classes. The following figure 1 illustrates steps of this approach.

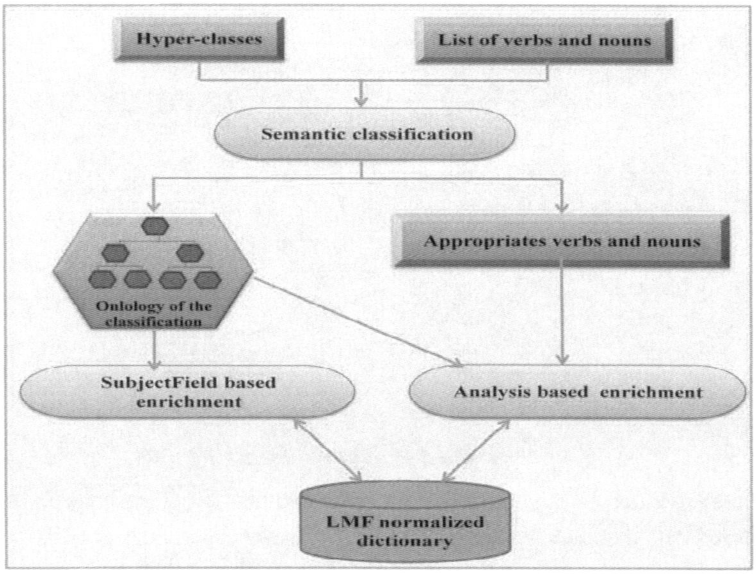

Figure 1: Proposed approach

The proposed approach is composed of three steps: a semantic classification and two phases of automatic enrichment. To accomplish the aims of the semantic classification, this step requires the hyper-classes of the Gaston Gross classification and a list of verbs and nouns of the studied language in input. The results of the semantic classification step are the ontology of the classification and a list of appropriate verbs and nouns characterizing this classification. Whereas, the SubjectField based enrichment uses the ontology of the classification to enrich the LMF normalized dictionaries by identifying semantic classes. The analysis based enrichment requires achieving the enrichment of the LMF normalized dictionary, both the ontology of the classification and the list of appropriates verbs and nouns identified previously.

4.1. Semantic classification

4.1.1. Basic concept

Our semantic classification is based on the studies of the Gaston Gross (Gross, 1994) semantic classification (see section 2). This classification uses the predicate-argument structure to classify lexical units. Thus, the simple sentence represents the minimum unit of analysis. Indeed, two major semantic classes characterize this classification namely: the semantic classes of predicates and the semantic classes of arguments. However, prior to the object classes, and based on syntactic features, the classification maintains classes that regroup all predicates that share the common syntactic behaviors named Hyper-classes. Thus, hyper-classes of predicates, specified by this classification are: "ACTION, EVENT, STATE and PREDICATIVE HUMAN." While hyper-classes of arguments are: "HUMAN, CONCRETE, PLANTS, ANIMALS, TIME, RENTAL and ABSTRACT." These hyper-classes are subject to sub classifications by means of arguments permutations (distributional criteria) appearing in one or more positions of arguments related to a given predicate. Thus, if a permutation of a noun by another contributes to a rupture of the meaning of a predicate sense, then a new object class is required to be created. These object classes allow highlighting the different uses of a polysemous predicate.

[2] www.isocat.org

4.1.2. Steps of the semantic classification

We propose in figure 2 the general semantic classification process.

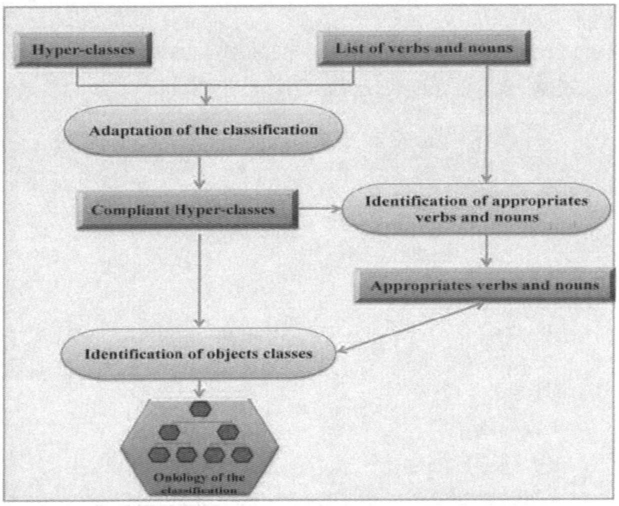

Figure 2: Semantic classification

The process of the proposed semantic classification is realized manually by a linguist. It composed by three steps: (i) Adaptation of the classification, (ii) Identification of appropriates verbs and nouns and (iii) Identification of object classes.

i. Adaptation of the classification:

Hyper-classes of the Gaston Gross studies (see section 4.1.1) and a *list of verbs and nouns* of the studied language perform together in order to accomplish the adaptation of the adaptation of the classification step. Considering that the semantic classification is performed by a linguist, this step requires the abilities of this expert and the syntactic features of the studied language in order to study the possibility of the adaptation of the semantic classification on the studied language. On the basis of syntactic features of the studied language, the expert can identify new hyper-classes appropriate to the treated language, delete or rename the existing semantic hyper-classes. Therefore the *compliant hyper-classes* represent the result of this step.

ii. Identification of appropriates verbs and nouns:

On the basis of the novel list of *hyper-classes* identified in the previous step, related to the specific studied language, the identification of appropriates verbs and nouns take place. This step aims to detect the *appropriate list of verbs and nouns* characterizing each hyper-classes of the proposed semantic classification.

iii. Identification of object classes:

The object class concept represents the characteristic of the proposed semantic classification. Thus, the aim of this step is the *identification of object classes* for each semantic class. To accomplish this objective, this step requires the *compliant hyper-classes* of the studied language and the list of *appropriates verbs and nouns* recognized in the last step. The results of this step affect predicates-semantic classes to as well as arguments. Indeed, the expert benefits from the syntactic features of the studied language in order to identify objects classes relating respectively to hyper-semantic classes of predicates and arguments. As hyper-classes, the identification of the object classes outcomes a list of verbs and nouns characterizing each object class. This list performs to update the list of appropriates verbs and nouns of the classification. An *ontology of the classification* that's regroups all complaint hyper-classes and object classes related to the studied language represent the result of this step.

4.2. Enrichment of LMF standardized dictionaries

After developing a semantic classification, the enrichment process of the standardized LMF dictionaries with semantic classes will take place. It composed of two main phases: (i) the Subject Field based enrichment that benefited from the LMF dictionaries structure, particularly from the uses domains related to meanings of lexical entries (ii) the analysis based enrichment that uses features of the obtained semantic classification.

4.2.1. Subject Field based enrichment

This enrichment is based on the field "SubjectField" according to the LMF model. As shown in figure 3, it consists of two steps described as follow:

i. Searching senses with "SubjectField": the domains of uses for each *"Senses"* of lexical entries in *LMF normalized dictionary* are represented through a class named "SubjectField". The aim of this step is the extraction from the dictionary, *Senses* related to treated lexical entry containing the "SubjectField" field.

ii. Identification of semantic classes: a pretreatment realized on the obtained semantic classification and the existed "Subjectfield" in an LMF stadardized dictionary can made a directly correspondence between the hyper-semantic classes or the object classes with the "SubjectField". If this is the case, this step identifies the semantic class from the *ontology of the classification* related to the founded *"SubjectField"* and updates the LMF standardized dictionary by the addition of the retained semantic class to the corresponding *Sense*.

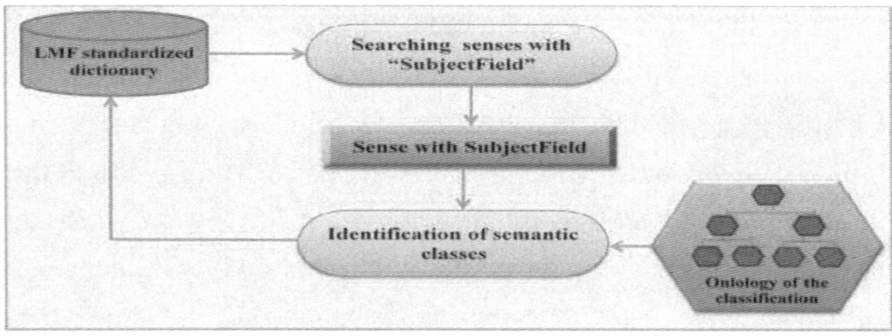

Figure 3: Subject Field based enrichment

4.2.2. The analysis based enrichment

The analysis based enrichment uses the features of the retained semantic classification. The following figure 4 illustrates the steps of this kind of enrichment.

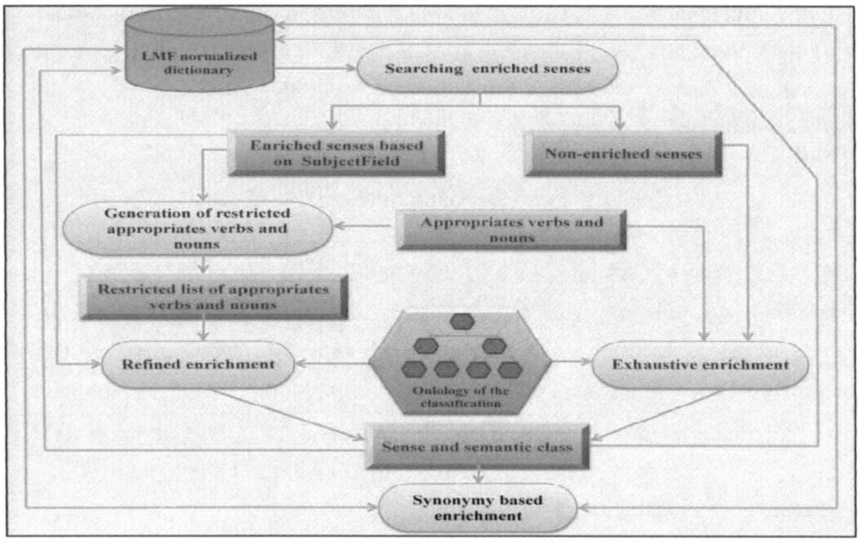

Figure 4: Analysis based enrichment

The list of appropriates verbs and nouns and the ontology of the classification represent the input of analysis based enrichment. It is composed by the following five steps:

i. <u>Searching enriched senses:</u> this step aims to search from *LMF normalized dictionary* the *enriched senses* with semantic classes based on the SubjectField based enrichment and in the same time the *non-enriched senses*. A specific treatment will be affected to those senses in the next step.

ii. <u>Generation of restricted appropriates verbs and nouns:</u> the assignment of the semantic class identified by the SubjectField based enrichment is not a definitive assignment. Indeed, in order to achieve the definitive enrichment, this step requires for the realization of its process both the *Appropriates verbs and nouns* and the *Enriched senses based on SubjectField. The restricted appropriates verbs and nouns* represent the result of the generation of restricted appropriates verbs and nouns phase.

iii. <u>Refined enrichment:</u> the *restricted list of verbs and nouns* identified in the last step, *the sense already enriched based on SubjectField* and *the ontology of the classification* represents the input of this step. Indeed, this step uses the *restricted list of verbs and nouns* to analyze the textual content of the enriched "Sense" in order to refine the semantic class assignment. Thus a relevant *semantic class* is identified based on the ontology of the classification and will definitive be attribute to the treated *Sense*.

iv. <u>Exhaustive enrichment:</u> the exhaustive enrichment concerns the *non-enriched senses*. In fact, a specific treatment is performed to those non-enriched senses by the means of the *Appropriates verbs and nouns identified* by the retained semantic classification. This treatment consist of an analyze of the *"Contexts"* and the *"Definitions"* field related to a Sense of a lexical entry in the *LMF dictionary* using the appropriate verbs and nouns. This analyze identify the relevant semantic class from *the ontology of the semantic classification* which will be affected to the Sense in order to enrich semantically the LMF dictionary.

v. <u>Synonymy based enrichment:</u> in this step we have identified and affected a semantic class to the treated Sense. After that, the synonymy based enrichment takes place, it aims to search the synonymy senses related to the treated sense. Then, the same semantic class identified by the exhaustive or the refined enrichment will be affected to the synonymy senses. At the end of this step, we obtain an enriched sense with the relevant semantic class and also the related synonymy senses enriched by the same semantic class.

5. Experimentation on the Arabic language

This section focuses an experimentation of the proposed approach of the automatic enrichment of standardized dictionaries by semantic classes. An Arabic LMF dictionary is used to test the performance of this approach.

5.1. Choice of the Arabic language

With respect to the Arabic language and to our knowledge there has been no works treated effectively an Arabic semantic classification. In fact, in literature available works are limited to some attempts of specialized dictionaries without related to any theoretical semantic classification. We can note for example, the " فقه اللغة وسر العربية / *fiq.hu all~uyaħi wa sir~u alçarabiy~ati*" dictionary created by " أبو منصور الثعالبي / *Aabuw mansuwr alθ~açaAlibiy*" which groups lexical units into thirty chapters. Each chapter is subdivided into sub-chapters grouping together lexical units sharing the same semantic meaning. The chapter " في اللباس وما يتصل به والسلاح وما ينضاف إليه وسائر الأدوات والآلات وما يأخذ مأخذها / fiy al~*ibaAs wa maA yat~asilu bihi wa als~ilaAH wa maA yan.DaAfu Ăilay.hi wa saAŷiri alAadawaAti wa alĀlaAti wa maA yuA.xaDu maA.xaDahaA*" includes forty-nine sub-chapters as *"*في تقسيم النسيج*fiy taq.siym aln~asiyj"* "the division of tissues", *"*في تقسيم الخياطة*fiy taq.siym alHiyaATaħi "* "the division of sewing ", *"* في تقسيم الخيوط وتفصيلها*fiy taq.siym alxuyuwT wa tafSiyluhaA "* "the division of thread and its peculiarities "....

" المعجم العربي لأسماء الملابس*almuç.jam alçarabiy lias.maA'i almalaAbis"* is another Arabic dictionary specialized in the classification of Arabic nouns of clothes. *"* رجب عبد الجواد إبراهيم */ rajab çabd Aib.raAhiym"* the writer of this lexical resource grouped more than 1250 clothes Arabic nouns.

5.2. Illustration of the Arabic semantic classification

5.2.1. Classification of Arabic arguments

In this section, we experiment the process of the semantic classification (see section 4.1) on the Arabic language. We were interested in this experimentation on the "CONCRETE" hyper-class of arguments. This hyper-class is also retained for the Arabic language from the classification of Gaston Gross. Among the object classes belonging to the "CONCRETE" hyper class we note the "Clothes" class. Indeed, the Arabic verb "لَبِسَ" "to wear", represent the appropriate verb characterizing this object class. Thus, one meaning of this verb describe an "ACTION" realized by a first "HUMAN" argument and highlighting another "CONCRETE" argument. The example bellow illustrates three sentences detailed the mean of the "لَبِسَ" "to wear" verb:

(1)	لَبِسَ التِّلْمِيذُ القُبَّعَةَ	Labisa alt~*il.miydu alqub~açaha*	The pupil wears the hat
(2)	لَبِسَ التِّلْمِيذُ التُّفَّاحَ	Labisa alt~*il.miydu* alt~*ufaHaha*	The pupil wears the apple
(3)	لَبِسَ المَاءُ القُبَّعَةَ	Labisa almaA*'u alqub~açaha*	The water wears the hat

All sentences (1), (2) and (3) are syntactically correct. But, only the sentence (1) is semantically acceptable. Indeed, in sentence (1), a *"pupil"* can *"wear a hat"*, while in sentence (2) a *"Pupil"* cannot wear an *"apple"* because an *"apple"* is an "Aliment" so it can be eaten but not wean. Whereas, in sentence (3) the *"water"* is an "Aliment/ water" and cannot be wean. Those examples explicate the requirement of the creation of the "Clothes" and the "Aliment" objects classes under the "CONCRETE" hyper-class. Thus, he "Clothes" object class includes all nouns that can be worn by a "HUMAN". Arabic verbs such as: *"خلع/xalaça/to undress" "ارتدى/Air.tady'/to dress"," لبس/labisa/to wear"*, and nouns like: *"كساء/kisaA''/cloth"*, "لباس/libaAs/wear", *"ثوب/θaw.jbũ/dress"* characterize the "Clothes" object class.

Arguments instances of the "Clothes" object class can be: *"حذاء/HidaA'/shoes"*, *"نعل/naç.l/sock"*, *"خف/xuf~ũ/slipper"*, *"قبعة/qub~açahũ/hat"*, *"سروال/sir.waAlũ/pant"*, *"قميص/qamiuSũ/shirt"*. Thus, the appropriate verbs of the "Clothes" object class like *"خلع/xalaça/to undress" "ارتدى/Air.tady'/to dress"" لبس/labisa/to wear"* can be correctly introduces the arguments instances list before. But in Arabic language, some verbs select from the "Clothes" arguments instances a specific ones but cannot use all of them. For example, the (انتعل / Ain.taçala / to wear shoes, احتذى/AiH.tady /to wear shoes) verbs cannot precede allof the arguments instances "Clothes" but only <shoes> <حذاء>. Thus, the sentence (انتعل القميص) (he wear shoes shirt) is semantically incorrect because (انتعل /Ain.taçala / to wear shoes) is an appropriate verb to <shoes> <حذاء> class and (القميص/*alqamiuSũ/shirt*) does not represent <shoes> <حذاء> but rather <fringues> <ثياب>. Therefore, it is necessary to create two objects classes under the "Clothes" namely <shoes> <حذاء> and < fringues > <ثياب>.

The table 1 in following summarizes the previous idea:

Table 1: Appropriate verbs for the <shoes> <الحذاء> and <fringues> <ثياب> object class

		Examples of nouns / verbs	لبس *labisa* *to wear*	احتذى AiH.tady to wear shoes	خلع *xalaça* *to undress*	ارتدى *Air.tady'* *to dress*	انتعل Ain.taçala to wear shoes
<Clothes> object class	<shoes><الحذاء>	خف/*xuf~ũ/* *slipper*	👍	👍	👍	👍	👍
		حذاء/*HidaA'/* *shoes*	👍	👍	👍	👍	👍
		نعل/*naç.l/* *sock*	👍	👍	👍	👍	👍
	<fringues><ثياب>	قميص/*qamiuSũ/* *shirt*	👍	👎	👍	👍	👎
		سروال/*sir.waAlũ/* *pant*	👍	👎	👍	👍	👎
		قبعة/*qub~açahũ/* *hat*	👍	👎	👍	👍	👎

5.2.2. Results of the Arabic semantic classification

In this section we present an example of the semantic classification ontology for Arabic language. The below figure 5 illustrates some recognized hyper-classes and object classes using the proposed process of the semantic classification (see section 4.1). This figure is created with the OWL ontology.

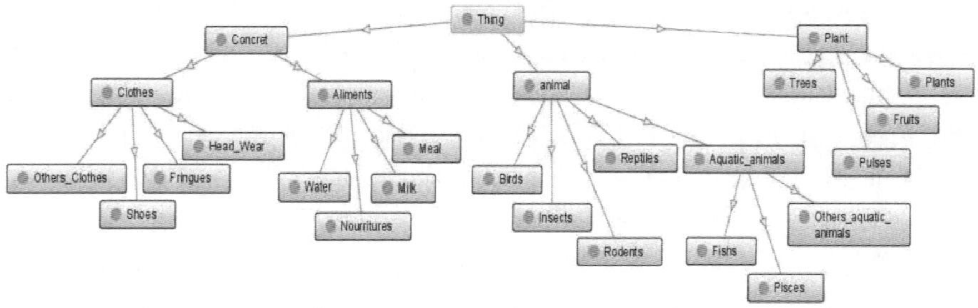

Figure5: Examples of Arabic hyper-classes and object classes of arguments

As presented in the figure 5, a "CONCRETE" is a hyper class. Among the object classes founded under the "CONCRETE" hyper class we note the "Clothes" and the "Aliments" subclasses. The "Clothes" object class is subdivided into the following object-sub-classes: "Head_wear", "Fringues", "Shoes" and "Others_Clothes". And so on for the other hyper and object classes.

Table 2 present the list of appropriate verbs and nouns related to the "CONCRETE" <clothes> class:

Table2: Appropriate verbs and nouns of the <clothes> object class

			Appropriate										
	Object classes		Verbs			Nouns							
CONCRETE hyper-class	Clothes		لبس labisa	خلع xalaça	ارتدى Air.taday	لباس libaAs	ألبسة Aal.bisah	ثوب θaw.jb	أثواب Aθ.waAb	كساء kisaA'	أكسية Ak.siyah	رداء ridaA'	أردية Ardiyah
			to wear	to undress	to dress	wear(s)		dress(es)		clothe(s)		apparel(s)	
	Sub-object-classes	<fringues> <ثياب>	تبرنس tabar.nasa	تجلبب tajal.baba	تبرقع tabarqaça	فضفاض faD.faAD				واسع waAsiç			
			to wear the burnous	to wear	to wear the veil	widish				ample			
		<shoes> <الحذاء>	احتذى Ain.taçala	انتعل AiH.tady		حذاء HidaA'		أحذية AH.diyah		نعل naç.l		نعال niçaAl	
			to wear shoes	to wear shoes		shoes				sock(s)			
		<head wear> <أغطية الرأس>	تعمم taçam~ama			رأس raA.s	رؤوس ruwius	حاسر Hasir		حاف HaAf			
			to wear a hat			head		bare		unshod			
		<others wear> <غيرها>	درز daraza	بكل bakala		رجل rij.l	رجلين rijlay.n	أرجل Arjul	يد yad	يدين yadayn	أيدي Ay.dy	كف kaf	كفين kaf~ay.n
			to sew	to buckle		foot			hand(s)			forehand(s)	

5.3. Illustration of the enrichment of the Arabic LMF dictionary

5.3.1. Arabic LMF standardized dictionary

The Arabic LMF standardized dictionary is a lexical resource conforms to the LMF standard ISO-24613. The model of this dictionary (khemakhem et al 2013) covers all lexical levels: morphological, syntactic, semantic and syntactico-semantic. This dictionary contains about 37000 lexical entries among them 10800 verbs and 3800 roots.

5.3.2. Experimentation of the "SubjectField" based enrichment

In Arabic LMF standardized dictionary, three classes namely *Definition*, *Context* and *SubjectField* characterize the *sense* of lexical entry. The *Definition* determines the meaning of sense. While the *Context* gives an example of using sense. Regarding the *SubjectField* it describes the use's domain related to a given sense of a lexical entry. The table below contains some examples of domains available in the Arabic LMF standardized dictionary.

Table3: Examples of available Subject Field in the Arabic standardized dictionary

Subject Field		
In Arabic	**Transliterated**	**In English**
حَيَوَان	HayawaAn	Animal
حَشَرَة	Hašarah	Insect
نَبَات	nabaAt	Plant
هَنْدَسَة	han.dasah	Geometry
طَبْخ	Tab.x	Culinary
جُغْرافيا	juɣ.raAfãyaA	Geography
مُوسِيقَى	musiyqaA	Music
رِيَاضَة	riyaADah	Sport
طِب	Tib	Medicine
عَسْكَر	ɕas.kar	Military

In the Arabic LMF normalized dictionary, the "ايَّ " "Animal" "HayawaAn" and the "اشرج" "Hašarah" "Insect" *SubjectFields* can be grouped into the "animal" hyper-class. It is important to indicate that the "اشرج" "Hašarah" "Insect" *SubjectField* corresponds directly to the object class named "Insect" and the "ايَّ " "HayawaAn" "animal" *SubjectField* may correspond to the object classes: "Bird", "Rodents", "reptiles" and "Aquatic-animals" as shows in figure5.

The following figure 6 illustrates an example of the SubjectField based enrichment.

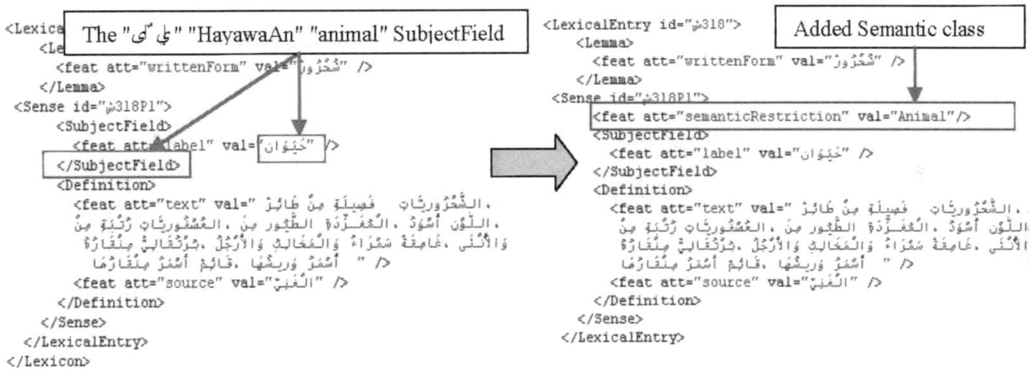

Figure 6: The SubjectField based enrichment applied to a sense of lexical entry

5.3.3. Experimentation of the analysis based enrichment

The analysis based enrichment is subdivided into two kind of enrichment. The first enrichment appointed refined enrichment requires for the progress of its process the restricted list of verbs and nouns in order to refine the primary enrichment carried out in the SubjectField based enrichment. Or the second enrichment is exhaustive, concerning only non-enriched senses, uses the appropriate verbs and nouns of the semantic classification in order to realize the semantic enrichment of the dictionary.

The table 4 given in the following, contains the restricted list of appropriates verbs and nouns related to the "ايَّ " "HayawaAn" "animal" arguments hyper-class.

Table4: Restricted list of appropriate verbs and nouns of "Animal" hyper-class

Hyper class	Restricted list of appropriate nouns and verbs	Object classes	Restricted list of appropriate nouns and verbs	Sub-Object-classes
Animal	عصفّر اوام طيّر طَؤز طِيز	Bird		
	سأاف س‌اف	Rodents		
	ارض طّن	Reptiles		
	الهَحَار هاء تحزي يّاه	Aquatic-animals	لّرواك س‌ول	Fish
			التّدْييَّات حوت جِيتان	Pisces
			هحَايّا خ رَخيّح القشْيّا خ	Others-aquatic-animals

The application of the process of the refined enrichment by using the restricted list of verbs and nouns (table5 in yellow) on the last extracted fragment used in the SubjectField based enrichment (figure 6) can give the enrichment presented in the following figure 7.

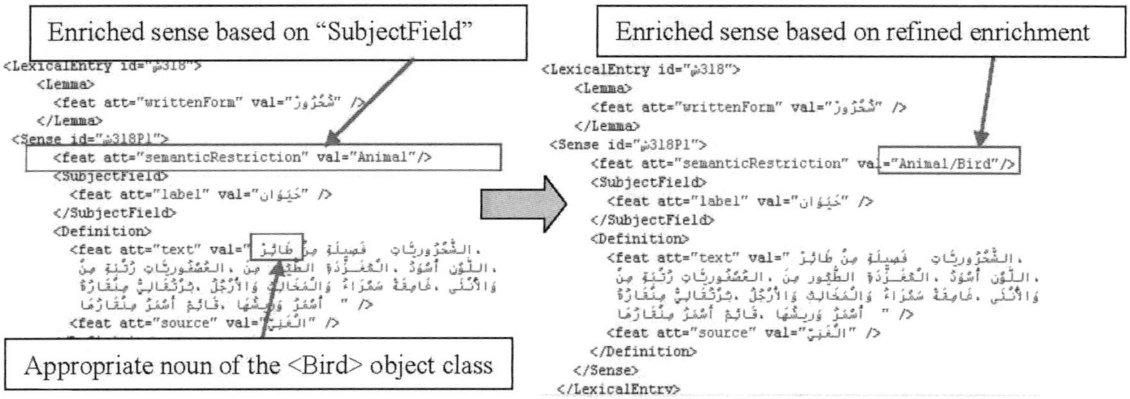

Figure 7: The refined enrichment applied to a sense of lexical entry

In the following, we present an experimentation of the exhaustive enrichment using the appropriate verbs and nouns applied to non-enriched senses. The analysis of *Contexts* and *Definitions* of senses related to a lexical entry in the Arabic LMF standardized dictionary by using the appropriate verbs and nouns (table4) can identify the relevant semantic class.

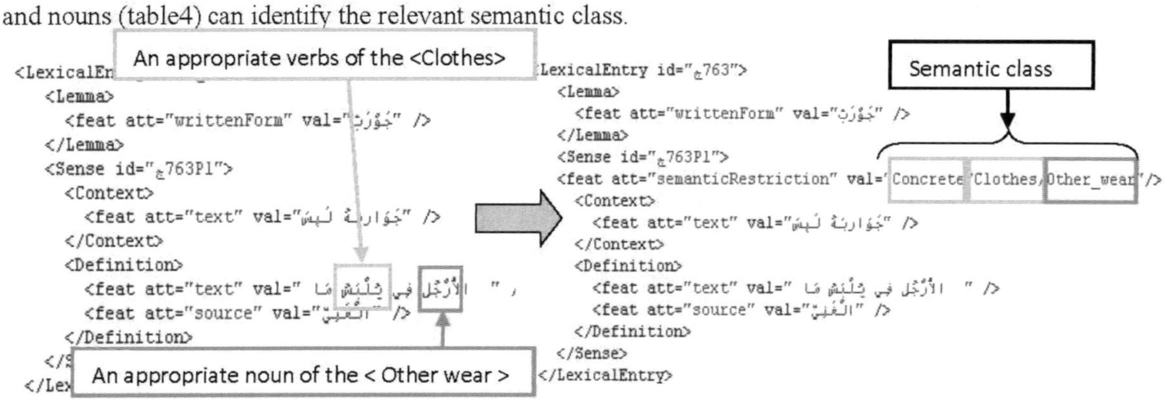

Figure 8: The exhaustive enrichment applied to a sense of lexical entry

5.4. Results

To test the performance of the carried out experimentation, we have realized a statistical evaluation.

Our Arabic standardized dictionary contains in total 34000 lexical entries including 62157 senses. Concerning the SubjectField based enrichment experimentation; we have used 4 "SubjectField" (Animal, Insect, Plant and Culinary) among the 19 available in the Arabic dictionary. And for the analysis based enrichment we have choice only the "CONCRETE" hyper class and specially the "Clothes" object class to experiment the process of this kind of enrichment.

The table 5 below gives the statistical evaluation of the "SubjectField" and the analysis based enrichment.

Table 5: Evaluation of the enrichment

		SubjectField based enrichment	Analysis based enrichment (exhaustive step)
Number of Subject Field	Animal	197	
	Insect	19	
	Plant	242	
	Culinary	39	
Total		**497**	
Correct assignment		454	90
Incorrect assignment		43	52
Recall		91,34 %	26 %
Precision		98 %	63 %

6. Conclusion and perspectives

In this paper, we have proposed an approach for the automatic enrichment of LMF standardized dictionaries with semantic classes. This approach is composed of a semantic classification based on the Gaston Gross studies and two types of enrichment. The first enrichment named SubjectField based enrichment, takes advantages from the structure of an LMF dictionary where meanings contain the domain of use of a lexical entry. The second enrichment called analysis based enrichment, uses the features of the proposed semantic classification based on appropriates verbs and nouns specifying each semantic class and applied to the available text components in the dictionary.

We carried out experimentation, by using an available Arabic standardized dictionary. The obtained results are satisfying concerning the SubjectField based enrichment. The synonymy based enrichment can reduce the enrichment effort at thirds because on average, the synonymy relation connects three or more senses.

In the future, we opted to achieve the experimentation on the others semantic classes of the proposed semantic classification for Arabic language and to complete the rest of SubjectField existed in the Arabic LMF standardized dictionary. In addition, we consider improving the analysis based enrichment by adding more efficient syntactic-semantic analysis. Finally, we foresee that the enrichment can offer the flexibility to create new oriented versions of the semantic knowledge needed for different NPL applications.

Reference

Cohen, D. (1996). Law, social policy, and violence: The impact of regional cultures. *Journal of personality and Social Psychology,* 70.961-978.

Condamines A. (2005). Sémantique et corpus, quelles rencontres possibles ? Sémantique et corpus, A. Condamines, éd., Paris : Hermès.

Dichy, J. (2000). Morphosyntactic Specifieers to be associated to Arabic lexical Entries- Methodological and Theoretical Aspects. *Proceddings of ACIDA'2000. Monastir, Tunisia, 22-24 March 2000. Corpora ans Natural Language Processing. Volume, p.55-60.*

Dorr, B. (1997). Large-scale dictionary construction for foreign language tutoring and interlingual machine translation. *Machine Translation,* 12(4):271–325.

Dubois, J. & Dubois-Charlier, F. (1997). Les verbes français (LVF) . *Jean Dubois et Dubois-Charlier Françoise Diffuseur exclusif. Larousse Bordas, Paris.*

Dziczkowski, G. & Wegrzyn-Wolska, K. An autonomous system designed for automatic detection and rating of film reviews. Extraction and linguistic analysis of sentiments. *In IEEE/WIC/ACM International Conferences on Web Intelligence*. WI'08, Australie.

Fellbaum, C. (1999). The organization of verbs and verb concepts in a semantic net. In P. Saint-Dizier, editor, *Predicative Forms in Natural Language and in Lexical Knowledge Bases,* pages 93–110. Kluwer Academic Publishers, Netherlands.

Fillmore, C.J. (1985). Frame and the semantics of understanding.Quaderni di semantica, 6(2):222–254.

Francopoulo, G. & George, M. (2008). ISO/TC 37/SC 4 Rev.16. *Language resource management- Lexical markup framework (LMF).*

Fuchs, C., Habert, B., éd. (2004). Traitement automatique et ressources numérisées pour le français, Le français moderne, Vol. 72, n°1.

Gross, G. (1994). Classes d'objets et description des verbes. *Langages,* 115, 15-30.

Gross, M. (1975). Méthodes en syntaxe : Régimes des constructions complétives. Hermann, Paris, France.

Habash, N., Soudi, A., Buckwalter, T., et al. (2007*). In Arabic Computational Morphology: Knowledge-based and Empirical Methods*. ISBN: 978-1-4020-6045-8

Hatzivassiloglou, V., McKeown, K. (1997). Predicting the Semantic Orientation of Adjectives. *ACL '98 Proceedings of the 35th Annual Meeting of the Association for Computational Linguistics and Eighth Conference of the European Chapter of the Association for Computational Linguistics.* Pages 174-181.

Jackendoff, R. (1990). *Semantic Structures.* MIT Press, Cambridge, Massachusetts.

Khemakhem, A., Gargouri, B., Haddar K. Ben Hamadou, A, et al. (2013). LMF for Arabic, chapter in the book *"LMF:Lexical Markup Framework".* Wiley Editions, ISBN: 9781848214309, pp.83-96, March 2013.

Kipper, K., Dang, H. T., Palmer, M., et al. (2000). Classbased construction of a verb lexicon. In *Proc. of the 17th National Conference on Artificial Intelligence.* Austin, TX.

Levin, B. (1993). *English Verb Classes and Alternations.* Chicago University Press, Chicago.

Miller, G. A. (1990). WordNet: An on-line lexical database. *International Journal of Lexicography,* 3(4):235–312.

Pinker, S. (1989). *Learnability and Cognition: The Acquisition of Argument Structure.* MIT Press, Cambridge, Massachusetts.

Rastier, F. (2001). Arts et sciences du texte. Paris : PUF.

Schapire, R. E. & Singer, Y. (2000). BoosTexter: A Boosting-based System for Text Categorization. *Machine Learning*, 39, 135–168, 2000

Stede, M. (1998). A generative perspective on verb alterntions. *Computational Linguistics*, 24(3):401–430.

Valette, M., Estacio-Moreno, A., PetitJean, E., Jacquey, E. (2006). Eléments pour la génération de classes sémantiques à partir de définitions lexicographiques. Pour une approche sémique du sens. Verbum ex machina, Actes de la 13ème conférence sur le traitement automatique des langues naturelles (TALN 06). Piet Mertens, Cédrick Fairon, Anne Dister, Patrick Watrin (éds).

Wilson, G.V., Gorda, B., Lu, P., et al. (1994). Twelve Ways to Make Sure Your Parallel Programming System Doesn't Make Others Look Bad. *IEEE Computer*, 27(10), 1994.

The 2014 Conference on Computational Linguistics and Speech Processing
ROCLING 2014, pp. 110-124

Collaborative Ranking between Supervised and Unsupervised Approaches for Keyphrase Extraction

Gerardo Figueroa*, **Yi-Shin Chen***

Abstract

Automatic keyphrase extraction methods have generally taken either supervised or unsupervised approaches. Supervised methods extract keyphrases by using a training document set, thus acquiring knowledge from a global collection of texts. Conversely, unsupervised methods extract keyphrases by determining their relevance in a single-document context, without prior learning. We present a hybrid keyphrase extraction method for short articles, HybridRank, which leverages the benefits of both approaches. Our system implements modified versions of the TextRank (Mihalcea and Tarau, 2004)—unsupervised—and KEA (Witten *et al.*, 1999)—supervised—methods, and applies a merging algorithm to produce an overall list of keyphrases. We have tested HybridRank on more than 900 abstracts belonging to a wide variety of subjects, and show its superior effectiveness. We conclude that knowledge collaboration between supervised and unsupervised methods can produce higher-quality keyphrases than applying these methods individually.

Keywords: Keyword extraction, Keyphrase extraction, Hybrid approach, Supervised methods, Unsupervised methods

1. Introduction

Keyphrases—also called keywords[1]—are highly condensed summaries that describe the contents of a document. They help readers know quickly what a document is about, and are generally assigned by the document's author or by a human indexer. However, with the massive growth of documents on the Web each day, it has become impractical to manually assign keywords to each document. The need for software applications that automatically assign keywords to documents has therefore become necessary.

---

* Institute of Information Systems and Applications, National Tsing Hua University, Hsinchu, Taiwan
E-mail: {gerardo.ofc, yishin}@gmail.com

[1] A keyphrase is a phrase composed of one or more keywords. We will use the terms keyphrase and keyword interchangeably in this paper.

In this work we apply efficient and effective practices from supervised and unsupervised methods to produce a hybrid system *HybridRank*. On the supervised side, we implement an extension of the Na¾e Bayes classifier originally proposed in KEA (Witten *et al.*, 1999). This classifier has shown to be practical to implement and can be extended for improved effectiveness. On the unsupervised side, we apply the well-known TextRank (Mihalcea and Tarau, 2004) algorithm with some modifications. TextRank is similarly practical to implement, and can effectively extract keyphrases from texts regardless of their size or domain.

Each method contributes by providing a list of keyphrases for a particular text, sorted by their rank or relevance as seen from each approach. Finally, a collaborative algorithm is executed, in which the two keyphrase lists are merged to create an overall list of keyphrases for that text. The merging algorithm thus takes into account the ranks given by both approaches to each keyphrase and produces a final, collaborative score reflected by these ranks.

We have tested HybridRank on a large number of abstracts belonging to scientific papers across different domains. The results of our experiments show the effectiveness of the proposed method and of the improvements made to the KEA and TextRank algorithms. Our system obtained a higher precision and recall than both KEA and TextRank in most cases, and obtained a higher precision and recall than at least one of these two methods in all the cases. The evaluation of our system also shows how knowledge from supervised and unsupervised approaches can be shared to produce keyphrases of better quality.

2. Related Work

Recent work on the automatic generation of keyphrases has been categorized as either *supervised* or *unsupervised*.

Supervised methods for keyphrase extraction, in essence, make use of training datasets´ a large corpus consisting of texts and their corresponding (previously assigned) keyphrases´ to classify candidate terms as keyphrases. Two traditional methods in this category are KEA (Witten *et al.*, 1999) and GenEx (Turney, 2000). KEA uses a Na¾e Bayes classifier constructed from two features extracted from phrases in documents: the TFIDF and the relative position of the phrase. GenEx uses a steady-state genetic algorithm to build an equation consisting of 12 low-level parameters. Even though KEA and GenEx perform similarly well, KEA has shown to be more practical to implement, and has served as the base for other supervised keyphrase extraction methods (Turney, 1999; Hulth, 2003; Nguyen and Kan, 2007).

Other innovative supervised approaches have been proposed in recent years, ranging from the application of neural networks (Jo, 2003; Wang *et al.*, 2006; Jo *et al.*, 2006; Sarkar *et al.*, 2010) to conditional random fields (Zhang, 2008). Yih *et al.* (Yih *et al.*, 2006) proposed a multi-class, logistic regression classifier for finding keywords on web pages.

Unsupervised methods for keyphrase extraction rely solely on implicit information found in individual texts. Simple approaches are based on statistics, using information such as term specificity (Kireyev, 2009), word frequency (Luhn, 1957), n-grams (Cohen, 1995), word co-occurrence (Matsuo and Ishizuka, 2004) and TFIDF (Salton *et al.*, 1975). Other approaches are graph-based, where a text is converted into a graph whose nodes represent text units (e.g. words, phrases, and sentences) and whose edges represent the relationships between these units. The graph is then recursively iterated and *saliency scores* are assigned to each node using different approaches.

Mihalcea and Tarau (Mihalcea and Tarau, 2004) developed TextRank, a graph-based ranking model that applies the PageRank (Brin and Page, 1998) formula into texts for assigning scores to phrases and sentences. Wan *et al.* (Wan *et al.*, 2007) proposed a method that fuses three kinds of relationships between sentences and words: relationships between words, relationships between sentences, and relationships between words and sentences. Wan and Xiao (Wan and Xiao, 2008) also developed CollabRank, which improves the keyphrase extraction task by making use of mutual influences of multiple documents within a cluster context.

To our knowledge, all previous work has been either supervised or unsupervised. Supervised methods have the advantage of learning from an already classified collection of documents in order to find keyphrases for a new document, but in essence make no analysis of individual text structure as done by unsupervised methods. HybridRank leverages the benefits of both approaches for keyphrase extraction, applying a supervised keyphrase extraction algorithm (KEA) and an unsupervised graph-based algorithm (TextRank).

3. Background

HybridRank makes use of two well-known and effective keyphrase extraction methods: KEA (Witten *et al.*, 1999) and TextRank (Mihalcea and Tarau, 2004). Each of these methods extracts a list of keyphrases ranked according to each method's approach. A final list of keyphrases is constructed from the collaboration between these two methods and the application of a merging algorithm.

This section will explain the general frameworks for the KEA and TextRank algorithms. The modifications made for these two methods in our work will be described in Section 4. For briefness purposes, we present only a brief explanation of each algorithm, and suggest the reader to refer to the original papers for more details.

3.1 The KEA Algorithm

The KEA algorithm consists of a Na¾e Bayes classifier that ranks phrases in order of their probability of being keyphrases as learned from a training document set. KEA is divided into four stages: *candidate phrase generation*, *feature extraction*, *training* and *ranking*.

3.1.1 Candidate phrase generation

The first stage in the KEA algorithm is the selection of phrases that are suitable for training and extraction. To avoid overfitting, this filtering process is applied on both the training document set and the input text to be analyzed.

3.1.2 Feature extraction

The features extracted from the candidate phrases generated in the previous stage are the heart of the KEA algorithm; they serve as the learning base for the Na¾e Bayes classifier and are used for the extraction of keyphrases. The features originally extracted by Witten *et al.* (Witten *et al.*, 1999) for each phrase in their KEA algorithm were the *TFIDF* and the *relative position* in the text.

3.1.3 Training

The training stage uses the training document set, which is composed of a collection of documents with their manually-assigned keyphrases. First, phrases are generated from each document in the set. The features for each phrase are then extracted and stored in a training model.

3.1.4 Ranking

With the model having been trained, the Na¾e Bayes classifier can extract keyphrases from a new text by first selecting its candidate phrases and then extracting each phrase's features. The model determines the probability of each phrase being a keyphrase using Bayes' formula with the two extracted features.

The probability that a phrase is a keyphrase given that it has TFIDF T and relative position R is then calculated as:

$$P(k \mid T, R) = \frac{P(T \mid k) \cdot P(R \mid k) \cdot Y}{Y + N}, \qquad (1)$$

where $P(T|k)$ is the probability that a keyphrase has TFIDF score T and $P(R|k)$ is the probability that it has relative position R. Y is the number of phrases that were manually assigned as keyphrases in the training document set and N is the number of phrases that were not. An expression similar to equation (1) is used to calculate the probability that a phrase is *not* a keyphrase ($P(\neg k|T,R)$).

The overall probability that a phrase is a keyphrase is then calculated with the following formula:

$$P = \frac{P(k|T,R)}{P(k|T,R) + P(\neg k|T,R)} \qquad (2)$$

The phrases are finally sorted in descending order of their probability scores.

3.2 The TextRank Algorithm

The TextRank algorithm was proposed by Mihalcea and Tarau (Mihalcea and Tarau, 2004). It is a graph-based, unsupervised method for keyphrase extraction. We have divided the TextRank algorithm into two stages to allow an easier comparison with our modifications: *graph construction* and *phrase ranking*.

3.2.1 Graph construction

The first step carried out in the TextRank algorithm is the construction of a graph that represents a text. The resulting graph is an interconnection of words and phrases ¯ the vertices ¯ with significant relations ¯ the edges.

3.2.2 Ranking

With the constructed graph in hand, a recursive algorithm is applied on it which assigns scores to each node on the graph on each iteration until convergence is reached. This algorithm is derived from Google's PageRank (Brin and Page, 1998), which determines the importance of a vertex within a graph by recursively taking into account global information. In other words, the score of one vertex in the graph will affect the scores of all vertices connected to that vertex, and vice-versa.

Before starting the recursive ranking algorithm, all vertices in the graph are initialized with a score of 1. Next, the algorithm is run on the graph for several iterations until it converges within a certain threshold. In each iteration, the original PageRank formula is calculated for each vertex V_i in graph G, as follows:

$$S(V_i) = (1-d) + d \cdot \sum_{j \in In(V_i)} \frac{1}{|Out(V_j)|} S(V_j), \quad (3)$$

where $In(V_i)$ is the set of vertices that point to V_i, $Out(V_i)$ is the set of vertices that V_i points to, and d is a damping factor, which is usually set to 0.85.

With final scores assigned to each vertex, they are sorted in descending order of this score.

4. Framework

HybridRank is divided into four main components:

1. **Preprocessing**
2. **Supervised Ranking**
3. **Unsupervised Ranking**
4. **Merging**

This section will describe the *Preprocessing* and *Merging* components in detail. For the *Supervised ranking* and *Unsupervised ranking* components, only the specific modifications made in our work will be detailed.

4.1 Preprocessing

All documents in the training document set, as well as the input text, are cleaned before being processed by the other components. The following steps are performed in this stage:

1. HTML tags are removed.
2. All non-alphanumeric characters are removed, with the exception of punctuation marks relevant to text structure and word meaning.
3. The cleaned text is sent to the supervised and unsupervised components.

4.2 Supervised Ranking

The supervised component of our system consists of a modified and extended version of the KEA algorithm proposed by Witten *et al.* This section will describe the modifications we made in each of the stages of KEA.

4.2.1 Candidate phrase generation

The way candidate phrases are selected in HybridRank has some variations from the procedure followed by the original KEA method. We have carefully inspected the training document set and have used this knowledge to construct a more effective filter for phrase selection (as is later shown in the experimental evaluation). The following procedure is carried out:

1. Phrases composed of 1 to 4 words are extracted from each sentence when they comply with the following criteria:

    a. They do not contain any of a list of 539 predetermined stopwords.

    b. They are composed of nouns, adjectives and/or verbs in their gerund or past participle forms.

    c. They do not contain words with less than 3 letters.

    d. They do not contain words composed only of numbers and/or other non-letters.

    e. They do not end with an adjective.

    f. One-word phrases cannot be an adjective or a verb.
2. Each word in the extracted phrases is then converted to its stemmed form.
3. The phrases are passed as candidate phrases to the Feature Extraction stage.

4.2.2 Feature extraction

We have included two additional features to the learning scheme as proposed in other works: the *keyphrase frequency* in the whole collection of texts (Frank *et al.*, 1999) and the *PoS tag pattern* (Hulth, 2003). Adding these two features produced better overall results in our experiments.

Keyphrase frequency

The keyphrase frequency of phrase P in document D is the number of times P is manually assigned as a keyphrase in the training document set G, excluding D.

PoS tag pattern

The PoS (Part-of-Speech) tag pattern of a phrase P is the sequence of PoS tags that belong to P. These tags are assigned to each word in P using a Part-of-Speech Tagger.

4.2.3 Training

Unlike the original KEA method, we do not discretize real-valued features (TFIDF and relative position) into numeric ranges; we instead round these values to one decimal place. Experiments with both discretization tables and rounding to one decimal gave similar results, so we decided to use rounding due to its simpler implementation and faster performance.

4.2.4 Ranking

With the two additional features (keyphrase frequency and PoS tag pattern) used in HybridRank, an expression similar to equation (1) can be constructed. The probability that a phrase is a keyphrase using all four features would then be calculated as:

$$P(k \mid T, R, S, F) = \frac{P(T \mid k) \cdot P(R \mid k) \cdot P(S \mid k) \cdot P(F \mid k) \cdot Y}{Y + N}, \quad (4)$$

where $P(S \mid k)$ is the probability that it has PoS tag pattern S and $P(F \mid k)$ the probability that it has keyphrase frequency F. An expression similar to equation (4) is used to calculate the probability that a phrase is *not* a keyphrase ($P(\neg k \mid T, R, S, F)$).

The TFIDF and relative position values are rounded to one decimal place in both the trained model and in the current phrase. Since the keyphrase frequency is a non-negative integer, no rounding is performed. Finally, the PoS tag pattern value has to be an exact string match with the one in the trained model.

4.3 Unsupervised Ranking

The unsupervised ranking component of HybridRank is an implementation of the TextRank algorithm proposed by Mihalcea *et al.* for keyphrase extraction. This section will detail the configuration used in our system for the first stage (graph construction) of the TextRank algorithm. No modifications were made to the ranking stage described in Section 3.2.2.

4.3.1 Graph construction

The parameters we have used for the graph construction in our implementation of TextRank presented the best results in our experiments. The following configuration was used:

- The graph is unweighted and undirected.
- Two types of vertices are added to the graph: words and phrases.
- Maximum phrase size is 4 words; they can only be composed of nouns and adjectives.
- The words added to the graph and those in the phrases cannot be any of the 539 predetermined stopwords.
- The relation between words and phrases is the co-occurrence, i.e. the maximum distance

(in words) between two text units. The value used for co-occurrence is 2.

4.4 Merging

The merging component is the core of HybridRank. Once the two keyphrase lists are generated by KEA and TextRank, they are combined into a single list using a merging algorithm. The overall list is the result of the collaboration between a supervised and an unsupervised approach for keyphrase extraction.

The two main stages in the merging component are *keyphrase list merging* and *post-processing*. We illustrate the procedure with an example for easier understanding.

4.4.1 Keyphrase list merging

The first step performed in the merging stage is to add missing keyphrases to each keyphrase list, which results in two lists of the same size and with the same keyphrases, but in different order. In other words, keyphrases that appear in the KEA list which are not in the TextRank list are appended to the TextRank list, and vice-versa. Missing keyphrases are added to each list in the same order of their original list; their corresponding scores are marked with a flag to indicate that these phrases were not in that list before.

Next, a reordering of the two lists is done by giving more priority to those phrases that appear in both lists. Assuming that the two lists are already sorted, the reordering is done by applying the following algorithm to each list L:

```
reorderedK = {}
existentK = {}
inexistentK = {}
for each phrase P in L P do
    if exists in both lists then
        existentK .append( P )
    else
        inexistentK .append( P )
    end if
end for
reorderedK .append( existentK )
```

$reorderedK$ .append($inexistentK$)

$L \leftarrow reorderedK$

The previous algorithm partitions each list into two sections, leaving phrases that appear on both lists on top, and phrases that only appear in one list on the bottom. It is worth pointing out that the original order of the phrases is maintained in each partition.

Finally, the two keyphrase lists are merged into a single list based on the order in which each phrase appears in both lists. Given phrase P with position i in the KEA list and with position j in the TextRank list, three different merging methods can be used to assign an overall position k to P:

- **Average:** $k = (i + j)/2$
- **Min:** $k = Min(i, j)$
- **Max:** $k = Max(i, j)$

Once the new HybridRank position k has been calculated for every phrase in the text, the phrases are sorted according to this new position. If two phrases have the same value for k, as it often occurs, then a tie-breaker is used. The tie-breakers have the following precedence: KEA score, TextRank score, TFIDF value, and finally alphabetical order.

4.4.2 Post-processing

In the final stage of HybridRank, a post-processing filter is applied on the final list of keyphrases. First, any phrase that is a subphrase of a higher-ranking phrase is removed from the list. For example, if the phrase *bass diffusion* has a higher ranking than the phrase *bass*, then the latter is eliminated.

Second, any phrase that exists in a predetermined *stop-phrase* list is removed. The stop-phrase list is a list of words and phrases that will rarely or never be keyphrases by themselves. We have identified 28 stop-phrases, which consist of frequent nouns and noun phrases found in the training documents that were never assigned as author keyphrases. These phrases are different to stopwords in the way that when combined with other words they may become keyphrases. Stopwords, on the other hand, are removed in a previous stage because they will rarely or never be part of a keyphrase. For example, the words *research* and *method* are stop-phrases and not stopwords, because they are too general to be keyphrases, unless combined with other word(s), such as in *photonics research* or *kernel method*.

5. Experiments

5.1 The Corpora

Two different document collections were used for our experiments: the *IEEE Xplore* collection (1,606 documents) and the *Hulth 2003* collection (2,000 documents). The documents consist of abstracts in English from journal and conference papers of various disciplines with their corresponding, manually-assigned keyphrases. Of the total number of abstracts, 1,822 were used for training (to construct the trained model), 917 for testing, and 867 for validation (to evaluate different parameters in the methods used and select the values with the best performance); this assignation was made by random sampling.

Some statistics relevant to the analysis of our experiments were extracted from the collections used. The statistics show that ‒ in general ‒ only 51% of the manually-assigned keyphrases are actually contained in the abstract text in their stemmed forms. With this knowledge, it can be deducted that the precision of any keyphrase extraction method will rarely surpass this percentage on these corpora, which presents a difficulty for adequate evaluation. For the purpose of carrying out a fairer evaluation, a *utopian subset* was selected from the testing set. Each of this subset's abstracts must contain at least one of the manually-assigned keyphrases in the text. Additionally, an average of 7 keyphrases were manually assigned for each abstract by either authors or other human annotators, which correspond to roughly 6% of the total number of words per abstract.

5.2 Experimental Setup

For evaluating the performance of HybridRank, we have performed experiments on the utopian subset using two other keyphrase extraction methods: KEA and TextRank. HybridRank has been separated into three different merging methods, which we evaluate individually: *average*, *min* and *max*.

To further break down our evaluation, we have performed experiments using the original procedures stated in the KEA and TextRank papers, and compared their performance with our modified versions. Additionally, we separated the evaluation of the KEA and HybridRank methods by using two different feature sets for the Naïve Bayes classifier: the *Base Feature Set (New)* and the *PoS Tag Feature Set*.

Base Feature Set (New)

Only the TFIDF, relative position and keyphrase frequency are taken into account when calculating equation 4 in Section 4.2.4.

PoS Tag Feature Set

Only the TFIDF, relative position and PoS tag pattern are taken into account when calculating equation 4 in Section 4.2.4.

The three measures used in our evaluation were the precision, recall and F-score. We compare the output keyphrases of each method with those in the manually-assigned list; the keyphrases in each list are previously stemmed. The number of keyphrases extracted per abstract corresponds to 6. This way of selecting the number of output keyphrases presented the best results.

5.3 Evaluation and Discussion

The results for the Hulth 2003 dataset are shown in Figure 1. For this dataset, HybridRank obtained the highest precision, recall and F-score when using the Max merging method. This best performance was obtained when applying either the Base Feature Set (New) or the PoS Tag Feature Set on KEA. It can also be observed in Figure 1 that our modified versions of both KEA and TextRank performed better than the original ones.

Figure 2 displays the results for the IEEE Xplore dataset. In this dataset, when applying the Base Feature Set (New) on KEA and using the Min merging method, HybridRank performed better than the other methods. However, when applying the PoS Tag Feature Set, the original KEA method outperformed the others. This is probably due to the fact that the IEEE Xplore dataset has a greater variety of subjects than the Hulth 2003 dataset. This wide range of subjects causes the Keyphrase Frequency attribute ¯ applied on the Base Feature Set (New) ¯ to become less meaningful (Frank *et al.*, 1999), thus allowing the PoS Tag Feature Set to predict a phrase's class (keyphrase or non-keyphrase) with higher accuracy. Overall, our method performed better than either KEA or TextRank in all of the cases.

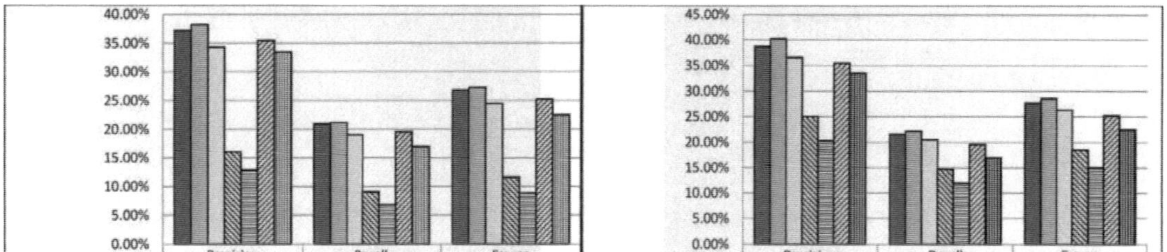

	Precision	Recall	Fscore
HybridRank (Avg)	37.14%	21.01%	26.84%
HybridRank (Max)	38.20%	21.21%	27.27%
HybridRank (Min)	34.28%	19.07%	24.51%
KEA (modified)	16.09%	9.11%	11.63%
KEA (original)	12.90%	6.77%	8.88%
TextRank (modified)	35.44%	19.61%	25.25%
TextRank (original)	33.46%	17.00%	22.55%

	Precision	Recall	Fscore
HybridRank (Avg)	38.76%	21.53%	27.68%
HybridRank (Max)	40.20%	22.19%	28.60%
HybridRank (Min)	36.57%	20.54%	26.30%
KEA (modified)	25.04%	14.74%	18.56%
KEA (original)	20.37%	11.94%	15.05%
TextRank (modified)	35.44%	19.61%	25.25%
TextRank (original)	33.46%	17.00%	22.55%

Figure 1. Precision, recall and F-score on the Hulth 2003 dataset. The left corresponds to the Base Feature Set (New), the right to the PoS Tag Feature Set.

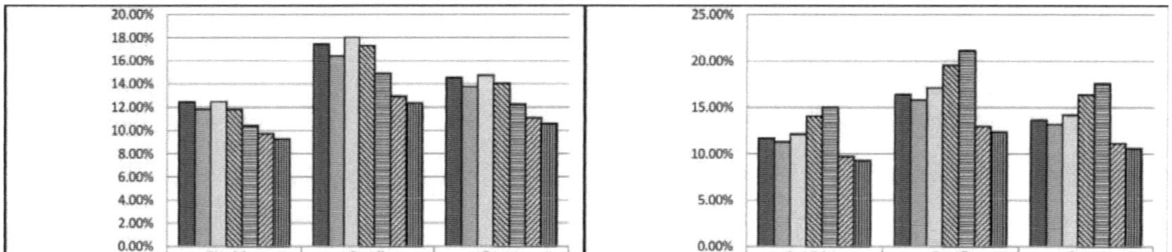

	Precision	Recall	Fscore
HybridRank (Avg)	12.46%	17.46%	14.54%
HybridRank (Max)	11.83%	16.44%	13.76%
HybridRank (Min)	12.47%	18.03%	14.74%
KEA (modified)	11.81%	17.32%	14.05%
KEA (original)	10.42%	14.89%	12.26%
TextRank (modified)	9.73%	12.92%	11.10%
TextRank (original)	9.28%	12.35%	10.60%

	Precision	Recall	Fscore
HybridRank (Avg)	11.66%	16.39%	13.63%
HybridRank (Max)	11.28%	15.79%	13.16%
HybridRank (Min)	12.12%	17.09%	14.18%
KEA (modified)	14.02%	19.58%	16.34%
KEA (original)	15.01%	21.13%	17.55%
TextRank (modified)	9.73%	12.92%	11.10%
TextRank (original)	9.28%	12.35%	10.60%

Figure 2. Precision, recall and F-score on the IEEE Xplore dataset. The left corresponds to the Base Feature Set (New), the right to the PoS Tag Feature Set.

6. Conclusions and Future Work

In this paper, we have described and evaluated a hybrid keyphrase extraction method: HybridRank. Our results show that collaboration between a supervised and an unsupervised approach can produce high-quality keyphrase lists for short articles. We have compared the performance of HybridRank with two other well-known keyphrase extraction methods ‾ KEA and TextRank ‾ and showed that HybridRank obtained a higher precision, recall and F-score when applied on the Hulth 2003 dataset.

On our second dataset (IEEE Xplore), the original KEA algorithm performed better than HybridRank and TextRank when using PoS Tag Patterns because this dataset contains a wide range of domains, affecting the performance of the Na¾ve Bayes classifier when using the Base Feature Set (New). Our method, however, outperformed in all cases either the supervised (KEA) or unsupervised (TextRank) approaches. Furthermore, doing some modifications to KEA and TextRank improved their performance in most cases as compared to the original methods proposed by their authors.

We can conclude that HybridRank performs the best when the unsupervised component outperforms the supervised component. Additionally, merging KEA's and TextRank's keyphrases with the Min or Max methods produced better results than using the Average.

Among our planned future work is adopting a weighting mechanism to both components, so as to have biased merging, either towards the supervised component or towards the unsupervised one. Another approach we have considered is to implement different (and newer) methods for the supervised and unsupervised components (see Section 2), so as to maximize the overall performance of the HybridRank system.

References

S. Brin and L. Page. The anatomy of a large-scale hypertextual Web search engine. *Computer networks and ISDN systems*, 30(1-7):107--117, 1998.

Eibe Frank and Gordon W. Paynter and Ian H. Witten. Domain-specific keyphrase extraction. *IJCAI*, 1999.

Anette Hulth. Improved automatic keyword extraction given more linguistic knowledge. *Proceedings of the 2003 conference on Empirical methods in natural language processing*, :216--223, 2003.

R. Mihalcea and P. Tarau. TextRank: Bringing order into texts. *Proceedings of EMNLP*, :404--411, 2004.

T.D. Nguyen and M.Y. Kan. Keyphrase extraction in scientific publications. *Proceedings of ICADL2007*, 2007.

Peter D. Turney. Coherent Keyphrase Extraction via Web Mining. *Proceedings of the Eighteenth Research Council*, 1999.

Peter D. Turney. Learning Algorithms for Keyphrase Extraction. *Inf. Retr.*, 2(4):303--336, 2000.

X. Wan and J. Xiao. CollabRank: towards a collaborative approach to single-document keyphrase extraction. *Proceedings of the 22nd International Conference on Computational Linguistics*, 1:969--976, 2008.

X. Wan and J. Yang and J. Xiao. Towards an iterative reinforcement approach for simultaneous document summarization and keyword extraction. *Annual Meeting-Association for Computational Linguistics*, 45(1):552, 2007.

Ian H. Witten and Gordon W. Paynter and Eibe Frank and Carl Gutwin and Craig G. Nevill-Manning. KEA: practical automatic keyphrase extraction. *DL '99: Proceedings of the fourth ACM conference on Digital libraries*, :254--255, 1999.

J. D. Cohen. Highlights: Language- and domain-independent automatic indexing terms for abstracting. *JASIS*, 46(3):162--174, 1995.

T. Jo. Neural based approach to keyword extraction from documents. In *Computational Science and Its Applications--ICCSA 2003*, pages 456--461. Springer, 2003.

T. Jo, M. Lee, and T. M. Gatton. Keyword extraction from documents using a neural network model. In *Hybrid Information Technology, 2006. ICHIT'06. International Conference on*, volume 2, pages 194--197. IEEE, 2006.

H. P. Luhn. A statistical approach to mechanized encoding and searching of literary information. *IBM Journal of research and development*, 1(4):309--317, 1957.

Y. Matsuo and M. Ishizuka. Keyword extraction from a single document using word co-occurrence statistical information. *International Journal on Artificial Intelligence Tools*, 13(01):157--169, 2004.

G. Salton, C.-S. Yang, and C. T. Yu. A theory of term importance in automatic text analysis. *Journal of the American society for Information Science*, 26(1):33--44, 1975.

K. Sarkar, M. Nasipuri, and S. Ghose. A new approach to keyphrase extraction using neural networks. *arXiv preprint arXiv:1004.3274*, 2010.

W. tau Yih, J. Goodman, and V. R. Carvalho. Finding advertising keywords on web pages. In *Proceedings of the 15th international conference on World Wide Web*, pages 213--222. ACM, 2006.

J. Wang, H. Peng, and J. song Hu. Automatic keyphrases extraction from document using neural network. *In Advances in Machine Learning and Cybernetics*, pages 633--641. Springer, 2006.

C. Zhang. Automatic keyword extraction from documents using conditional random fields. *Journal of Computational Information Systems*, 2008.

The 2014 Conference on Computational Linguistics and Speech Processing
ROCLING 2014, pp. 125-138

Semantic Representation of Ellipsis in the Prague Dependency Treebanks

Marie Mikulová*

Abstract

This article answers the question what is and what is not ellipsis and specifies criteria for identification of elliptical sentences. It reports on an analysis of types of ellipsis from the point of view of semantic representation of sentences. It does not deal with conditions and causes of the constitution of elliptical positions in sentences (when and why is it possible to omit something in a sentence) but it focuses exclusively on the identification of elliptical positions (if there is something omitted and what) and on their semantic representation in a treebank, specifically on their representation on the deep syntactic level of the Prague Dependency Treebanks. The theoretical frame of the approach to ellipsis presented in this article is dependency grammar.

Keywords: Ellipsis, Semantic Annotation, the Prague Dependency Treebanks.

1. Introduction

The analysis of well-formed sentences, some of whose constituents are missing, has been of central concern to computational linguists at least since the beginnings of the work in formal grammar. There has been a considerable amount of research on ellipsis from a variety of perspectives. Different approaches to an explanation of the procedures involved in assigning representations to sentences containing deletions have been developed (see, for example, Berman ¯ Hestsvik, 1992 and Lappin ¯ Benmamoun, 1999) but they have been mostly designed within the framework of constituency grammar.

The theoretical frame of our approach to ellipsis is dependency grammar. The dependency-based approach offers a totally different perspective on ellipsis. The constituency-based approach assigns more empty positions. The so-called gaps are assigned particularly when two constituents cannot be bracketed because they do not occur one next to the other in the surface form of a sentence. This discontinuity of two constituents does not impede the construction of a dependency tree. Only those gaps are perceived as ellipses when

* Charles University in Prague, Faculty of Mathematics and Physics, Institute of Formal and Applied Linguistics, Czech Republic; E-mail: mikulova@ufal.mff.cuni.cz.

one of the constituents is not expressed at all in the surface form of the sentence. Thus, only a small part of the gaps (identified by constituency-based approaches) overlaps with the types of ellipses that have been defined by means of dependency syntax.

This article answers the question what is and what is not ellipsis in dependency grammar. It reports on an analysis of types of ellipsis from the point of view of semantic representation of sentences in a dependency treebank. We identify a boundary between the grammatical ellipses on the one hand and the accidental omissions on the other. We will distinguish morphological, surface and deep syntactic features of ellipses.

2. What is Ellipsis?

In attempting to characterize elided sentences in natural language we are faced with the problem of explaining how speakers or recipients are able to represent and interpret linguistic objects which, at least on the surface, are not present. We believe that one of the major questions is related to the reason why we suppose that something is missing in a sentence. There is an expectation of a certain lexical position to be realized, but this expectation is not fulfilled. However, who is the subject/bearer of the expectation? The speaker, the recipient, or the linguist? Such questions are also asked by Hlavsa (1981) who offers convincing reasons, saying that the subject that performs an analysis of ellipsis in a sentence can only be the linguist. Neither the speaker nor the recipient are aware of the presence of ellipsis (in terms of information that is being communicated). Sentences that are incomplete from the grammatical viewpoint (e.g. *Mary likes Bach, Susan Beethoven.*) still maintain their information value. Thus, the basic characteristics of ellipsis can be defined as incompleteness from the perspective of the grammatical system of the language. We do not claim that sentences cannot be analyzed from the viewpoint of their informational completeness. However, we refer to the types of elision that are supported by the grammatical system of the language and distinguish them from those that lack such a support (accidental omissions caused by a sudden interruption of a dialog for example).

If we say that ellipsis is a grammatical incompleteness, we have to specify the corresponding grammatical representation for each sentence. Therefore, we are going to analyze surface form of a sentence and search for a theoretical representation of this sentence in the grammatical system. Then it will be possible to give an unambiguous and reliable definition of ellipsis based on the relation between a particular surface form of a sentence and its description in the grammatical system. Our representation of a sentence is based on a solid, well-developed dependency syntax theory which is known as Functional Generative Description (for a detailed account of this framework, see e.g. Sgall et al. (1986)). This formal theoretical approach has already been applied to an analysis of multifarious linguistic phenomena, mostly concentrated on Czech but also in comparison with English, Russian or some other languages. In the Functional Generative Description, the grammar has been described as a system of several layers. We work with three layers: morphological layer and two structural layers (surface and deep syntactic layer). Each layer has its own syntax. At each layer, the elementary units combine into complex units. In a simplified way, a complex unit of each layer consists of an autosemantic (lexical) base and function elements. At the syntactic layers, each complex unit of a sentence is classified as a governor or a dependent in relation to another one.

In our approach, ellipsis is an empty, non-expressed position in a sentence representation at the given grammatical layer (and what is beyond the boundary of the grammatical system, what is not defined in that system, it cannot be (grammatical) ellipsis; we treat accidental omissions, etc. here). Ellipsis is a relation; something is missing, because something else in the given sentence representation needs it for building complete complex unit or complete dependency structure. For example, at the morphological layer, a suffix or prefix cannot exist without a base word. Therefore, in the example *pre- and post-election discussion*, we analyze ellipsis of base word to the expressed prefix.

At the syntactic layers, we distinguish two pairs of ellipses:

A. Forming unit ellipses:

1. Ellipsis of an autosemantic base to a function element
2. Ellipsis of a function element to an autosemantic base

B. Dependency structure ellipses:

1. Ellipsis of a governing unit to a dependent (structural ellipses)
2. Ellipsis of (an obligatory) dependent to a governing unit (valency ellipses)

We define forming unit ellipses at both syntactic layers. At the surface syntactic layer, a complex unit consists of an autosemantic verb with its auxiliary verbs; prepositions are connected with nouns. So, we analyze ellipsis of an autosemantic verb to an auxiliary verb (type A.1) and ellipsis of an auxiliary verb to an autosemantic verb (type A.2); ellipsis of a noun to a preposition (type A.1) and ellipsis of a preposition to a noun (type A.2). As one deep complex unit, we treat idioms and connections of an autosemantic verb with a modal or phase verb.

The ellipsis of a governing unit to a dependent (type B.1) is the main type of ellipses at the surface syntactic layer. The ellipsis of an (obligatory) dependent to a governing unit (type B.2) is the main type of ellipses at the deep syntactic layer. Here, the ellipsis is a matter of valency (we work with the theory of valency that was treated particularly by Panevov®(see Panenov® 1980; see also Urepov® 2011, about valency in the Prague Dependency Treebank).

3. Types of Ellipses

Ellipses are classified (as morphological, surface and deep syntactic) according to the layer of the grammatical system that has been assigned to the empty position. Table 1, 2 and 3 include a brief summary of the defined types of ellipsis with some simple examples that give a sufficient illustration of these types (the elided text is in square brackets).

Table 1. Morphological ellipses.

Word ellipses	
Ellipsis of end of word to prefix	*pre-*[election] *and post-election discussion*
Ellipsis of beginning of word to suffix	*in terms of the context(*[context]*s)*
Ellipsis of part of composite word	*two-*[seater] *or four-seater car*

Table 2. Surface syntactic ellipses.

Forming unit ellipses	
Ellipsis of auxiliary verb to autosemantic verb	*Peter will go to Prague and* [will] *visit his mother there.*
Ellipsis of autosemantic verb to auxiliary verb	*(Will you go?) Yes, I will* [go].
Ellipsis of noun to preposition	*in front of* [camera] *and behind the camera*
Ellipsis of preposition to noun	*in Prague and* [in] *Pilsen*
Ellipsis of verb to subordinating conjunction	*We know, when* [she came] *and why she came.*
Ellipsis of subordinating conjunction in dependent clause	*He said, that they would come and* [that they would] *stay the night.*
Ellipsis of second paratactic element	*Go away otherwise...* [?]
Structural ellipses	
Ellipsis of governing verb	*Mary likes Bach, Susan* [likes] *Beethoven.*
Ellipsis of governing noun	*Central* [Europe] *and Eastern Europe*

Table 3. Deep syntactic ellipses.

Forming unit ellipses	
Ellipsis of modal verb to autosemantic verb	*Peter wants to relax and* [wants to] *listen to music.*
Ellipsis of autosemantic verb to modal verb	*(Stay the night.) I could not* [stay].
Ellipsis of part of idiom	*They buried* [the hatchet] *and then dug up the hatchet again.*
Valency ellipses	
Textual ellipsis	*(Did the shop assistant pack the book?) Yes, he did* [what-the book].
General argument	*Jane sells at Bata* [what] [to whom].
Control	*The company planned* [who-the company] *to increase production.*
Reciprocity	*John a Mary met* [who-each other].

4. The Prague Dependency Treebanks

The Prague Dependency Treebank (PDT) is the first complex linguistically motivated treebank capturing also the deep syntactic structure of sentences. It is based on a dependency syntactic theory, on the Functional Generative Description. The treebank consists of continuous Czech texts mostly of the journalistic style analyzed at three layers of annotation: morphological (m-layer); surface syntactic (analytical, a-layer) and deep syntactic (tectogrammatical, t-layer). In addition to these three annotation layers there is also one non-annotation layer, representing the `raw-text_. At this layer, called word layer (w-layer), the text is segmented into documents and paragraphs and individual tokens are recognized and associated with unique identifiers. At the m-layer each sentence is provided with morphological categories (lemma, tag). At the a-layer, a dependency tree captures surface syntactic relations such as Subject, Object, and Adverbial. The highest t-layer contains all the information that is encoded in the structure of the sentence and its lexical items. So, this layer captures the deep, semantico-syntactic structure, the functions of its parts, the `deep_ grammatical information, coreference and topic-focus articulation including the deep word order. Figure 1 displays the relations between the neighboring layers as annotated and represented in the data. Thus, for example, the Czech sentence *Byl by šel dolesa*, literally in English: :He-was would went toforest.˘ contains past conditional of the verb *jít* (*byl by šel* :he-was would went˘) and a typo (*dolesa* :toforest˘).

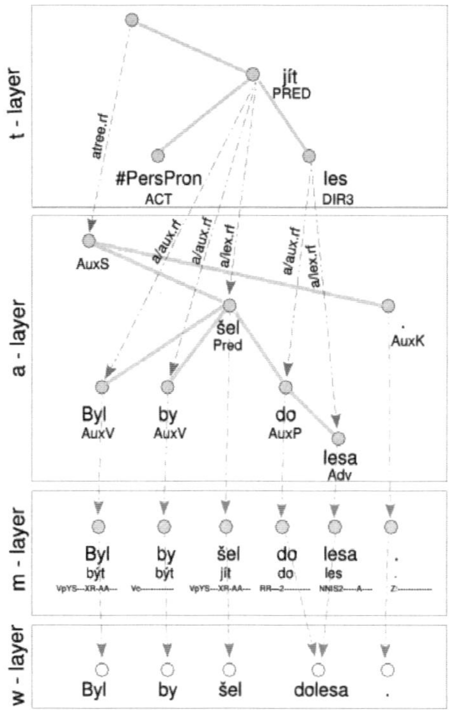

Figure 1. Linking the layers in PDT.

The total number of sentences annotated at all the three layers is 49,442, amounting to 833,357 (occurrences of) nodes. The PDT version 1.0 (with the annotation of the first two layers; HajiT et al., 2001) is available from the Linguistic Data Consortium, as is the version 2.0 (with the annotation of the third, deep syntactic layer; HajiT et al., 2006). The latest version PDT 3.0 (BejTek et al., 2013) with some additions (textual coreference, discourse relations, genre specification, multiword expressions) is available from the LINDAT/CLARIN repository. A similarly based annotation has been used for other Prague treebanks. The Prague Czech-English Dependency Treebank (HajiT et al., 2011) contains parallel PDT-like annotations of English texts (Wall Street Journal part of Penn Treebank) and of their professional translation to Czech. The Prague Dependency Treebank of Spoken Czech (it is planned to be released at the end of 2014) contains spontaneous dialogue speech, transcribed, reconstructed and further annotated in the PDT style.

5. Capturing Ellipsis Techniques

In the Prague Dependency Treebanks, ellipsis is treated at the highest t-layer. All types of ellipses given in Section 3 (excluding some minor exceptions) are captured at this layer. The principles of the build-up of the lower layers in PDT (namely that the number of nodes at these layers is identical to the number of tokens in the sentence) do not allow capturing ellipsis by an addition of a node (which is the most intuitive way of capturing ellipsis in corpora). Therefore, at the m-layer and a-layer, ellipsis is indicated only by a special attribute at such an expressed node that cannot be annotated according to usual rules because of an ellipsis in the sentence. At the t-layer, ellipses are represented by the linking the nodes of the highest t-layer with the nodes of the lower a-layer (Section 5.1) and by added nodes at the t-layer (Section 5.2).

5.1 Links of the t-layer to the a-layer

The relation between the t-layer and a-layer is rather complex. The linking between the layers is not only a technical question, but it carries a piece of linguistic information. It captures the transition from the (linguistic) meaning of a sentence to its form, transition from the deep syntactic structure to the surface expression. The basic principle of linking is as follows: there is a link from the t-node (node at the t-layer) to each a-node (node at the a-layer) that influences the value of some of its attribute. Based on the type of attribute that is influenced by the a-node two types of links to the a-layer are differentiated:

- **lex** = link to the a-node from which the t-node got its lexical meaning (or its biggest part). The a-node influences the value of the *lemma* attribute. Usually it is an a-node that represents an autosemantic word (noun, adjective, verb, adverb).
- **aux** = links to remaining a-nodes that influence values of attributes of the given t-node. Typically, the a-nodes affect values of syntactic and morphological attributes, such as *functor* (deep syntactic function), *subfunctor* (detailed classification of functors) and *gram* (the structure of attributes, the so-called grammatemes, which capture deep grammatical correlates of the morphological categories). These are usually a-nodes representing prepositions, conjunctions, auxiliary verbs, supporting expressions.

For example, in Figure 1, there are three links from the t-node representing the verb *jít* :to_go˘: to the a-node representing word *šel* :went˘, to the a-node representing word *by* :would˘ and to the a-node representing the word *byl* :he-was˘. The link to the first mentioned a-node (*šel* :went˘) is *lex* type; the other two links are *aux* types.

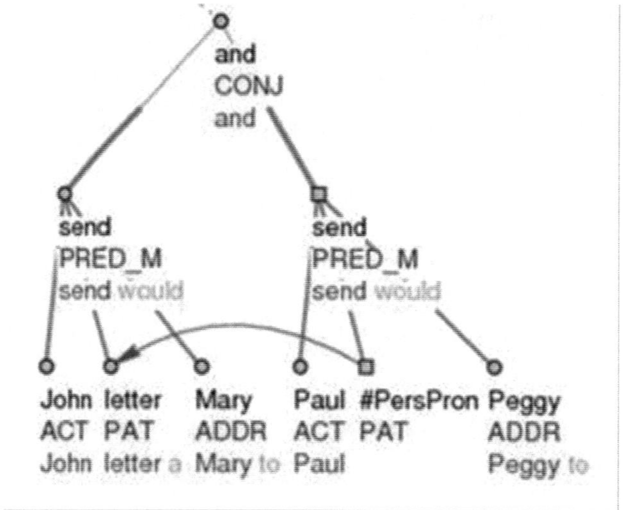

Figure 2. PDT-annotation: John would send a letter to Mary and Paul to Peggy.

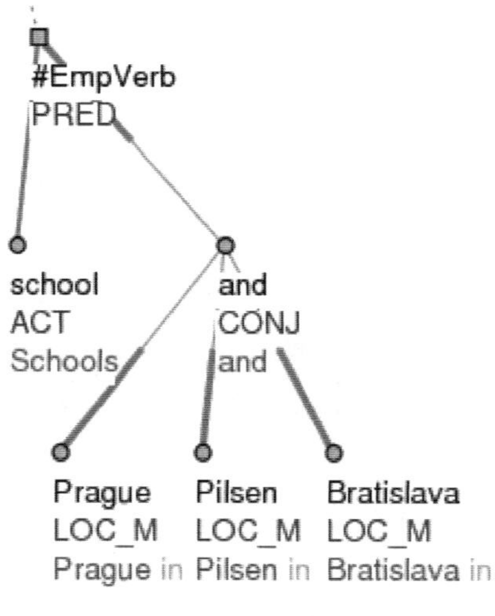

Figure 3. PDT-annotation: Schools in Prague, Pilsen and Bratislava.

There may be more links to one a-node ¯ from various t-nodes. It happens in case of an ellipsis. For example, in the second clause of the sentence *John would send a letter to Mary, Paul to Peggy.*, a t-node will be added for the elided governing verb and there will be a lex-link from this added t-node to the a-node representing the word *send* and aux-link to the a-node representing the word *would*. The identical links will also be used in case of the t-node that represents a governing verb in the first clause. Thus there are two double links to a-nodes representing the words *send* and *would* from the t-layer and this is the way we capture the textual ellipsis of a governing unit (along with the addition of the t-node). In this case, the main indicator of ellipsis in the sentence is of course the added t-node. However, the textual ellipsis itself is captured by the double links to the a-layer (by the lex-link to the a-node from the added t-node). See Figure 2; the linking a-nodes are written in green (lex-link) and orange (aux-link) color by each t-node.

Some types of ellipses are only captured via links to the a-layer. For example, the fact that prepositions in the fragment *Schools in Prague, Pilsen and Bratislava*. are not repeated, is represented only by an aux-link to the expressed preposition from each of the t-nodes that represent the names of cities (there is a link to the preposition *in* from three t-nodes; see Figure 3).

5.2 Addition of Nodes

In order to capture the whole meaning of a sentence, it is sometimes necessary to add t-nodes that lack their direct counterpart at surface form of sentence (at the a-layer). We distinguish two basic types of added t-nodes:

- **copy** = a t-node that has the same values of certain attributes (lemma, some grammatemes and valency frame) as an expressed t-node. We call this added t-node a `copy_ of that t-node. There are double lex-links to the a-node that represents expressed copied word.

- **substitute** = an artificial t-node to which one of the following lemma substitutes has been assigned:

  a. *#EmpNoun*; *#EmpVerb*

  b. *#Cor*, *#Gen*, *#Oblfm*, *#PersPron*, *#Rcp*

Various types of ellipsis are captured by various types of added t-nodes. The textual ellipsis of governing verb or noun is captured using `copy_ t-nodes. The system ellipsis (with no antecedent) of governing verb or noun is captured using `substitute_ t-node with a lemma substitute mentioned in the list a) above. The various types of valency ellipses are captured using t-nodes with a lemma substitute mentioned in the list b). In case of textual ellipsis, there is a coreference (anaphora) arrow from the added t-node to the t-node representing expressed unit (anaphor).

In the tree, t-nodes representing expressed words are drawn as circles; added t-nodes are drawn as squares. In Figure 2, there is an example of capturing a textual ellipsis of the governing verb. In the second clause, there is an added t-node representing the governing verb and this t-node is a copy of the t-node representing the expressed verb in the first clause. The system ellipsis of the governing verb is captured in Figure 3. There is an added t-node with *#EmpVerb* lemma substitute on the governing verb position.

In Figure 2, there is also an example of textual valency ellipsis. The elided Patient *letter* (in the second clause) is captured using an added t-node with *#PersPron* lemma. There is a coreference arrow from the added t-node to the expressed Patient in the first clause. A similar example of textual valency ellipsis is also in Figure 4.

6. Summary of Representation of Ellipsis

This section brings an overview of the ways the defined ellipses (see the summary in Section 3) are represented at the t-layer. Structural ellipses (type B.1 in Section 2) are always captured by an addition of a `copy_ or a `substitute_ t-node (see Table 4; if the ellipsis is captured by a t-node with a lemma substitute, only the lemma is mentioned in the table). Valency ellipses (type B.2 in Section 2) are always captured by an addition of a t-node with a lemma substitute; the overview of valency types of ellipses and their lemmas substitute is presented in Table 5.

Table 4. Representation of structural ellipses in PDT.

	Textual ellipsis	**System ellipsis**
Ellipsis of governing verb	copy t-node lex-link	*#EmpVerb* no lex-link
Ellipsis of governing noun	copy t-node lex-link	*#EmpNoun* no lex-link

Table 5. Representation of valency ellipses in PDT.

Obligatory argument	*#PersPron* coreference arrow
Controlled argument	*#Cor* coreference arrow
Reciprocity	*#Rcp* coreference arrow
General argument	*#Gen* no coreference arrow

At the t-layer, we also capture both types forming unit ellipses: surface syntactic (forming unit ellipses in Table 2) and deep syntactic (forming unit ellipses in Table 3). The method of capturing is similar for both types. The ellipsis of an autosemantic base to a function element (type A.1 in Section 2) is captured according to the same rules that apply to the ellipsis of a governing verb or noun, i.e. with the help of the `copy_ t-node (in case of textual ellipsis) or `substitute_ t-node with the *#EmpVerb* or *#EmpNoun* lemma (in case of system ellipsis). There are aux-links to a-nodes representing expressed function elements. For a clear overview, see Table 6. An example of capturing an ellipsis of an autosemantic base to a function element is in Figure 4. There is an ellipsis of the verb *obtain* to the modal verb *want* in the second clause.

Ellipses of a function element to an autosemantic base (type A.2 in Section 2) are always captured only by means of links to the a-layer. See the example *Schools in Prague, Pilsen and Bratislava* in Figure 3 where ellipsis of a preposition to nouns is captured.

Table 6. Ellipsis of autosemantic base to function element in PDT.

Textual ellipsis	**System ellipsis**
copy t-node	*#EmpVerb / #EmpNoun*
lex-link	no lex-link
aux-links	aux-links

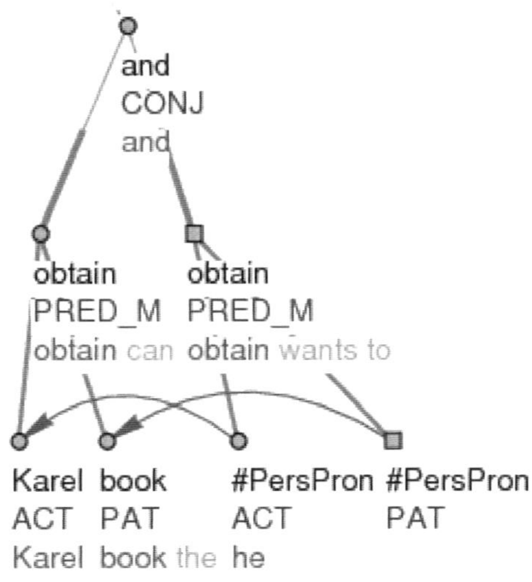

Figure 4. PDT-annotation: Karel can obtain the book and he wants to.

The majority of the defined types of ellipses (see their summary in Section 3) is captured in the PDT. However, the morphological word ellipsis (see Table 1) still remains unannotated. We suggest that special morphological tags should be implemented to resolve the cases when only a part of a word (prefix, suffix, ending, part of a composite word) is separated as an individual lexical unit based on the principle of tokenization `from a space to a space_. Next, we suggest capturing the word ellipses in a similar way to the representation of ellipsis of an autosemantic base to a function element (see Table 6). The lemma of the t-node representing the elided word should get a non-elided, full lexical form and the lexical and morphological attributes of this t-node should correspond to a non-elided reconstructed form. There should be a lex-link to a-node representing a non-elided word (in case of textual ellipsis) or there should be no link at all (in case of system ellipsis). The a-node representing the expressed part of a word (prefix, suffix, ending, part of a composite word) should be captured as an aux-linking a-node.

7. Conclusion

In the article, we delimitate the theoretical basis of ellipsis, bring a productive classification and describe its semantic representation in the Prague Dependency Treebanks.

The Prague Dependency Treebanks has already been used in many projects, both in linguistics research and for the development of NLP learning algorithms and software tools. The analytical and later the tectogrammatical layer has been used as a basis for conversion to the well-known CoNLL format in the 2007 and 2009 shared tasks (HajiT et al., 2009). In these shared tasks, over 30 parsers and SRL tools have been created, as described in the proceedings of CoNLL 2007 and CoNLL 2009 Shared Tasks. Parallel Czech-English Dependency Treebank has been also used for learning parsers and sematic role labelers, which have in turn been used for machine translation projects (Bojar et al., 2009; Tamchyna et al., 2014; MareTek, Popel, σabokrtskω 2010). Based on the data and experience with the PDT, a new multilingual treebank HamleDT with 30 treebanks in different languages have been converted to a uniform format and made available (Rosa et al., 2014).

Acknowledgments

The research reported in the article was supported by the Ministry of Education, Youth and Sport of Czech Republic within the project LINDAT-Clarin LM2010013. The participation on ROCLING 2014 conference was also supported by the πkoda Auto company.

Reference

BejTek, E. et al. (2013). *Prague Dependency Treebank 3.0*. Data/software, Institute of Formal and Applied Linguistics, Charles University in Prague, Prague. URL: http://ufal.mff.cuni.cz/pdt3.0/

Berman, S. ¯ Hestvik, A. (eds.) (1992). *Proceedings of the Stuttgart Ellipsis Workshop*. Arbeitspapiere des Sonderforschungsbereichs 340, Bericht No. 29, University of Stuttgart, Stuttgart.

Bojar O., Callison-Burch Ch., HajiT J., Koehn P. (2009): Special Issue on Open Source Machine Translation Tools, *The Prague Bulletin of Mathematical Linguistics*, Charles University in Prague, Prague, No. 91, ISBN 978-80-904175-1-9, ISSN 0032-6585.

BØhmov® A., HajiT, J., HajiTov® E., Hladk® B. (2003). The Prague dependency treebank: a 3-level annotation scenario. In *Treebanks: Building and using parsed corpora,* ed. A. Abeill¶ Kluwer, Dordrecht, 103-128.

HajiT J, Ciaramita M., Johansson R., Kawahara D., Mart° M. A., Marquez L., Meyers A., Nivre J., PadÆS., πtap®nek J., Straκ®k P., Surdeanu M., Xue Nianwen, Zhang Yi (2009): The CoNLL-2009 Shared Task: Syntactic and Semantic Dependencies in Multiple Languages. In: *Proceedings of the Thirteenth Conference on Computational Natural Language Learning (CoNLL): Shared Task,* Association for Computational Linguistics, Boulder, CO, USA, ISBN 978-1-932432-29-9, 1-18.

HajiT, J. et al. (2006). *The Prague Dependency Treebank 2.0.* CD-ROM. Cat. No. LDC2006T01, Linguistics Data Consortium, Philadelphia.

HajiT, J., HajiTov® E., Panevov® J. et al. (2012). Announcing Prague Czech-English Dependency Treebank 2.0. In *Proceedings of the 8th International Conference on Language Resources and Evaluation (LREC 2012)*, European Language Resources Association, Istanbul, ISBN 978-2-9517408-7-7, 3153-3160.

HajiT, J. et al. (2011). *Prague Czech-English Dependency Treebank 2.0*. Data/software, Institute of Formal and Applied Linguistics, Charles University in Prague, Prague.

HajiT, J. et al. (2001). *Prague Dependency Treebank 1.0 (Final Production Label)*. CD-ROM. Cat. No. LDC2001T10, Linguistic Data Consortium, Philadelphia, ISBN 1-58563-212-0.

Hlavsa, Z. (1981). On Syntactical Ellipsis. In *Satzsemantische Komponenten und Relationem im Text*, eds. Danep F., Viehweger, D., ΩJC CSAV, Prague, 119-128.

Lappin, S. ¯ Benmamoun, E. (eds.) (1999). *Fragments. Studies in Ellipsis and Gapping.* Oxford University Press, New York, ISBN 0-19-512302-6.

MareTek D., Popel M., σabokrtskω Z. (2010). Maximum Entropy Translation Model in Dependency-Based MT Framework. In: *Proceedings of the Joint Fifth Workshop on Statistical Machine Translation and MetricsMATR*, Association for Computational Linguistics, Uppsala, Sweden, ISBN 978-1-932432-71-8, 201-201.

Mikulov® M. et al. (2006): *Annotation on the tectogrammatical level in the Prague Dependency Treebank. Annotation manual*. Technical report no. 2006/30, Institute of Formal and Applied Linguistics, Charles University in Prague, Prague.

Marcus, M. et al. (1995). *Treebank 2*. CD-ROM. Cat. No. LDC95T7, Linguistics Data Consortium, Philadelphia.

Rosa R., Mapek J., MareTek D., Popel M., Zeman D., σabokrtskω Z. (2014). HamleDT 2.0: Thirty Dependency Treebanks Stanfordized. In: *Proceedings of the 9th International Conference on Language Resources and Evaluation (LREC 2014)*, European Language Resources Association, Reykjav%k, Iceland, ISBN 978-2-9517408-8-4, 2334-2341.

Sgall, P. et al. (1986). *The Meanings of the Sentence in Its Semantic and Pragmatic Aspects.* Dordrecht, D. Reidel Publishing Company - Praha, Academia, Prague.

Tamchyna A., Popel M., Rosa R., Bojar O.: CUNI in WMT14 (2014). Chimera Still Awaits Bellerophon. In: *Proceedings of the Ninth Workshop on Statistical Machine Translation*, Association for Computational Linguistics, Baltimore, MD, USA, ISBN 978-1-941643-17-4, 195-200.

Urepov®Z. (2011): *Valenční slovník Pražského závislostního korpusu (PDT-Vallex).* Institute of Formal and Applied Linguistics, Charles University in Prague, Prague., ISBN 978-80-904571-1-9.

The 2014 Conference on Computational Linguistics and Speech Processing
ROCLING 2014, pp. 139-152

Sketching the Dependency Relations of Words in Chinese

Meng-Hsien Shih* and Shu-Kai Hsieh*

Abstract

We proposes a language resource by automatically sketching grammatical relations of words based on dependency parses from untagged texts. The advantage of word sketch based on parsed corpora is, compared to Sketch Engine (Kilgarriff, Rychly, Smrz, & Tugwell, 2004), to provide more details about the different usage of each word such as various types of modification, which is also important in language pedagogy. Although some language resources of other languages have attempted to sketch words based on parsed data, in Chinese we have not seen a resource for dependency sketch of words in customized texts. Therefore, we propose such a resource and evaluate with Chinese Sketch Engine (Huang et al., 2005) in terms of corresponding thesaurus function.

Keywords: Dependency grammar, Grammatical relation, NLP tools/resources.

1. Introduction

Syntagmatic relational information has been the focus of the interface studies of syntax and semantics. With the rapid development of corpora, various corpus query, profiling and visualization tools have emerged quickly over the past years. Among these tools, Word Sketch Engine (Kilgarriff et al., 2004; Huang et al., 2005) has provided an effective approach to quantitatively summarize grammatical and collocation behavior [1]. The provided functions include Concordancer, Word Sketch, Sketch Diff, Thesaurus, and other web corpus crawling and processing tools.

Previous literatures have revealed that corpus linguistics has benefited greatly from Chinese Sketch Engine (Hong & Huang, 2006). Although proprietary, Word Sketch Engine system is popular among corpus linguists and language teachers because of its functions in language analysis. However, the construction of Sketch Engine is time-consuming due to the

---

* Graduate Institute of Linguistics, National Taiwan University, Taipei, Taiwan
E-mail: {simon.xian, shukai}@gmail.com

[1] http://www.sketchengine.co.uk

manually edited sketch grammar. Here we propose an alternative approach to sketch the grammar profile of words automatically from a text corpus.

The paper is organized as follows: Section 2 reviews the current design of related language resources. Section 3 describes the proposed method of sketching words in a parsed corpus. Section 4 presents the results from the proposed approach and evaluation. In the final section, we have a brief conclusion for this paper.

2. Review

Word Sketch Engine (WSE) provides a set of corpus query tools that aims to help users reveal linguistic patterns in language use. Among these tools, word sketch function gains the most popularity and has widely applied in the studies of corpus linguistics and language pedagogy (Kilgarriff, 2007).

Given the preprocessed corpus data, the available WSE system in most languages makes use of regular expressions to extract grammatical information from a POS-tagged corpus. The so-called *sketch grammars*, mostly manually crafted by linguists, describe the relation between a target word and its dependent, constrained on the surrounding context. In its design of grammar engineering, the sketch grammars are used for finite-state shallow parsing to extract the different grammatical relations [2]. Typical relations in English WSE include: [OBJECT_OF], [ADJ_MODIFIER], [NOUN_MODIFIER], [MODIFIES], [AND/OR], [PP_INTO], etc.

In terms of corpus linguistics, the *sketch* for a word presents a candidate set of its *collocates* organized by their grammatical relations they stand in to the target word. These collocates are sorted according to certain statistic measure of co-occurrence, as illustrated in the case of 打`hit_[3]:

[2] http://www.sketchengine.co.uk/documentation/wiki/SkE/Help/CreateCorpus

[3] http://wordsketch.ling.sinica.edu.tw

Home | Concordance | Word Sketch | Thesaurus | Sketch-Diff

打 **sinica freq = 2695**

PP_在 59		5.4
臉	8	19.07
身	6	14.45

Object	1834	3.4
電話	92	32.92
折	30	32.3
籃球	42	32.29
高爾夫球	23	31.69
零工	14	29.41
仗	15	26.76
招呼	16	24.74
折扣	18	24.03
交道	7	23.57
呵欠	8	23.5
勝仗	6	21.95
太極拳	9	21.74
冷顫	6	21.33
寒顫	6	21.33
寒噤	5	20.96
高爾夫	11	20.16
嗝	6	19.68
預防針	6	19.53
敗仗	6	19.53
盹	5	19.44
虎	14	19.35
場	33	19.22
羽毛球	6	19.11
排球	9	19.11
強心針	5	18.92

SentObject_of 122		3.3
敢	13	21.23
開始	12	16.41
喜歡	10	15.84
怕	6	14.05
繼續	7	13.95
知道	8	11.88

Modifier 776		2.6
去	49	19.95
要	55	18.61
愈	9	17.32
就	41	16.82
先	18	16.78
再	26	15.86
不會	15	15.2
該	9	14.87
一起	10	14.11
不能	14	13.88
會	31	13.7
連	7	13.35
一直	10	13.35
一	17	13.17
亂	5	13.11
不要	10	12.84
不	42	12.58
各	6	11.37
能	20	11.23
可以	18	10.93
還	15	10.39
別	5	9.76
又	11	9.6
只	11	9.18
都	15	8.98

Subject 1173		2.2
武松	13	28.39
棍子	5	16.55
球	9	14.15
我	99	13.91
你	49	13.54
他	66	11.62
爸爸	9	11.06
雨	5	9.77
電話	8	9.63
人	47	8.49
人家	5	8.11
老師	10	7.46
妳	7	7.22
他們	16	7.1
她	22	7.05
門	5	6.98
誰	5	5.86
媽媽	5	5.26
同學	5	5.21
學生	10	4.71
我們	15	4.67
孩子	6	4.55
自己	10	3.44
時候	5	3.28

Figure 1. Word sketch of 打"hit"

The core component in WSE system is the *sketch grammar*, which defines the linear patterns with regular expression for the system to automatically identify possible relations to the target word. For instance, one of the sketch grammar rules defined in the huge Chinese corpus (zhTenTen11, with 2.1 billion tokens) provided by WSE are concerned with modification. That is, we can identify the cases of modification relation where the target word (indicated by the prefix `1:_) can be any noun followed by non-nouns. And the collocates, i.e., that words we want to capture (marked with the prefix `2:_) is taken to be any verb followed by a word 的:

**DUAL*

=A_Modifier/Modifies

2:[tag="V.*"] [word="的"] [tag="N.*"]{0,**1:**[tag="N.*"] [tag!="N.*"]

The sketch grammar can be more complicated with the granularity of POS. The following grammar shows the classification relation developed by Huang et al. (2005) and implemented in the Chinese WordSketch system[4], i.e., the target word can be a noun preceded by a measure word (tagged by Nf):

=Measure

2:"Nf.*" ("A"|"VH11"|"VH13"|"VH21"|"V.*" "DE") [tag="N[abcd].*" & tag!="Ncd"]
1:[tag="N[abcdhf].*" & tag!="Nbc.*" & tag!="Ncd.*" & word!="者" & word!="們"]
[tag!="N[abcdhef].*"|tag="Nbc.*"|tag="Ncd.*"]

However, the writing of grammar is time-consuming, running risk of :low recall˘, so we turn to exploit the dependency parser for enriching the relational information. Unlike phrase-structure grammar, dependency grammar concentrates on the *typed dependency* between words, rather than constituent information. It is highly advantageous to our study, for it is linguistically-rich - capturing not only syntactic information such as *nsubj* (nominal subject) but also abstract semantic ones such as *loc* (localizer) - and can be further applied to other syntactic-semantic interface tasks (Chang, Tseng, Jurafsky, & Manning, 2009).

The Stanford lexicalized probabilistic parser (Levy & Manning, 2003) works out the grammatical structure of sentences with a factored product model efficiently combing preferences of PCFG phrase structure and lexical dependency experts. In addition to phrase structure tree, the parser also provides Stanford Dependencies (SD)[5] that are known as grammatical relations between words in a sentence. Take the following Chinese sentence for example: 我 很 喜歡 兩 則 惜福 與 惜緣 的 故事。 The *head* 喜歡 has a *dependent* of 我 as its nominal subject, and another dependent of 故事 as direct object (Fig. 2).

---

[4] http://wordsketch.ling.sinica.edu.tw

[5] http://nlp.stanford.edu/software/stanford-dependencies.shtml

```
(ROOT
(IP
  (NP (PN 我))
  (VP
    (ADVP (AD 很))
    (VP (VV 喜歡)
      (NP
        (DNP
          (NP
            (NP (NR 兩))
            (NP (NN 則) (NN 惜福) (NN 與) (NN 惜緣)))
          (DEG 的))
        (NP (NN 故事)))))
  (PU 。)))
```

```
nsubj(喜歡-3, 我-1)
advmod(喜歡-3, 很-2)
root(ROOT-0, 喜歡-3)
nn(惜緣-8, 兩-4)
nn(惜緣-8, 則-5)
nn(惜緣-8, 惜福-6)
nn(惜緣-8, 與-7)
assmod(故事-10, 惜緣-8)
assm(惜緣-8, 的-9)
dobj(喜歡-3, 故事-10)
```

Figure 2. Dependencies in a Chinese sentence with PCFG: **我很喜歡兩則惜福與惜緣的故事。**

The SD has been widely used in NLP-related fields such as sentiment analysis (Meena & Prabhakar, 2007), textual entailment (Androutsopoulos & Malakasiotis, 2010). The Chinese version of SD (Chang et al., 2009) is also available on the Stanford Dependencies page[6]. The SD can even distinguish 45 typed dependencies among Chinese words, as shown in Table 1.

6 http://nlp.stanford.edu/software/stanford-dependencies.shtml#Chinese

Table 1. Chinese dependency relations (Chang et al., 2009)

abbreviation	short description	Chinese example	typed dependency	counts	percentage
nn	noun compound modifier	服务 中心	nn(中心, 服务)	13278	15.48%
punct	punctuation	海关 统计 表明 ，	punct(表明, ，)	10896	12.71%
nsubj	nominal subject	梅花 盛开	nsubj(盛开, 梅花)	5893	6.87%
conj	conjunct (links two conjuncts)	设备 和 原材料	conj(原材料, 设备)	5438	6.34%
dobj	direct object	浦东 颁布 了 七十一 件 文件	dobj(颁布, 文件)	5221	6.09%
advmod	adverbial modifier	部门 先 送上 文件	advmod(送上, 先)	4231	4.93%
prep	prepositional modifier	在 实践 中 逐步 完善	prep(完善, 在)	3138	3.66%
nummod	number modifier	七十一 件 文件	nummod(件, 七十一)	2885	3.36%
amod	adjectival modifier	跨世纪 工程	amod(工程, 跨世纪)	2691	3.14%
pobj	prepositional object	根据 有关 规定	pobj(根据, 规定)	2417	2.82%
rcmod	relative clause modifier	不 曾 遇到 过 的 情况	rcmod(情况, 遇到)	2348	2.74%
cpm	complementizer	开发 浦东 的 经济 活动	cpm(开发, 的)	2013	2.35%
assm	associative marker	企业 的 商品	assm(企业, 的)	1969	2.30%
assmod	associative modifier	企业 的 商品	assmod(商品, 企业)	1941	2.26%
cc	coordinating conjunction	设备 和 原材料	cc(原材料, 和)	1763	2.06%
clf	classifier modifier	七十一 件 文件	clf(文件, 件)	1558	1.82%
ccomp	clausal complement	银行 决定 先 取得 信用 评级	ccomp(决定, 取得)	1113	1.30%
det	determiner	这些 经济 活动	det(活动, 这些)	1113	1.30%
lobj	localizer object	近年 来	lobj(来, 近年)	1010	1.18%
range	dative object that is a quantifier phrase	成交 药品 一亿多 元	range(成交, 元)	891	1.04%
asp	aspect marker	发挥 了 作用	asp(发挥, 了)	857	1.00%
tmod	temporal modifier	以前 不 曾 遇到 过	tmod(遇到, 以前)	679	0.79%
plmod	localizer modifier of a preposition	在 这 片 热土 上	plmod(在, 上)	630	0.73%
attr	attributive	贸易额 为 二百亿 美元	attr(为, 美元)	534	0.62%
mmod	modal verb modifier	利益 能 得到 保障	mmod(得到, 能)	497	0.58%
loc	localizer	占 九成 以上	loc(占, 以上)	428	0.50%
top	topic	建筑 是 主要 活动	top(是, 建筑)	380	0.44%
pccomp	clausal complement of a preposition	据 有关 部门 介绍	pccomp(据, 介绍)	374	0.44%
etc	etc modifier	科技 、 文教 等 领域	etc(文教, 等)	295	0.34%
lccomp	clausal complement of a localizer	中国 对 外 开放 中 升起 的 明星	lccomp(中, 开放)	207	0.24%
ordmod	ordinal number modifier	第七 个 机构	ordmod(个, 第七)	199	0.23%
xsubj	controlling subject	银行 决定 先 取得 信用 评级	xsubj(取得, 银行)	192	0.22%
neg	negative modifier	以前 不 曾 遇到 过	neg(遇到, 不)	186	0.22%
rcomp	resultative complement	研究 成功	rcomp(研究, 成功)	176	0.21%
comod	coordinated verb compound modifier	颁布 实行	comod(颁布, 实行)	150	0.17%
vmod	verb modifier	其 在 支持 外商 企业 方面 的 作用	vmod(方面, 支持)	133	0.16%
prtmod	particles such as 所, 以, 来, 而	在 产业化 所 取得 的 成就	prtmod(取得, 所)	124	0.14%
ba	"ba" construction	把 注意力 转向 市场	ba(转向, 把)	95	0.11%
dvpm	manner DE(地) modifier	有效 地 防止 流失	dvpm(有效, 地)	73	0.09%
dvpmod	a "XP+DEV(地)" phrase that modifies VP	有效 地 防止 流失	dvpmod(防止, 有效)	69	0.08%
prnmod	parenthetical modifier	八五 期间 （ 1990 – 1995 ）	prnmod(期间, 1995)	67	0.08%
cop	copular	原 是 自给自足 的 经济	cop(自给自足, 是)	59	0.07%
pass	passive marker	被 认定 为 高 技术 产业	pass(认定, 被)	53	0.06%
nsubjpass	nominal passive subject	镍 被 称作 现代 工业 的 维生素	nsubjpass(称作, 镍)	14	0.02%

On the other hand, most semantic resources like PropBank (Palmer, Gildea, & Kingsbury, 2005) and FrameNet (Baker, Fillmore, & Lowe, 1998) either provide coarse-grained information or with limited coverage. In this paper, we propose a lexical resource tool to describe more detailed information for all words in a text corpus. We choose Sinica Corpus (Chen, Huang, Chang, & Hsu, 1996) as our texts and evaluate the results with Chinese Sketch Engine in terms of corresponding thesaurus function.

3. Method

In this case study, untagged texts of 567,702 sentences from Sinica Corpus 3.0[7] were parsed with dependency relations by the Stanford Parser (Chang et al., 2009). We obtained 574,552 dependency relations (of 23 types) between 44,257 words.

To sketch a word, we make use of the dependency tuples from the parsed corpus (see the right panel of Fig. 2) to extract the relations of each word with its dependents, and obtain the sketch of words such as 打 `hit_ shown below:

Table 2. Dependency sketch of* 打 *"hit"

(Matches with Chinese Sketch Engine are marked in red bold face)

prep	dobj	advmod/mmod	nsubj	asp	conj
在	**電話**	**去**	**武松**	了	重建
到	**折**	**要**	**棍子**	著	是
自	**籃球**	**就**	**球**		鬧
	高爾夫球	**先**	**我**		
	硬仗	**不會**	**你**		
	招呼	**該**	**他**		
	折扣	**一起**	**爸爸**		
	哈欠	**會**	**雨**		
	太極拳	連續	**人**		
	麻藥針	**一**	**老師**		
	盹兒	**能**	**他們**		
	虎	**可以**	**她**		
	羽毛球	還要	**學生**		
	排球	**都**	**自己**		
	蛇	雖然	湖人		
	起來	仍然	來		
	秋千	而	政		

[7] www.sinica.edu.tw/SinicaCorpus

Since the Stanford Parser still suffers from parsing difficulty in Chinese (Levy & Manning, 2003), the grammatical relations automatically required, though impressive, may contain heterogeneous errors originating from mistagging errors [8], syntactic ambiguities and other dependency parsing issues, so we have observed some minor sketch errors in the result. However, it˘s hard to evaluate the results in an automatic way as conventionalized in the field of NLP. The main reasons are:

[1]. Currently, there is no gold-standard (in Chinese). It is particularly hard to measure recall for the set of :correct answer˘is not available.

[2]. An overall evaluation of the sketch performance will have to rely on the assessment of each module (word segmentation, POS tagging, sketch grammar and/or dependency parsing, etc.) separately. A comparative table is shown in Table 3.

Table 3. Comparison of Different Word Sketch Systems

Word Sketch System	word segmentation	pos tagging/tagset	sketch grammar	dependency parser
CWSE.sinica	CKIP	CKIP/ASBC	hand-crafted rules	*
zhTenTen.11	Stanford Chinese Word Segmenter	Stanford Log-linear Part-Of-Speech Tagger / Chinese Penn Treebank standard	hand-crafted (2 rules)	*
Proposed	Stanford Chinese Word Segmenter	*	*	Stanford dependencies

[8] In this study, since Stanford Parser takes manully tokenized input from Sinica Corpus, the segmentation error may be less than that from an automatic segmenter and be omitted here.

In addition, from the perspective of language resources construction as well as applied lexicography, as the system aims to identify highly salient candidate patterns, the noisy data should not constitute a serious problem for the task. The position is also well-articulated and proposed in (Kilgarriff, Kov®p Krek, SrdanoviP, & Tiberius, 2010), where a variant of evaluation paradigm (user/developer-oriented paradigm) is required.

Different from Ambati, Reddy, and Kilgarriff (2012) and Reddy, Klapaftis, McCarthy, and Manandhar (2011) where an external evaluation task such as *topic coherence* or *semantic composition* were adopted, we evaluated the proposed method with the task of automatic construction of thesaurus, for our main concern is the construction of language resource rather than NLP system performance.

The thesaurus in WSE is called **distributional thesaurus**, and can be built for any language if the word sketches data of the language is available. The thesaurus is constructed by computing the similarity between words based upon the overlapping rate of their word sketches. Our method instead, follows the **distributional semantic model** (Dinu, Pham, & Baroni, 2013; Turney & Pantel, 2010) and anchors on two manually constructed resources of the **Chinese Wordnet**[9] and Chilin (Chao & Chung, 2013)[10].

4. Evaluation

The dependency data of five selected synonym sets (經常, 原因, 按照, 相當, and 快樂) from Chinese Wordnet were converted into multi-dimensional (to avoid sparseness, only dependents shared by both synonyms were included) in order to calculate distributional similarity between synonyms. Five synonym sets from Chinese Wordnet were examined. For example, the dependency data of 高興 and 快樂 are converted as follows (disregarding the dependency type):

	不	也	了	他	可以
高興	7	1	5	5	1
快樂	1	4	1	3	2

[9] http://lope.linguistics.ntu.edu.tw/cwn2

[10] http://code.google.com/p/tw-synonyms-chilin

Then we adopt one of the common measures for similarity in distributional models, *cosine similarity*, to calculate the similarity between two words (e.g., 高興 and 快樂). The meaning of a word is determined by its collocation, and represented as a vector of its co-occurrence with other words in multiple dimensions. In this model, the similarity between two word vectors, w_1 and w_2, can be calculated by their cosine value:

$$CosSimilarity(w_1, w_2) = \frac{w_1 \cdot w_2}{|w_1||w_2|} \quad (1)$$

To illustrate, consider only the first two dimensions of 高興 and 快樂, the cosine similarity between the two words would be $(7,1)\cdot(1,4)/\sqrt{(7^2+1^2)}/\sqrt{(1^2+4^2)}=0.377$, and the calculation can be extended to even more dimensions. If two words have similar collocation with other words, the value of cosine similarity will approach the upper bound of 1.0 and could be considered a pair of synonyms.

Finally, to obtain a synonym list, the dependents of a target word are ranked by their similarity with the target word, regardless of their dependency relations. The results for the selected five synonym sets in Chinese Wordnet and Chilin[11] are shown in Table 4.

Table 4. Comparison of the results with Sketch Engine

	快樂	經常	原因	按照	相當
Cilin	高興,愉快,樂,…	時常,常常,時時,常..	因,故,緣故,緣由,ǔ	依照,比照,遵照,ǔ	頂,相當於,ǔ
Chinese Wordnet	樂,愉快,愉	時常,勤,常常,常,恆	關係,肇始,因, 故,導因,緣	按,依照,依據,根據,ǔ	很,相當於,具體
Proposed Method	有趣,愉快,美好,ǔ	時常	關係	按,依照	具體, ǔ
Sketch Engine	愉快,美好,ǔ	n/a	因素,背景,條件,環境,理由,..	n/a	莫大,重大,重要,直接,ǔ

[11]Although WordNet is more used in natural language processing, Chilin is considered a more appropriate resource designed for thesaurus. Here we present the comparison with both.

For a brief look, we observed that the proposed method is capable of extracting more synonyms from a text corpus, which might be absent in the Sketch Engine, although we still cannot perform as accurately as does the manual *sketch grammar* of Sketch Engine.

We also built a web interface considering the friendly access for potential users from TCSL (Teaching Chinese as Second Language) and linguistics[12]. Figure 3 shows a snapshot of the prototype. The sketch page first shows the frequent roles of the query word ranked by their frequency, followed by the collocation in each role. The page also shows, as the classical Word Sketch does, an analysis of the types of words which the query word collocates with. For example, in Figure 3 we can know that 快樂 `happy_ frequently serves as an associative modifier (14.3%) and modifies 笑容 `smile_ twice in this corpus. We believe that such word sketch information is useful in TCSL application. The scripts and data has been put on Github[13] for open access and further collaboration.

[12] http://140.112.147.131:8000/sketch

[13] http://github.com/mhshih/sketch

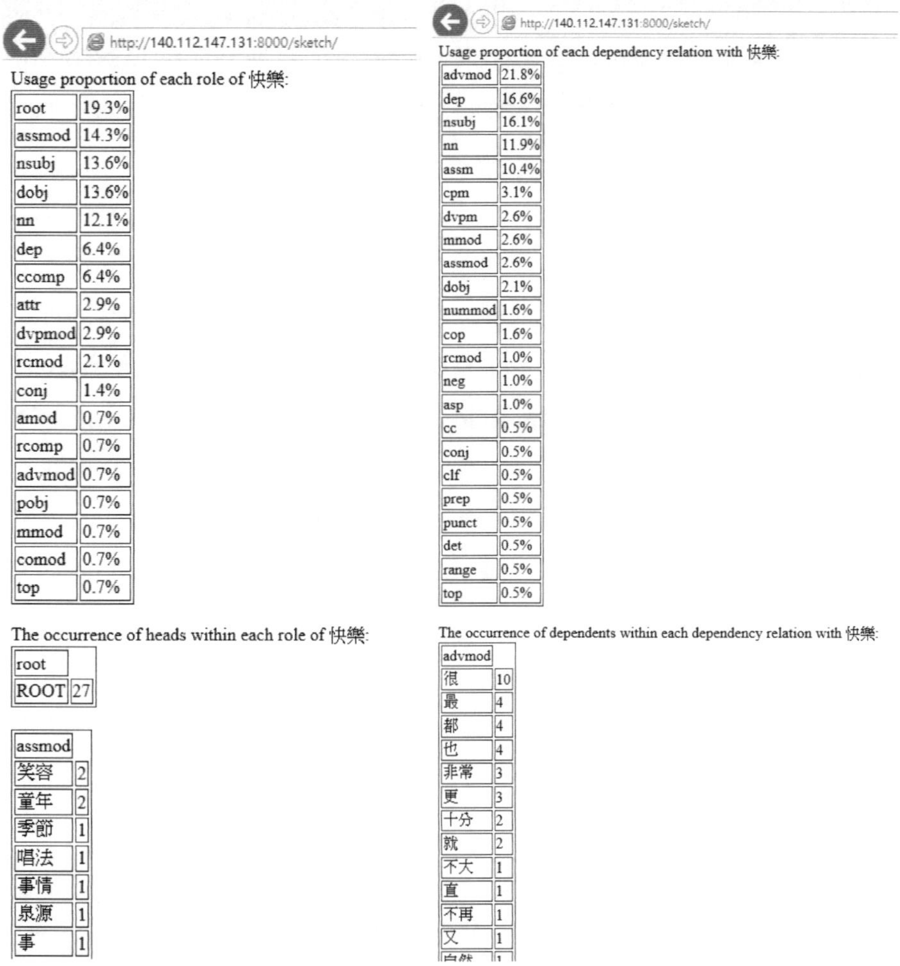

Figure 3. Snapshot of the sketch function

5. Conclusion

Word sketch is a corpus-based automatic summary of a word`s grammatical and collocational behavior. Based on the hand-crafted finite-state sketch grammar over a POS-tagged corpus, word sketch system can identify the collocates with grammatical relations to the target word. However, the grammar engineering is time-consuming and requires experts, in this paper, we propose an alternative by leveraging an existing dependency parser. The results were evaluated based on the comparison of distributional thesaurus with significance.

This paper serves as the first attempt to create an open-sourced word sketch-like corpus profiling system for Chinese linguistics and Teaching Chinese as Second Language. The proposed method is pipelined and can be applied to user-created corpus. The extracted relation triples <w1, R, w2> can be used to enrich our on-going Chinese BIGLEX database. Future works include exploring other dependency parsing algorithm, incorporating advanced statistics to single out salient collocations, and an open evaluation platform for the further improvement of the resource are in progress.

Acknowledgements

The authors would like to thank reviewers of ROCLING 2014 for their insightful comments that help improve the manuscript.

References

Ambati, B. R., Reddy, S., & Kilgarriff, A. (2012). *Word Sketches for Turkish.* Paper presented at the LREC.

Androutsopoulos, I., & Malakasiotis, P. (2010). A survey of paraphrasing and textual entailment methods. *J. Artif. Int. Res., 38*(1), 135-187.

Baker, C. F., Fillmore, C. J., & Lowe, J. B. (1998). *The Berkeley FrameNet Project.* Paper presented at the Proceedings of the 36th Annual Meeting of the Association for Computational Linguistics and 17th International Conference on Computational Linguistics - Volume 1, Montreal, Quebec, Canada.

Chang, P.-C., Tseng, H., Jurafsky, D., & Manning, C. D. (2009). *Discriminative reordering with Chinese grammatical relations features*. Paper presented at the Proceedings of the Third Workshop on Syntax and Structure in Statistical Translation, Boulder, Colorado.

Chao, F. A., & Chung, S.-F. (2013). A Definition-based Shared-concept Extraction within Groups of Chinese Synonyms: A Study Utilizing the Extended Chinese Synonym Forest. *IJCLCLP, 18*(2).

Chen, K.-J., Huang, C.-R., Chang, L.-P., & Hsu, H.-L. (1996). *Sinica corpus: Design methodology for balanced corpora.* Paper presented at the The 11th Pacific Asia Conference on Language, Information and Computation (PACLIC-11).

Dinu, G., Pham, N., & Baroni, M. (2013). *DISSECT-DIStributional SEmantics Composition Toolkit.* Paper presented at the 51st Annual Meeting of the Association for Computational Linguistics.

Hong, J.-F., & Huang, C.-R. (2006). *Using chinese gigaword corpus and chinese word sketch in linguistic research.* Paper presented at the The 20th Pacific Asia Conference on Language, Information and Computation (PACLIC-20).

Huang, C.-R., Kilgarriff, A., Wu, Y., Chiu, C.-M., Smith, S., Rychly, P., . . . Chen, K.-J. (2005). *Chinese Sketch Engine and the extraction of grammatical collocations.* Paper presented at the Proceedings of the Fourth SIGHAN Workshop on Chinese Language Processing.

Kilgarriff, A. (2007). Using corpora in language learning: the Sketch Engine. *Optimizing the role of language in Technology-Enhanced Learning, 22*, 21.

Kilgarriff, A., Kov®p V., Krek, S., SrdanoviP, I., & Tiberius, C. (2010). *A quantitative evaluation of word sketches.* Paper presented at the Proceedings of the 14th EURALEX International Congress, Leeuwarden, The Netherlands.

Kilgarriff, A., Rychly, P., Smrz, P., & Tugwell, D. (2004). Itri-04-08 the sketch engine. *Information Technology, 105*, 116.

Levy, R., & Manning, C. (2003). *Is it harder to parse Chinese, or the Chinese Treebank?* Paper presented at the Proceedings of the 41st Annual Meeting on Association for Computational Linguistics - Volume 1, Sapporo, Japan.

Meena, A., & Prabhakar, T. V. (2007). *Sentence level sentiment analysis in the presence of conjuncts using linguistic analysis*. Paper presented at the Proceedings of the 29th European conference on IR research, Rome, Italy.

Palmer, M., Gildea, D., & Kingsbury, P. (2005). The Proposition Bank: An Annotated Corpus of Semantic Roles. *Computational Linguistics, 31*(1), 71-106. doi: 10.1162/0891201053630264

Reddy, S., Klapaftis, I. P., McCarthy, D., & Manandhar, S. (2011). *Dynamic and Static Prototype Vectors for Semantic Composition.* Paper presented at the IJCNLP.

Turney, P. D., & Pantel, P. (2010). From frequency to meaning: vector space models of semantics. *J. Artif. Int. Res., 37*(1), 141-188.

The 2014 Conference on Computational Linguistics and Speech Processing
ROCLING 2014, pp. 153-162

使用中文字筆畫構形資料庫校正字形相似之別字

Using Chinese Orthography Database to Correct Chinese Misspelling Words With Graphemic Similarity

張道行[1]　陳學志[2]　鄭健良[1]

摘要

中文別字自動偵測與校正是個相當重要的工具，許多分析別字類型的研究指出，「字音混淆」、「字形混淆」與「字義混淆」是別字產生的主要原因，因此近年來許多別字自動校正的研究也都採取分別針對字音、字形、字義造成的混淆進行探討。但對於字形相似別字的校正正確率仍不夠好，主要原因之一是因為在中文字字形結構的資訊不夠完整。本文的目的是利用中文部件組字與形構資料庫的筆畫結構資料提出一個演算法，計算兩個中文字筆畫結構序列的相似程度，並用於字形相似類別字的偵測與校正。實驗結果顯示筆畫結構用在偵測與校正字形相似別字的效能較原先以部件的方法來得有效。

關鍵字：別字偵測；別字校正；字形相似；筆畫；中文部件組字與形構資料庫；LCS 演算法

1. 緒論

中文別字自動偵測與校正是個相當重要的工具，在資訊應用中也具有相當的價值。例如許多文書處理軟體都有提供別字檢查與校正建議。但由於中文別字的偵測與校正較困難，這些軟體在中文別字校正效能上仍有不足。因此除了英文的別字校正研究[1][7]之外，一直以來也有許多研究[4][6][8][11][13][15][16]提出不同的方法試圖解決中文別字偵測與校正的問題。

早期別字自動偵測方法大多是透過建立混淆字集方式搭配語言模型運作。例如 Chang[2]將欲處理語句中的每個字視為別字，並以該字混淆字集中的字逐一替換原字，組合出多種可能的句子。再利用 bi-gram 語言模型計算所有句子的分數，選出最可能的句子。

[1] Department of Computer Science and Information Engineering, National Kaohsiung University of Applied Sciences, Kaohsiung, Taiwan
[2] Department of Educational Psychology and Counseling, National Taiwan Normal University, Taipei, Taiwan
Email: changth@gm.kuas.edu.tw

許多研究也提出了類似的方法，但改用不同的語言模型，如 tri-gram[17]、混合規則式與機率式的模型[12]。此類方法相當容易實作，也可同時適用於字音相似與字形相似兩類別字的偵測與校正。但這種方法的主要缺點為適當的混淆字集建立不易，如果廣泛蒐集所有可能的混淆字，很容易造成誤報率(false alarm)提高。但若只蒐集常見別字，則會遺漏不在混淆字集中的字。

許多分析別字類型的研究[18][19][20]指出，「字音混淆」、「字形混淆」與「字義混淆」是別字產生主要原因，因此近年來許多別字自動校正的研究也都採取分別針對字音、字形與字義造成的混淆進行分析、再加以整合的策略。這些研究在字音造成的別字部分都有相當好的校正正確率，但對於字形與字義造成的別字的校正正確率仍不夠好。對於字形造成的別字校正效能有限，主要原因之一是因為在中文字字形結構的資訊不夠完整，導致建立某些中文字字形混淆字集時容易產生相似度誤差使得字集不夠精確。

陳學志等人[22]建立的「中文部件組字與形構資料庫」是一個解決這個問題的可能線索。該資料庫於 2010 年起提供每個中文字的部件組字資料，又於 2013 年進一步擴充，將每個部件進一步拆解為筆畫結構的組合，得到每個字以筆畫為基本單位的構形資料，我們稱為筆畫結構序列。本文的目的就是利用這個中文字筆畫結構資料庫處理字形相似度問題，並用於字形相似類別字的偵測與校正。但是筆畫結構資料是描繪基本筆畫單元間的空間關係，要如何使用於計算兩字間的字形相似度並不是個容易的問題。本文的主要貢獻在於提供一個演算法可計算兩個中文字筆畫結構序列的相似程度。

本文其餘內容將組織如下。第 2 節說明字形相似別字的相關研究以及所遭遇的問題。第 3 節介紹「中文部件組字與形構資料庫」中筆畫結構資訊的表達方式。第 4 節說明本文所提的字形相似度計算方法。第 5 節說明如何將字形相似度計算結果整合在別字預測工具中。第 6 節展示應用此方法於字形錯別字的實驗結果。最後提出未來可能的研究方向。

2. 相關研究

早期研究多使用混淆字集偵測與校正別字，然而這種方法未必能將真正字形相似字完整涵括。因此有些研究針對字形相似性設計自動建立混淆字集的方法。最早的相關研究是使用與字形相關的倉頡輸入法偵測字形相似別字。如 Lin 等人[9]利用倉頡碼建立混淆字集，再採用類似 Chang[2]的方法偵測與校正。實驗結果顯示校正的成功率有明顯提升且有較少的誤報率。Liu 等人[10]也是利用倉頡碼對形構相近字提出計算相似度的方法。[10]利用倉頡輸入法將中文字編碼，透過倉頡碼 26 個基本單位的組合比較兩兩中文字的相似性。然而倉頡輸入法為了維持每一個漢字輸入不超過五個碼的效率，因此某些部件較多或較複雜的漢字倉頡碼會被簡化，使得字與字之間的相似證據難以找出。於是[10]建構了一套「倉頡詳碼」完整地還原字的構形，將每個字以倉頡詳碼表示，可提供較精確的相似度訊息。

基本上使用倉頡碼建立混淆字集的概念是認為漢字可拆解成數個基本單元、或稱為部件(radical)，比對部件的使用可判斷字形相似性。而有一些研究[22][23]提出了更完整的中文字部件構形資料庫，例如[23]提出的「漢字構型資料庫」，以及 [22]建構的「中文部件組字與形構資料庫」。以後者為例，其蒐集了 6097 個常用字，從內拆解出 439 個基礎中文部件，並歸納出 11 種字形空間的結構關係。透過以上指標與部件跟結構關係的組合，可以更加瞭解字形的構成，進而觀察字與字之間的相似關係。與倉頡碼相比，使用中文字部件資料庫比較字形相似度是更為合理且精確的作法。

先前 Chang 等人[5]的研究也利用「中文部件組字資料庫」中的部件偵測與校正字形別字。該研究也發現使用部件偵測及校正字形相似字的確有效，但該研究也指出有些部件由於未能進一步拆解導致某些字的相似度計算有相當大的誤差。例如西本身是一個部件，因此當他和西計算相似度時因為沒有相同部件導致相似度非常低。這個問題突顯了以部件量測字形相似性的侷限所在，但也指出改良的方向，也就是應該以更基本的字形組成單元測量相似性。

3. 中文字筆畫結構表示法

在「中文部件組字與形構資料庫」中，所有漢字可歸納出 41 個基礎筆畫與 11 個字形結構關係。筆畫中包含基本的橫{一}、豎{|}、撇{丿}等。其中部分筆畫無法透過系統 unicode 編碼呈現，便會將其透過組合的方式表達，例如「國」的第二劃為橫豎，但橫豎無法以一般 unicode 編碼呈現，因此以筆畫{口 2}(代表「口」字書寫時的第二劃，也就是橫豎)表示。有些更複雜的筆畫必須透過結構關係描述，例如「大」的第三劃為撇捺，同樣無法以 unicode 呈現，因此會以筆畫{[尺/]}表示，其中筆畫內置於「尺」右側的「/」代表右下方的筆畫，即「尺」字右下方的那一劃，也就是撇捺。

字形結構部分則包含 10 種組合及其它結構。10 種組合包含：垂直組合(例如「二」字結構是由上下垂直組合而成)、水平組合(例如「林」字是由左右水平方式組合)、封閉組合(例如「國」字是由四面包圍方式組成)等。這些組合以符號表示，例如垂直組合為「-」、水平組合為「|」、封閉組合為「0」等。大多數字都可以用這 10 種組合結構表示，但有些字的結構不屬於任何一種組合，故這些字歸類為無字形組合之結構，例如「一」、「乙」字

都為單獨存在的形體結構，不屬於任何一種組合。

在資料庫中每一個漢字都是由筆畫、筆畫間連接關係、與字形結構三項所組合，稱為「基礎筆畫組合」。例如「二」字，其基礎筆畫組合為「-({一 s},{一})」，從中可看出垂直組合(-)是主結構，這個組合包含了兩個筆畫{一 s}與{一}，其中{一 s}代表書寫時較短的{一}。「二」字無筆畫連接關係，對於有筆畫連接關係的字也會在基礎筆畫組合以符號組合「+{a:b@c}」表示連接關係。此符號組合一般都會緊鄰在一筆畫之後，例如「{丨}+{a:b@c}」，表示會以筆畫{丨}為基準，本文稱為基本筆畫。符號組合中的 a 代表整個基礎筆畫組合中由左而右數來第 a 個筆畫和基準筆畫{丨}有連接關係，這第 a 個筆畫本文稱為連接筆畫。符號組合中的 b 代表基準筆畫在連接筆畫的 b 位置相接，「@c」則代表連接筆畫在基準筆畫的 c 位置相接。此資料庫將每一個基礎筆畫依照比例平均劃分為 10 等分，用來表示前述相接位置。符號組合中的「+」表示筆畫間的連接關係為相互交錯；若筆畫間為相接但非交錯的關係，則以「~」符號表示。筆畫間連接關係只有以上兩種。

圖 1 是一個基礎筆畫組合的範例。範例中的「十」字其基礎筆畫組合為「[{一},{丨}+(1:5@5)]」。「十」的筆畫連接關係表示為{一}在其 5 的位置(也就是正中間)與{丨}在其 5 的位置相互交錯。然而「十」的結構為單獨存在，故在筆畫組合裡面不會看到結構符號、只會有筆畫。但是兩個筆畫有連接關係，因此僅以「{丨}+(1:5@5)」表示。

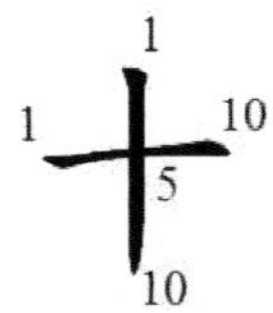

圖 1：基礎筆畫組合範例字「十」

4. 中文字筆畫結構相似度

由於前述的筆畫結構表示法不容易直接用來計算兩中文字筆畫結構的相似度，因此必須先將整體筆畫結構轉換為筆畫結構配對。轉換方法是先將每個漢字的基礎筆畫組合中以有連接關係的一組筆畫配對作為相似度計算的基本單位。例如「大」字，基礎筆畫組合為「[{一},{月 1}+(1:5@3),{[尺/]}~(1:5@0)~(2:3@0)]」，將其透過兩兩筆畫連接關係配對成({一},{月 1})、({一},{[尺/]})及({月 1},{[尺/]})三個筆畫配對，並以漢字書寫時的筆畫順序將配對排序，形成一個配對序列。

接著便可使用最長公共子序列(Longest Common Subsequences，LCS)演算法[7][14]計算兩個配對序列的相似度。LCS 演算法可以經由比對得到兩序列中最長相同的子序列，因此廣泛被使用於計算兩字串或序列之間的相似度。其計算方法是將序列中的所有子序列依照順序一個個與另一序列之子序列做比對，若相同則比較下一個子序列，不同則記錄比較至目前最長的相同子序列，接著再從頭比對另一序列的下一個子序列，重複上述動作直到所有子序列比較完成即可取得最長相似的子序列組合。例如比較兩字串「Look」與「Books」，會先以「Look」的 L 與「Books」的 B 比較，不同則比較「Books」下一個子字元 o，重複以 L 比對完「Books」所有字元後，再以「Look」的第二字元 o 重新比對「Books」。藉由不斷地循環比對便能得到最長的子字串為「ook」，長度為 3。

由於 LCS 演算法具備「擷取序列必須順序相同」的特性，符合漢字是依固定筆畫順序書寫的規則，因此我們採用 LCS 演算法作為兩字間筆畫配對序列相似計算的方法。以「大」和「太」兩字之相似度比較為例，其配對序列分別為({一},{月 1})、({一},{[尺/]})、({月 1},{[尺/]})與({一},{月 1})、({一},{[尺/]})、({月 1},{[尺/]})、({、})，兩字間除了配對({、})不一樣之外，其餘三個配對均相同，且其配對經由 LCS 演算法計算後，最長連續相似配對的配對數為 3。

上述的配對方法雖然依照順序的特性能有效計算大多數字之間的相似度，但有兩種特殊情況必須考慮。第一種情形是部件相同但部件位置不同的鏡寫字會造成相似度不足的問題。例如「部」與「陪」兩字，其筆畫配對完全相同，但出現的順序不同，若如果利用原本配對序列經由 LCS 演算法計算並無法得到合理的相似度。因為有鏡寫障礙的學生很容易寫出這類的別字，故我們修正前述配對序列產生的方式以改善 LCS 演算法的問題。

我們將欲比較的兩序列其中之一複製後連結在原先序列的後面，形成一個長度為原先兩倍的新序列，稱為複製倍增序列，再將複製倍增序列與另一序列做比較。以「abcdef」與「defabc」兩序列為例，由於兩序列僅「abc」與「def」順序顛倒，若使用原先 LCS 演算法計算，其最長相似長度為 3。因此我們將序列「abcdef」倍增為「abcdefabcdef」後，再與另一序列「defabc」比較，可得最長共同序列為「defabc」，長度為 6。但由於這種做法會使一個字與自己的最長共同序列的相似度會和它與鏡寫字間的相同，因此當兩字為鏡寫字時，必須在使用最長共同序列長度作為相似度評估時略做調整，才能有較合理的結果。

第二種情形則是配對序列省略了字形結構資訊導致某些字的相似性計算不合理。例如「昌」與「BB」兩字，其筆畫配對序列完全相同，若以 LCS 方法比較兩字，兩序列完全相同，但兩字並不是相同字，是屬於主字形結構不同的相異字。因此相似度公式必須考慮比較兩字之間的主結構關係，根據研究經驗給予不同的字形主結構的結構相似係數。在 LCS 計算相似性時須另外再乘上結構相似係數，作為兩字最後的字形相似分數。例如「昌」

與「田」字，其主字形結構分別屬於「垂直組合(-)」與「水平組合(|)」，這兩個結構關係差異較大，較容易分辨，因此兩結構的相似係數為 0.4。。

另外，本文使用筆畫評估字形相似性的原始動機之一，是因為有些相似的部件無法被有效判斷相似性。雖然用筆畫能將部件拆解成更小的比較單位，但筆畫與筆畫之間仍有相似的問題，例如筆畫{一}和筆畫{㇆ 2}、{㇗ 2}及{㇖}相當相似。為解決這個問題，我們使用[22]所提供的筆畫相似度資訊，[22]將所有筆畫分類為 21 個筆畫相似集。因此本文在計算筆畫配對序列相似度時，對於兩個筆畫配對，若對應的筆畫在同一個筆畫相似集中，即使筆畫不同仍視為相同筆畫配對。

綜合以上討論，對於兩個中文字 C_1 與 C_2，其筆畫配對序列分別為 S_1 與 S_2，則兩字的字形相似度公式如下:

$$sim(C_1, C_2) = sms(C_1, C_2) \times \frac{2 \times lcs(rep(S_1), S_2) - mirror}{num(S_1) + num(S_2)} \tag{1}$$

其中 *rep* 函數可產生輸入序列的複製倍增序列；*lcs* 函數計算兩序列的最長共同子序列的長度；*num* 函數計算該序列的配對數量；*sms* 函數計算兩字主字形結構的相似性；參數 *mirror* 在 *lcs* 函數值分別等於兩個 num 函數值且兩字相異時，其值為 1，否則為 0。

5. 別字校正模型

本文使用的別字訓練模型是以 Chang 等人[5]所提的方法為基礎。[5]利用訓練資料中別字所產生的候選詞的四個參數(字音相似度、字形相似度、字頻機率比值、詞性機率比值)建立一個線性迴歸公式作為預測模型，用來判別候選詞是否可以對原句的可疑字組進行替換校正。本文與[5]的差別就在於字形相似度的計算方法不同。為了建立預測模型，本文準備 650 筆含有別字的資料，在計算有別字的可疑字組與有正確字的候選詞間的四個參數後，成為一個 positive 樣本集合;另外準備 650 筆句子包含無別字句子與含有別字句子，在計算可疑字組與無正確字的候選詞間的四個參數後成為一個 negative 樣本。使用這兩個樣本集合共 1300 句可以建立線性迴歸公式。這個線性迴歸公式如下：

$$y = \beta_1 X_1 + \beta_2 X_2 + \beta_3 X_3 + \beta_4 X_4 \tag{2}$$

其中X_i為候選詞與可疑字組間的四個參數，β_i為四個參數的迴歸係數，將候選詞對應可疑字組的四個參數及各項迴歸係數代入上述公式可得到 y 值。當候選詞代入公式所得之 y 值越大時，其作為應替換的正確詞彙的可能性越高。相對地，若 y 值越小其作為可替換詞的機會也相對減少，因此可以利用 y 值作為候選詞應替換原字組可能性的依據。

本文從訓練的 1300 句 positive 及 negative 樣本集合裡候選詞與可疑字組間四個參數代入公式所得之 y 值找出最佳分類正確率，並以此 y 值作為預測模型的門檻值。若候選詞是應替換原字組的可能性分數大於門檻值即會被判定為可替換之正確詞彙而進行校正，反之若一個候選詞是應替換原字組的可能性分數小於門檻值，該候選詞則會被判定為無法替換詞彙而被捨棄。

6. 實驗

本文採用 SIGHAN-7 Bake-off 2013: Chinese Spelling Check[15]所提供的資料集作為實驗的測試資料。資料集內包含 SubTask1 與 SubTask2 各 1000 份文本。其中 SubTask1 只提供含有別字的文本與別字位置的資料，因此本文僅採用 SubTask2 資料作為量測中文別字偵測與校正效能使用。SubTask2 的 1000 份文本是來自於蒐集學生寫作常見的錯誤類型，每一份文本內至少含有一個以上的別字及數句未包含別字的句子，全部共包含 1265 個別字。本文保留含有別字的句子作為測試資料，合計共 1219 筆句子。由於我們是測試字形相似度的效能，因此只採用字形相似以及形音相似實驗的別字。另外，實驗使用的別字偵測工具只能擷取 WECAn[3]斷詞系統將詞彙中別字分成單字詞者，因此我們只使用符合上述兩項條件的 451 個別字作為測試資料。

本文別字校正實驗將以第 5 節所提方法設計兩個預測工具，一個是使用 Chang 等人[5]所提出的部件相似度計算方法，另一個則是使用本文所提筆畫結構相似度計算方法。兩個工具分別針對 451 筆測試資料進行測試。另外由於測試的別字有些為字音與字形皆相似的別字，為了評估字形相似計算之結果差異，在系統提出可替換候選字時會淘汰僅字音相似的正字詞彙，只比較字形混淆與形音同時混淆的別字。結果於表 1 所示。

表 1、使用部件相似與筆畫相似方法之校正結果

	校正字數	Recall	Precision	False Alarm
部件相似法	250	55.43%	63.29%	0.93%
筆畫相似法	417	92.46%	79.58%	0.60%

由表 1 的結果可知，在只比較形別字與形音別字的情況下，使用本文所提之筆畫相似方法能有效提升校正成功率。從本文所提方法的三項評估指標均遠優於使用組字部件的方法，可以得知筆畫計算字形相似的方法確實能改善部件相似性不足的問題。

7. 結論

本文提出了一個使用中文字筆畫結構資料的字形相似評估方法，並將其與現有別字偵測方法整合。從實驗結果可以證實本文所提方法用於字形相似別字的偵測與校正效能較原先以部件相似的方法來的好，其原因可以推論是本文所提方法讓字形相似度計算變得更加精確所導致。但受限於實驗材料沒有明顯區分字形別字以及形音均相似別字，因此無法證實本文所提方法在次分類別字上的效果，後續研究可以進一步加以證實。

另外，字形相似度計算的正確性評估可以考慮先建立真人相似度評估的標準，用以檢驗各種方法所得字形相似度與人類認知結果的一致性。我們目前正在進行這項工作。若是這項工作得以確認本文所提方法在計算字形相似度的正確性，本文所提方法可廣泛應用於漢字教學以及提供漢字習得理論研究相當有效的工具。

誌謝

本文作者感謝科技部計畫編號 NSC 102-2511-S-151-002 及 NSC 103-2911-I-003-301 的支持，同時也感謝教育部及國立台灣師範大學「邁向頂尖大學計畫」的支持。

参考文獻

[1] Bressan, S. (2004). Morphologic non-word error detection. Proceedings of IEEE 15th International Workshop on Database and Expert Systems Applications. 31-35

[2] Chang, C. H. (1995). A New Approach for Automatic Chinese Spelling Correction. Proceedings of Natural Language Processing Pacific Rim Symposium'95, Seoul, Korea. 278-283.

[3] Chang, T. H., Sung, Y. T., & Lee, Y. T. (2012). A Chinese word segmentation and POS tagging system for readability research. Paper presented at 42nd Annual Meeting of the Society for Computers in Psychology, Minneapolis, MN, USA.

[4] Chang, T. H., Su, S. Y., & Chen, H. C. (2012). Automatic Correction for Graphemic Chinese Misspelled Words. Proceedings of the 24th Conference on Computational Linguistics and Speech Processing, Taoyuan, Taiwan. 125-140.

[5] Chang, T. H., Chen, H. C., Tseng, Y. H., & Zheng, J. L. (2013). Automatic Detection and Correction for Chinese Misspelled Words Using Phonological and Orthographic Similarities. Proceedings of the Seventh SIGHAN Workshop on Chinese Language Processing (SIGHAN-7), Nagoya, Japan. 97-101.

[6] Chiu, H. W., Wu, J. C., & Chang, J. S. (2013). Chinese Spelling Checker Based on Statistical Machine Translation. Proceedings of the Seventh SIGHAN Workshop on Chinese Language Processing (SIGHAN-7), Nagoya, Japan. 49-53.

[7] Friedman, C., & Sideli, R. (1992). Tolerating spelling errors during patient validation. Journal of Computers and Biomedical Research, 25(5), 486–509.

[8] Huang, C. M., Wu, M. C., & Chang, C. C. (2007). Error Detection and Correction Based on Chinese Phonemic Alphabet in Chinese Text. Proceedings of the Fourth Conference on Modeling Decisions for Artificial Intelligence(MDAIIV). 463-476.

[9] Lin, Y. J., Huang, F. L., & Yu, M. S. (2002). A Chinese Spelling Error Correction System. Proceedings of the Seventh Conference on Artificial Intelligence and Applications. 207-212.

[10] Liu, C. L., Lai, M. H., Tien, K. W., Chuang, Y. H., Wu, S. H., & Lee C. Y. (2011). Visually and Phonologically Similar Characters in Incorrect Chinese Words: Analyses, Identification, and Applications. Journal of ACM Transaction on Asian Language Information Processing, 10(2), 10:1-39.

[11] Liu, X., Cheng, F., Luo, Y., Duh, K., & Matsumoto, Y. (2013). A Hybrid Chinese Spelling Correction Using Language Model and Statistical Machine Translation with Reranking. Proceedings of the Seventh SIGHAN Workshop on Chinese Language Processing (SIGHAN-7), Nagoya, Japan. 54-58.

[12] Ren, F., Shi, H., & Zhou, Q. (2001). A hybrid approach to automatic Chinese text checking and error correction. Proceedings of 2001 IEEE International Conference on Systems, Man, and Cybernetics. 1693-1698.

[13] Varol, C. (2011). Pattern and Phonetic Based Street Name Misspelling Correction. Proceedings of 2011 IEEE Conference on ITNG, Las Vegas, NV. 553-558.

[14] Vachharajani, V. (2012). Effective Label Matching for Automatic Evaluation of Use – Case Diagrams. Proceedings of 2012 IEEE Fourth International Conference on Technology for Education, Hyderabad. 172-175.

[15] Wu, S. H., Lin, C. L., & Lee, L. H. (2013). Chinese Spelling Check Evaluation. Proceedings of the Seventh SIGHAN Workshop on Chinese Language Processing (SIGHAN-7), Nagoya, Japan. 35–42.

[16] Yeh, J. F., Li, S. F., Wu, M. R., Chen, W. Y., & Su, M. C. (2013). Chinese Word Spelling Correction Based on N-gram Ranked Inverted Index List. Proceedings of the Seventh SIGHAN Workshop on Chinese Language Processing (SIGHAN-7), Nagoya, Japan. 43-48.

[17] Zhang, L., Huang, C., Zhou, M., & Pan, H. (2000). Automatic detecting/correcting errors in Chinese text by an approximate word-matching algorithm. In: Proceedings of the 38th Annual Meeting of the Association for Computational Linguistics, 248–254.

[18] 丘慶鈴 (民 92)。避免小學生寫錯別字之教學策略 (碩士論文)。國立新竹師範學院，新竹市。

[19] 陳思彧 (民97)。國民小學高年級別字矯誤教學研究 (碩士論文)。臺北市立教育大學，臺北市。

[20] 林佳儂 (民 98)。國中生錯別字教學策略研究 (碩士論文)。國立彰化師範大學，彰化縣。

[21] 張嘉惠、林書彥、李淑瑩、蔡孟峰、李淑萍、廖湘美、孫致文和黃鍔 (民 99)。以最佳化及機率分佈標記形聲字聲符之研究。中文計算語言學期刊，15(2)，70-84。

[22] 陳學志、張瓅勻、邱郁秀、宋曜廷、張國恩（民 100）。中文部件組字與形構資料庫之建立及其在識字教學的應用。教育心理學報。269-290。

[23] 莊德明、謝清俊（民 94）。漢字構形資料庫的建置與應用。漢字與全球化國際學術研討會，台北。

學術論文簡介的自動文步分析與寫作提示

黃冠誠 吳鑑城 許湘翎 顏孜曦 張俊盛

Abstract

近年來，英文逐漸變成全世界學術研究最主要的溝通的媒介。而學術英文寫作，也成為非常重要的研究與教學的領域。學者也很重視，如何透過電腦的輔助，幫助一般性的語言學習，甚或特定性的學術論文寫作。學術寫作包含許多的文節類型，包括研究論文、計畫申請書、回顧與評論文節等（Swales, 1990）。其中，研究論文占有最重要的角色。

在學術論文中，「簡介」是絕大部分論文都有的第一個節。現今，幾乎沒有學術論文，沒有「摘要」與「簡介」，而直接詳細地描述研究的目的、方法、結果。而且，對寫者和讀者而言，「簡介」在學術論文中都扮演非常重要的角色。一篇好的簡介，要能為整篇論文定調，抓住讀者的興趣，提供論文的扼要資訊。換言之，「簡介」 肩負重大責任──吸引讀者注意，讀完全文。

因此，有一些研究開始分析論文簡介如何達成其溝通的任務。Graetz (1985) 發現論文簡介似乎有共同的「問題─解法」修辭結構，依序包括問題（problem）、方法（solution）、評估(evaluation)、結論（conclusion）等部分。 Swales (1990) 分析大量的論文簡介，分析歸納出一套修辭的動機與模式：「創造研究空間」（Create A Research Space, CARS）。Swales 認為論文爭取研究得到讀者的認同，有如環境中生物爭取生存空間。為此，大部分作者依循三個修辭的步驟──也就是文步（moves）──來說服讀者。

CARS 文步	子文步與資訊內容
文步 I	1. 聲明研究領域的重要性，及/或
界定範圍	2. 聲明研究課題的廣泛性與普及性，及/或
	3. 回顧與評論前人研究
文步 II	1A. 提出與前人不同的聲明，或
建立利基	1B. 指出前人研究的缺口（gap），或
	1C. 提出本論文的研究議題（research question），或
	1D. 說明本研究所根據的典範與傳統
文步 III	1A. 概述本論文的目的，或
佔據利基	1B. 概述本論文的方法
	2. 宣布本論文的主要結果與發現
	3. 指出本論文的結構

圖 1. Swales (1990) 提出的 CARS 模式的文步與資訊內容

如圖 1 所示，這三個文步包括了「界定研究範圍」、「建立利基」、「佔據利基」。在每一個文步下，又需要描述若干必要或選項的內容。另外，美國國家醫學圖書館，也主張醫學論文作者，應提供分段有標題（labeled sections）的結構化摘要（structured abstract）。

目前已經有許多學術寫作教材，透過文步分析來教導英文非母語的學生，如何寫作學術論文（如 Swales and Feak, 2004; Glasman-Deal, 2010）。也有研究者開發軟體系統（例如，Marking Mate: writingtools.xjtlu.edu.cn:8080/mm/markingmate.html），分析學生 的作文，自動產生批改的建議與評分。但是很少有系統能夠在學生寫作中，依照文步的推進，適時地提供寫作提示與輔助。直覺上，如果我們能將大量的論文簡介加以處理，自動化分析其中每句的文步，繼而分析特定文步句子的常見片語或句型，我們將可以在寫作的過程，有效地協助學生。

然而，過去所提出的自動文步分析方法，都需費時費工標註大量論文。有鑑於此，我們提出新方法，以降低人工標註的工作量，運用於訓練統計式分類器，來預測論文簡介的句子的文步，並藉以開發一個線上輔助寫作系統 WriteAhead。在 *WriteAhead* 的開發過程，我們採用了比 CARS 更簡單的文步分類，如圖 2 所示。用了這一套分類方式，系統容易自動分類文步，而使用者比較容易掌握使用於寫作過程。

我們期望此一自動文步分析工具，以及 *WriteAhead* 系統，有助於提升英文非母語者（non-native speakers, NNS），寫作學術論文的能力。在本論文中，我們提出了一套監督式機器學習的方法，能夠自動地學習如何將語料庫內的簡介句子，大略地分類為幾個文步。有了分類的句子之後，我們就可以統計各文步的連續詞頻率（ngrams）。在 *WriteAhead* 系統，就參考使用者選擇的文步，以及游標之前的幾個字，提示接續片語。

WriteAhead 能夠提供與排列這些提示，是因為 *WriteAhead* 透過大量的論文原始資料以及少量的人工標示，學習如何辨識 OWN 文步的句子，以及這些句子內的常見片語及其頻率。我們將在第三節詳述 *WriteAhead* 所運用的文步分類器的訓練過程。

致謝詞

本研究承蒙科技部補助研究經費，計畫標號NSC 100-2511-S-007 -005 -MY3

The 2014 Conference on Computational Linguistics and Speech Processing
ROCLING 2014, pp. 165-174

以二維共振峰分布建立語者音色模型及其在語者驗證上之應用

Using 2D Formant Distribution to Build Speaker Models and Its Application in Speaker Verification

呂嘉穀 [1]，蕭志濱 [2]，李明慶 [2]，蒲長恩 [3]，吳家隆 [2,*]
[1] 國立台北大學資訊工程學系
[2] 法務部調查局鑑識科學處，[3] 法務部調查局通訊監察處
* 通訊作者

摘要

語音是重要的生物特徵之一，也是鑑識科學上的重要工具。在鑑識實務上常遭遇到的一個 挑戰，就是通訊線路及錄音裝置的多元性。不同的裝置與線路特性會對語音證物的頻譜產 生相當的影響，從而也會影響到鑑識的正確性。共振峰是語音中重要的要素，並且較不易 受到通道及裝置之頻率響應的影響。在本論文中我們提出一個從分析較長時間語料，所得 之二維共振峰的分布，來建立起一個語者之音色模型的方法。這個方法對於相同語詞及相 異語詞方式的語者驗證工作均適用。在實驗的部分，我們報告了對約七十人規模的語料分 別進行數位錄音及電話錄音的語者驗證測試。

關鍵詞: 語者驗證，線性預測方法(LPC)，共振峰，語者音色模型

1、目的與背景

語音是人類彼此間溝通最方便也最首要的方式。語音不但是用於傳播信息，也是一項重要的生物特徵(biometrics)，可以用來做身份識別之用。對於利用電腦來分析語音這方面的研究，大致可分為兩個領域：一是語詞識別（speech recognition），一是語者識別（speaker recognition）[1-4]。若是要分辨某一個語音 樣本是否來自某一個特定的語者，則又稱為語者驗證（speaker verification 或 speaker authentication）語者驗證又可細分為限定語詞（text dependent）與非限定語詞（text independent）兩種方式[5,6]。在限 定語詞的方式中，用來比對的兩段語音樣本，其語音之內容須為相同或相似。而在非限定語詞的方式下， 其語句之內容可為不同。後者之處理難度較高，但在取樣上較不受限，其應用也較為廣泛。本研究之內 容是屬於語者驗證性質，同時包括了限定語詞與非限定語詞的方式。

語音分析最基本的技術就是頻譜分析。由於每個人的口腔構造及發音習慣均有所不同，所以發出聲音的 共鳴結構就會有所不同，語音中較強的共鳴成分就會形成頻譜中的波峰，稱為共振峰(formants)。不同 的語者，因生理構造或口音上的差異，即使是發出同一個字音，其頻譜的形狀也會有所差異。所以藉著 分析頻譜，我們可以分辨語者，也可以辨識字音中之韻母。

在語音分析的工作上一個經常遇到的問題就是裝置或是通訊線路(channel)所帶來的影響。如果裝置或線 路的頻率響應為已知，我們尚可藉著演算還原出原音訊之頻譜，但是對於鑑識工作方面的實案而言，裝 置或線路的特性通常為未知。一般而言，裝置及線路的頻率響應呈現平滑的變化，通常是中頻部分高起 而高頻與低頻部分低下的情形。如下圖一所示。相對而言，發聲道的頻率響應，特別是共振良好時，其

變化較為複雜，從低頻到高頻會出現若干個高峰點，如圖二所示。

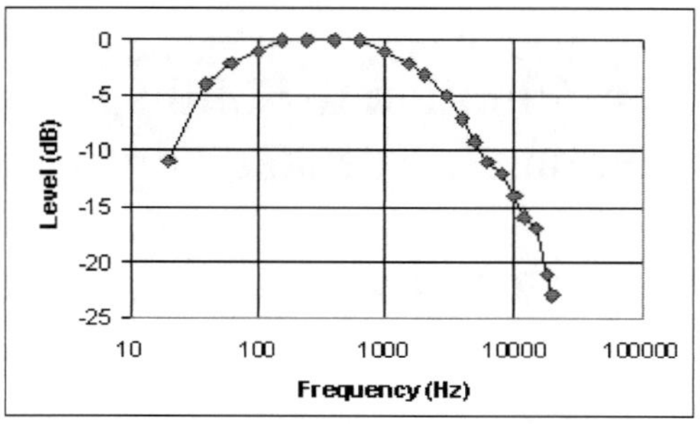

圖一、裝置或線路之頻率響應示意圖

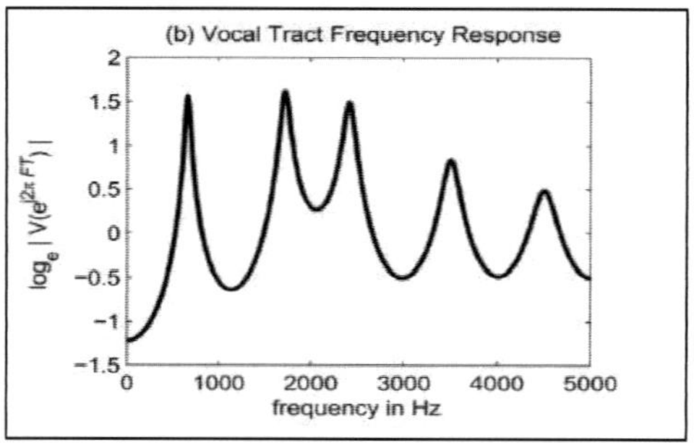

圖二、發聲道頻率響應例圖

當我們把較緩慢變化的裝置或通道的頻率響應，與較快速變化的發聲道頻率響應相乘(或相加)時，其結 果就是前者會影響到後者的整體起伏變化，但是較不會影響到個別高峰點的出現及位置。也就是說，雖 然語音之頻譜會受到裝置的影響，但是其中共振峰的位置相對穩定。本研究所提出之語者音色模型將以 共振峰的位置為主。我們將從語音中擷取出共振峰，然後以共振峰的分布來建立一語者的音色模型。

近年來有越來越多的研究指出觀察長時間共振峰分析(LTF, Long term formant analysis)在語者驗證上的重要性。所謂長時間共振峰分析就是累計整段語料中各共振峰出現的位置，通常是前四個共振峰。因為 是包含眾多不同的字音在內，所以各共振峰的位置並非固定，一段時間累積下來，就會得到一個分布曲 線。因為是來自於相同語者，所以語者的因素自然包含在其中。又因為是來自於許多不同的字音的混合， 所以字音的因素就會被淡化掉。因為語者驗證的重點是在語者的音色特徵而非語詞內容，所以長時間共 振峰分析會是一個可利用的工具。

英國的 Nolan 與 Grigoras 在 2005 年的一篇論文中報告，紀錄語音中前四共振峰的長時間分布，在語者鑑識實案上十分有效[7]。在後續的研究中他們進一步報告各共振峰的長時間分布多呈現出不對稱(skewed)的情形，並且其分布最高點(mode)之位置在鑑識上的重要性超過其平均位置[8]。歐洲學者 Becker、Jessen、及 Grigoras 在 2008 年提出將長時間共振峰分析所得之參數值套用到高斯混合模型(Gaussian mixture model)來進行語者識別[9]。他們假定各共振峰的長時間分布為高斯分布，並自各段語料估計出高斯分布的平均值與標準差值，以進行 likelihood 計算。他們對 68 位男性語者的語料，以前三個共振峰的位置及頻寬為參數(共六個)，達到了 EER 為 0.03 的驗證成績。

德國學者 Moos 對 71 位男性語者的行動電話錄音語料進行 LTF 分析[10]，他發現 F2 與 F3 合用時有優良的語者鑑別效果。他同時發現，F3 較 F2 有著更好的穩定性，也就是對同一個語者其變異性較低。在文章中也指出，LTF 也具有一些其他良好的特性，例如不易受到說話速度快慢及音調高低等因素的影響。中國學者 Xu 與 Kong 在 2012 年的一篇文章中報告他們以 LTF 分析進行跨語言的語者驗證[11]。他們以前四個共振峰的分布之 peak, kurtosis, 與 skewness 作為特徵值，發現能夠成功的以三種不同語言(中、英、韓)的語料進行跨語言的語者驗證。歐洲學者 Jessen 與 Becker 在 2010 也曾報告他們對德語、俄語、及阿爾巴尼亞語所進行的實驗，也有著相似的結論[12]。

前述學者所提出的長時間共振峰分析，多係對個別共振峰的分布一一的來進行，也就是屬於一個維度的 分析。本論文提出的方法是將前幾個共振峰做成對的分析，也就是求得二維的共振峰分布來進行分析。 又因為前二共振峰的分布與幾個主要單音韻母有很明確的對應，我們進一步將 F1-F2 平面分割為若干區 域，並分別分析落在這些區域中的音框以建立更細緻的語者音色模型。在下一節中我們將詳細介紹本研 究所提出建立音色模型的方法。在第三部分中我們會將這個音色模型應用到語者驗證的實驗上。

2、研究方法

本論文所提出的方法大致可分為以下幾個步驟。首先我們找出一段語音中具有共振的部分，也就是其中 的有聲字音(voiced sounds)部分。其次我們以線性預測方法，逐一分析這些有聲字音的音框，找出其中的共振峰。再根據所找出的共振峰的分布建立起該位語者的音色模型。最後，我們藉比對兩組共振峰分 布的相似度，來比對兩段語料之音色相似度。這些步驟分別敘述如下。

2.1、找出語料中之有聲字音部分

因為本方法是要找出語料中的共振峰分布，以建立起一語者之音色模型，所以首先我們就要找出語料中 具有明顯共振的部分，即是語料中的有聲字音。在本研究中，我們先將語料切割為 20ms 大小的音框， 相鄰的音框有 10ms (即為 50%)的重疊。我們對每一個音框計算出一個音量大小值，以及求取其 autocorrelation function (ACF)曲線，並找出其在合理之週期範圍所能達到的最高值。如果一個音框具有足夠的音量大小以及夠大的 ACF 峰值，我們就接受此一音框為一個有聲字音的音框。在語料量足夠的情形下，上述兩項門檻值可以做較嚴格之設定，以確保所找出的音框均有不錯的共振品質。

2.2、以線性預測法(LPC)找出音框之共振峰

本研究聲音樣本的取樣率(sampling rate)為 11,025 Hz，依據文獻的建議，階數 p 的設定大約是在 14 至 16 左右。在這個取樣率之下，音訊中的頻寬大約保留到 5K Hz，其中共振峰的數目因字音而異，大約有五到六個。本研究在建立語者音色模型時，將會利用到前四個共振峰，即 F1 到 F4。在推導這 p 個 LPC 係數方面我們所用的方法是常見的 Levinson- Durbin 演算法。這個演算法首先自一音框求出 p 個 autocorrelation function 的值，然後再藉由一個遞迴式的演算法解出模型的 p 個係數值來。在對一個音框求出一組係數值之後，我們會再將音框之音訊值帶入模型，並計算出預測值與實際值之誤差。倘若誤差 值過大，則表示其所找出的共振峰並不準確，或是該音框的共振仍為不佳，或是該音框受到了較大的雜 訊。當有此情形發生時，我們就會略過這些音框不用。一般而言在此一階段會被淘汰的音框大約占有聲 字音的 5%以內。

2.3、建立語者之音色模型

自一語者之語料找出有聲字音之音框，並推算出其中的共振峰之後，我們就可開始建立該語者之音色模 型。如果是使用於相同語詞式的語者驗證工作，無論語料多寡，我們都可以建立起音色模型，只是在語 料量少時，所建立起的音色模型也是與語詞內容相關。而當使用於相異語詞式的語者驗證時，我們就需 要有較多的語料才能建立起一個較為完整的音色模型。

在我們所建立的語者模型中，第一部分就是共振峰分布的情形。在上一個小節中我們提到，我們自每一 個音框找出其前四道的共振峰(F1- F4)。在此我們將自語料產生出三個二維(2D)的共振峰分布圖，分別是 F1 對 F2，F2 對 F3，以及 F3 對 F4。每一個有效的音框將會對應到這些圖中的一個點，語料的時間越長，則分布圖中的點也會越多。因為每個語者的音色有所不同，即使是在發出同一個音，其共振峰的 位置也會有所差異，反映在這些二維的分布圖上，就是這些點的集中位置會有所不同。

在圖二中我們顯示了兩位不同男性語者在約 60 秒的相同語詞語料所呈現出的 F1-F2 共振峰分布圖。從圖中我們可以很清楚的看出兩位語者的 F1 對 F2 在分布上的差異。因為是依據相同的語詞，所以這裡所反映出的差異主要是來自於二人在音色上的不同。圖四及圖五分別顯示出此二位語者之 F2-F3 與 F3-F4 的分布圖。

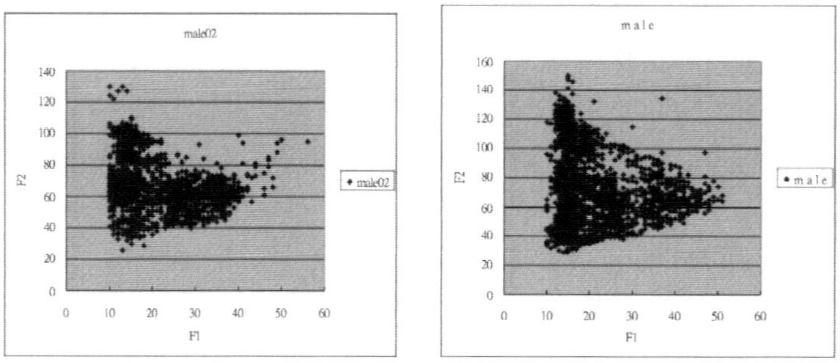

(a) (b)

圖三、兩位男性語者之 F1-F2 分布圖

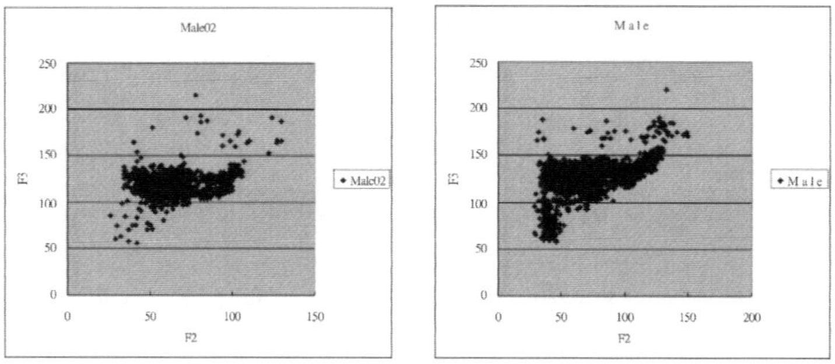

(a) (b)

圖四、兩位男性語者之 F2-F3 分布圖

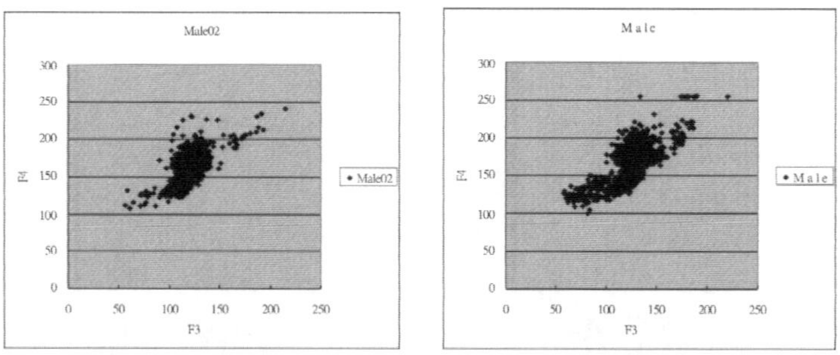

(a) (b)

圖五、兩位男性語者之 F3-F4 分布圖

在上二圖中我們同樣可以觀察到，此二位語者在共振峰分布上的差異。接下來我們要顯示的是，相同一 位語者對於不同的語詞其所呈現之共振峰的分布情形。在這裡我們將以 Male02 這位男性語者在兩段各約 60 秒，但語詞內容為不同的語料所得之共振峰分布圖來相比較。在下面的三個圖中我們分別比較此位語者在這兩段語料在 F1-F2，F2-F3，與 F3-F4 分布上的差異。

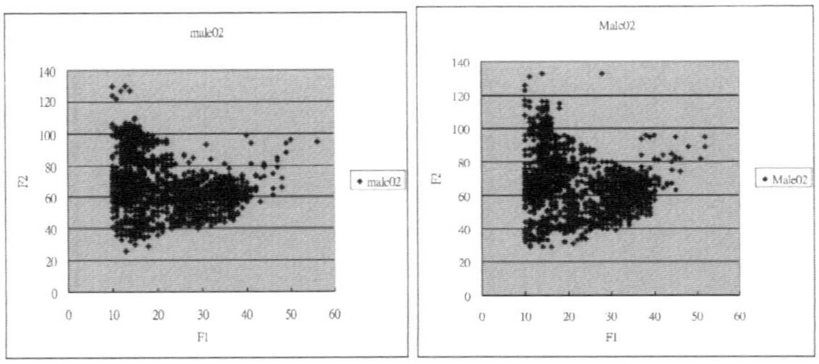

(a) (b)

圖六、同一位男性語者不同語詞語料之 F1-F2 分布圖

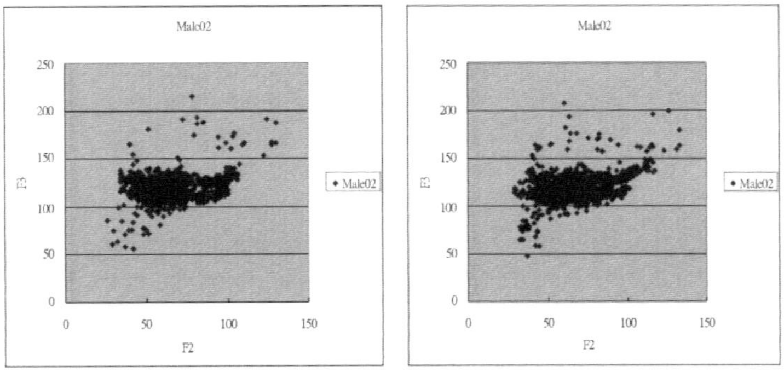

(a) (b)

圖七、同一位男性語者不同語詞語料之 F2-F3 分布圖

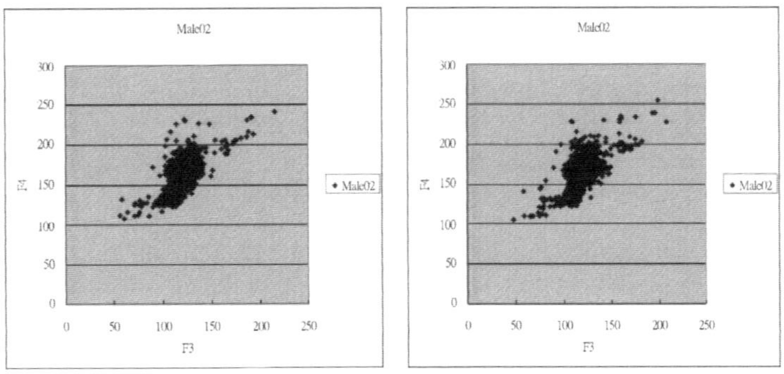

(a) (b)

圖八、同一位男性語者不同語詞語料之 F3-F4 分布圖

自以上三對共振峰分布圖我們可以清楚看出它們之間的相似性。即使在語詞內容為不同的情形下，因著 語料長度夠長，亦即字音重疊程度提高，相同語者之共振峰的累進分布也就趨近於相似。基於以上對不

同語者相同語詞，及相同語者不同語詞之共振峰分布所做的觀察，我們認為以共振峰之分布來建立語者 音色模型，將會是一個有效區分語者的工具。

除了以共振峰來建立語者音色模型外，我們也會為語者建立若干個頻譜模型。其原因為頻譜中能量變化 上下起伏，但共振峰只標示出其中高峰點的位置，而忽略了頻譜中下凹部分變化的資訊。這些下凹的部 分包含了實際發聲道系統中的零點(zeros)，但是 LPC 方法假定發聲道模型中只有極點，所以其所包含 的資訊並不完整。

我們為每個語者建立起十個平均頻譜作為其音色之頻譜模型。在此我們先將整個 F1-F2 平面分割為十個區域，其中之九個區域大致對應到一般(F1,F2)會落入的區域，而第十個區域就是對應(F1,F2)不可能出 現的區域，對應到此一區域即表示在共振峰的推算上發生了錯誤。對於每一個有聲字音的音框，我們除 了求取其前四個共振峰之外，我們也求出其對數功率頻譜(log power spectrum)。我們依其 F1 與 F2 的值 將其頻譜累計至前述之十個區域的平均頻譜之中。

本研究的目標是要發展出，一種能夠同時適用於相同語詞式、與相異語詞式語者驗證的方法。共振峰的 分布圖仍多少會受到語詞內容的影響，特別是當語料的量較少時。但是這九個區域中的平均頻譜，則較 不會受到語詞內容不同的影響。其原因為，當語詞內容為不同時，只會影響到落到各區域中音框的數目， 但是對於取自各區中音框之平均頻譜的影響則較輕。也就是說，由這些平均頻譜所組成的模型，能夠更 全面性的表現出一位語者的音色特徵。

下表顯示出對男聲我們分割 F1-F2 平面的方式。因為男女聲在共振峰分布上有著相當顯著的差異，所以在區域的分割上也有所不同。在我們的分割方式中，有部分的區域剛好與幾個主要的韻母有所對應，我 們也一併標示於表中。

表一、將男性語者之 F1-F2 平面分為 10 個區域

區域編號	F1 範圍 (Hz)	F2 範圍 (Hz)	所對應之單韻母音
1	258 – 387	580 – 1010	ㄨ
2	258 – 387	1010 – 1913	
3	258 – 387	1913 – 2687	一
4	387 – 688	580 – 1075	ㄛ
5	387 – 688	1075 – 1720	ㄜ
6	387 – 688	1720 – 2472	ㄟ
7	688- 1075	580 – 1075	
8	688- 1075	1075 – 1483	ㄚ
9	688- 1075	1483 – 2257	
0	其他頻率	其他頻率	屬錯誤情形

再接下來我們就對落在每一個區域內的音框進行分析，並擷取出一些描述語者聲音特色的參數。計有以 下各項：

A、各區域內音框之 FFT 平均頻譜

我們利用 LPC 頻譜來找出 F1 及 F2 共振峰，藉以將音框分群，其原因為 LPC 頻譜的長處就是在於找出主要之共振峰。但是聲音中除了共振峰外尚有其他的特徵及變化，FFT 頻譜就有較全面的紀錄。在此我們先求出各音框的 FFT 頻譜，再將這些頻譜作平均，以得到一個平均 FFT 頻譜。因為音框已經大致依照韻母經過分類，所以落在同一區域中的音框，其發音大致相近，頻譜也會相似。當我們將這些頻 譜加以平均時，其個別之差異將會淡化，而共有之特徵將會得到增強。未來在比對兩個語者模型時，我 們會將對應區域中之平均頻譜加以比對，以計算其相似度。

B、各區域內音框之 LPC 平均頻譜

LPC 頻譜係由線性預測之係數所推出，其特色在於較能顯出共振峰之位置。在比對語者之音色時，共振峰仍為最主要之資訊，因為共振峰位置是由發聲器官及發音習慣所決定。我們在此將一個區域內所有 音框之 LPC 頻譜加以平均，以得到一個平均頻譜。這個頻譜在高峰的部分與 FFT 平均頻譜十分相近， 但是在波谷的部分則有較大的差異。我們可藉比對 LPC 頻譜特別來檢視兩位語者在共振峰位置上的相似程度。

C、各區域內音框之共振峰的累加曲線

我們做完 LPC 分析之後，對於每個音框我們得到了一組的共振峰。目前我們是找出前五至六個，就是 F1 到 F6。不過在有效的頻寬範圍中我們可能只會看到四個共振峰，此時第五個共振峰就經常在有效頻寬之外，在比對時可忽略不看。在這裡我們將一個區域內，所有音框的所有共振峰，全部投到同一個頻 率軸線上。因為區域本身就是按 F1 與 F2 來劃分的，自然這些音框在 F1 與 F2 的頻率範圍會有相當高的一致性。但是我們發現這些來自同一語者的聲音，在 F3, F4, 甚至於 F5 也會有著相當好的一致性。這一項特徵參數也是用來反映出一位語者在發出不同字音時，其共振峰分布的情形。但是與前一項不同 之處是，在前一項中，我們是對 LPC 頻譜之強度值做平均，所以一個音強的音框，會較一個音弱的音框有著更大的影響。但是在這裡我們對每一個音框的共振峰都是以同一強度值紀錄，所以在意義上略有 不同。

2.4、藉比對音色模型決定二段語料之音色相似度

在前面的部分我們說明了如何自一段語料建立起其語者的音色模型，一個模型中包含了三個二維的共振 峰分布圖，以及將 F1-F2 平面分為十個區域後，在每個區域所累積出的 FFT 平均頻譜、LPC 平均頻譜、 以及共振峰分布累加曲線。在比，我們將比對兩個音色模型的內容，以估計兩段語料之語者在音色上的 相似程度。

我們進行比對兩個音色模型的基本方法為計算其相關係數值。在比對二維共振峰分布時，我們分別就三 對的二維共振峰分布(F1-F2, F2-F3, F3-F4)兩兩計算出其間之相關係數值。在比對兩個音色模型中對應之 FFT 頻譜、LPC 頻譜、及一維之共振峰累加曲線時，我們則兩兩計算其間之一維相關係數。在完成以上之計算後，我們將得到六個相關係數值。因為這些相關係數均具有不同的特性，之後我們可以依語料 的特性顯選擇使用，或是將這些相關係數做加權平均，以得到一個綜合相似指標值。

3、實驗與結果

在以相異語詞進行語者驗證之實驗部分，我們分別針對了男聲及女聲，並以數位錄音及電話錄音兩種方 式進行實驗。每一種的錄音方式又可分為比對同次錄音中之不同語句，以及比對不同次錄音中之不同語 句兩種方式。在實驗中，我們使用了 72 人的語音樣本，其中有男生 38 人及女生 34 人，均為 18 歲以上 之成年人。採樣分兩次進行，時間上的間隔為兩個月。實驗中所用到的國語語句每組的句數均是六十句， 每句有六至十個字不等。

每次的錄音因語者說話速度快慢不同，大約有三分鐘的長度。我們再將每份語料分為前後兩段，每段的 長度大約在 90 秒左右，其中包含一句與一句之間停頓的時間。倘若扣除掉語句間停頓所花的時間，每段錄音的長度約為 60 秒左右。因為前段與後段有著不同的語詞內容，所以我們可以用同次錄音中的前段與後段進行相異語詞之語者驗證。因為是取自於同一次的錄音，無論是錄音裝置、錄音環境、或是語 者的生理狀況都會極為相似，所以我們預期比對的結果(即驗證正確率)將會較好。

我們也將利用不同次錄音中的前後段落進行交叉的比對，例如將第一次錄音中的前半段，與第二次錄音

中的後半段進行比對；或是將第一次錄音的後半段與第二次錄音的前半段進行比對。這種的比對方式不 單是語詞不相同，就連錄音的裝置、錄音的環境、通訊的線路、以及語者的生理狀況都有可能不同。我 們預期驗證的正確率也將會下降。

在驗證所用的參數部分，如在前面一節中所述，我們有以下幾個，分別給予編號P1到P9：

P1	九個特徵區域中音框之 FFT 平均頻譜
P2	九個特徵區域中音框之 LPC 平均頻譜
P3	九個特徵區域中音框之共振峰分布曲線
P4	全域之 F1-F2 分布
P5	全域之 F2-F3 分布
P6	全域之 F3-F4 分布
P7	P1-P3 之綜合
P8	P4-P6 之綜合
P9	P1-P6 之綜合

其中 P1 到 P6 是個別的參數曲線或是分布圖，P7 是把前三個特徵曲線(P1-P3)加以綜合的結果。而 P8 是將 P4-P6 這三個分布圖加以綜合的結果，而 P9 則是再進一步把 P7 和 P8 加以綜合。接下來我們就依序表列不同條件下所得之驗證正確率。

A、以同一次數位錄音中之不同段落進行語者驗證

相對於電話錄音，數位錄音有著較大的頻寬，保存語者音色的能力較佳。又因為比對用的語料取自同一 次的錄音，在錄音裝置、錄音環境、通訊線路、以及語者生理狀態等多方面均為最相近，所以驗證的準 確率最高。

表二、以同次數位錄音中之相異段落進行語者驗證所得之驗證等錯誤率 EER (%)

參數	男聲	女聲
P1	0.3	0.0
P2	0.3	0.0
P3	1.3	0.1
P4	0.3	0.7
P5	5.4	4.3
P6	5.6	4.5
P7	0.2	0.1
P8	1.8	0.1
P9	1.1	0.0

從上表中可以看到，無論是男聲或是女聲，我們都達到了相當高的正確率。這就反映出這些特徵值確實 能夠掌握到一個語者的音色特徵。仔細的比較，我們可以發現 P1-P3 的表現略為優於 P4-P6，但是 P4 仍然是有著相當高的驗證正確率(EER 1%以下)。女聲的正確率略優於男聲，這也是因為女聲所使用的頻域較男聲為寬，其音色可有較大的差異度。

B、以不同次之數位錄音中之不同段落進行語者驗證

如前所述，兩次錄音之間間隔了兩個月的時間，在裝置及人員方面均有所變化，所得到的語者驗證正確 率也就有所下降。

表三、 以不同次數位錄音中之不同段落進行語者驗證所得之驗證等錯誤率 EER (%)

參數	男聲	女聲
P1	15.1	14.3
P2	6.2	9.2
P3	7.0	11.2
P4	19.4	21.3
P5	24.2	16.0
P6	18.8	21.0
P7	8.4	10.5
P8	12.4	11.5
P9	6.9	10.6

從上表中可以看到，所有特徵值的驗證 EER 值都有明顯的上升。但其中部分的參數，尤其是 P2 與 P3，表現相對穩定。因此之故，P7 與 P9 也有著較佳的表現。在這個部份我們看到對男聲的正確率略為優於女聲，一個可能的原因就是男聲相對受到隨時間變化因素的影響較小。

C、以同次之電話錄音中之不同段落進行語者驗證

電話錄音之頻寬為 3.5k Hz 左右，相當程度低於數位錄音之約 5.5k Hz 的頻寬。這個減少的頻寬對於語者的音色會產生一定程度的影響，這樣的影響也些微的反映在驗證的 EER 之上。

表四、 以同次電話錄音中之相異段落進行語者驗證所得之驗證等錯誤率 EER (%)

參數	男聲	女聲
P1	0.1	0.2
P2	0.3	0.4
P3	0.3	0.1
P4	1.9	2.1
P5	1.8	1.4
P6	3.0	1.5
P7	0.2	0.2
P8	0.2	0.4
P9	0.1	0.2

比較上表與表二，我們看到在男聲的部分差異不大，但是在女聲的部分正確率有略為下降。這個下降的情形主要是受到頻寬被壓縮的緣故，對女聲音色的影響較比對男聲明顯。與前兩表(表二及表三)相似的是，P1-P3 的表現仍是優於 P4-P6，但是當我們將 P4-P6 綜合起來用(即為 P8)，仍然是有著不錯的正確率。

D、以不同次之電話錄音中之不同段落進行語者驗證

在四種組合之中，此一組合之情形最接近鑑識工作的實際情況。此處所利用到的電話線路十分多元，包括固網、手機、長途等等。語者的發話環境也各為不同，年齡的範圍也較廣。所以這個部分的語料的品質較為接近實案中的情形。

表五、 以不同次電話錄音中之不同段落進行語者驗證所得之驗證等錯誤率 EER (%)

參數	男聲	女聲
P1	11.5	8.1
P2	12.5	9.0
P3	12.5	8.4
P4	7.7	11.4
P5	16.7	8.9
P6	24.6	15.6

P7	12.2	8.7
P8	15.5	6.3
P9	14.4	6.2

將上表與表四比較，我們可以發現驗證之EER有所上升。從P9可以看出來，女聲部分大約上升了六個百分點，但是男聲則上升約十個百分點。值得注意的是女聲部分P8的表現超越P7，這表示出當錄音之線路及裝置多元時，共振峰分布之特徵比頻譜特徵有著較佳的表現。此外男聲部分 P4 的表現也相對較佳。P6在電話錄音的部分表現較差的原因是，共振峰F4常常是高於截止頻。所以找到的F4經常並非真正的 F4。不同次(相隔兩個月)的電話錄音，又是在非實驗室的環境之下錄製，能夠達到 90%以上的驗證正確率，顯示本方法具有實用之潛力。

4、結論

在本論文中我們提出了一種可以以相異語詞語料進行語者驗證的方法。因為用來比對之語料的語詞可能為不同，我們無法逐句地來進行比對。我們所提出的方法，乃是自語料分析長時間共振峰的分布以建立起語者音色模型，然後再就兩個音色模型加以比對。這樣的一個音色模型，我們認為至少具有以下兩方面的優點。第一是頻譜本身的形狀相當容易受到通訊線路或錄音裝置的影響，從而影響到比對的結果，但是共振峰的位置卻是相對較為不會受到裝置或線路的影響。因為在鑑識實務上，線路及錄音裝置相當多樣化，也難以取得其頻率特性資料。使用共振峰特徵將有助於提升鑑識的穩定性。第二方面的優點是來自於我們將 F1-F2 平面分區之後，再就落在各區之中的音框，分別求取其平均頻譜和共振峰分布曲線，以建立語者音色模型。這些區域大致與不同的單韻母音對應，在語詞不同的情形下，各韻母出現的次數或為不同，但所建立起的語者音色模型仍屬完備。

5、參考文獻

1. R.D. Peacocke and D.H. Graf, "An introduction to Speech and Speaker Recognition," *IEEE Computer Magazine*, pp. 26-33, August 1990.
2. J.P. Campbell, "Speaker Recognition: A Tutorial," *Proceedings of the IEEE*, Vol. 85, pp. 1437-1462, September 1997.
3. Sadaoki Furui, *Digital Speech: Processing, Synthesis, and Recognition*, 2nd. Edition, Marcel Dekker, New York, New York, 2001
4. Thomas F. Quatieri, *Discrete-Time Speech Signal Processing principles and Practice*, Prentice Hall, 2002.
5. T. Dutta, "Text Dependent Speaker Identification based on Spectrograms," *Proceedings of Image and vision Computing New Zealand 2007*, pp. 238-243, December 2007.
6. F. Bimbot, J.-F. Bonastre, C. Fredouille, G. Gravier, I. Magrin-Chagnolleau, S. Meignier, T. Merlin, J. Ortega-Garcıa, D. Petrovska-Delacretaz, and D. A. Reynolds, "A Tutorial on Text-Independent Speaker Verification," *EURASIP Journal on Applied Signal Processing*, Vol. 4, pp. 430–451, 2004.
7. F. Nolan and C. Grigoras, "A case for formant analysis in forensic speaker identification," International Journal of Speech Language and the Law, Vol. 12, No. 2, pp. 143-173, 2005.
8. K. McDougall, P. Harrison, F. Nolan, and C. Kirchhubel, "Voice Similarity and Long Trem Formant Analysis," University of Cambridge report.
9. T. Becker, M. Jessen, and C. Grigoras, "Forensic Speaker Verification Using Formant Features and Gaussian Mixture Model," Proceedings of Interspeech 2008 Special Session: Forensic Speaker Recognition – Traditional and Automatic Approaches, Brisbane, Queensland, Australia, Sepember, 2008.
10. A. Moos, "Long-Term Formant Distribution (LTF) based on German spontaneous and read speech," Proceedings of IAFPA 2008, Swiss Federal Institute of Technology, Lausanne, 2008.
11. Y. Xi, "Vocal tract characteristics on long-term formant distribution," Proceedings of the 2012 International Conference on Computer Science and Network Tecnology (2012 ICCSNT), pp. 207-211, Dec. 29-31, 2012.
12. M. Jessen and T. Becker," Long-term formant distribution as a forensic-phonetic feature," Journal of Acoustical Society of America, Vol. 128, No. 4, p. 2378, 2010.

The 2014 Conference on Computational Linguistics and Speech Processing
ROCLING 2014, pp. 175-184

Unsupervised Approach for Automatic Keyword Extraction from Arabic Documents

Arafat Awajan *

Abstract

In this paper, we present an unsupervised two-phase approach to extract keywords from Arabic documents that combines statistical analysis and linguistic information. The first phase detects all the N-grams that may be considered keywords. In the second phase, the N-grams are analyzed using a morphological analyzer to replace the words of the N-grams with their base forms that are the roots for the derived words and the stems for the non-derivative words. The N-grams that have the same base forms are regrouped and their counts accumulated. The ones that appear more frequently are then selected as keywords. An experiment is conducted to evaluate the proposed approach by comparing the extracted keywords with those manually selected. The results show that the proposed approach achieved an average precision of 0.51.

Keywords: Keyword extraction, Keyphrase extraction, Arabic Language, N-gram.

1. Introduction

Keyword extraction is the process of identifying a short list of words or noun phrases that capture the most important ideas or topics covered in a document. Keyword extraction has been used in a variety of natural language processing applications, such as information retrieval systems, digital library searching, web content management, document clustering, and text summarization (Rose et al. 2010). Although keywords are very useful for a large spectrum of applications, only a limited number of documents with keywords are available on-line. Therefore, appropriate tools that can automatically extract keywords from text are increasingly needed with the continually growing amount of electronic textual content available online.

In this paper, an unsupervised two-phase approach for keyword extraction from Arabic

* Princess Sumaya University for Technology – Department of Computer Science, Amman – Jordan
E-mail: awajan@psut.edu.jo

documents is described. The proposed method combines the document's statistics and the linguistic features of the Arabic language to automatically extract keywords from a single document in a domain-independent way. In the first phase, all the N-grams are extracted and those considered as potential candidate keywords are retained. In the second phase, the candidate keywords are analyzed linguistically by a morphological analyzer that replaces each term with its base form, which are the roots of the derived words and the stems of the non-derivative words. The candidate keywords are then grouped in such a way that the keywords extracted from similar roots and stems are put together and their counts accumulated.

This paper is organized as follows. In section 2, we present related works and the main approaches to keyword extraction. Section 3 highlights the main Arabic language features used in our technique. A detailed description of the proposed technique and its two phases provided in Section 4 and Section 5. Section 6 consists of the experimental results and the main findings of the evaluation of the proposed method.

2. Related Work

Existing automatic keyword extraction methods can be divided into two main approaches: supervised and unsupervised (Pudota et al. 2010; Hasan and Ng 2010). In the supervised approach, the keyword extractor is trained to determine whether a given word or phrase is a keyword or not. An annotated set of documents with predefined keywords is always used in the learning phase. All the terms and noun phrases in the text are considered as potential keywords, but only those that match with keywords assigned to the annotated data are selected. The main disadvantages of this approach are its dependency on the learning model, the documents used as the training set, and the documents' domains. Furthermore, training data and learning processes are usually time-consuming (Turney 2000; Turney and Pantel 2010; Frank et al. 1999; Hulth 2003; Hulth 2004).

The unsupervised approach for keyphrase extraction avoids the need for annotated documents. It uses language modeling and statistical analysis to select the potential keywords. A candidate keyword is often selected based on features such as its frequency in the document, the position of its first occurrence in a document, and its linguistic attributes, such as its stem and part-of-speech (POS) tag (Matsuo and Ishizuka 2004; Mihalcea and Tarau 2004; Liu et al. 2009). The unsupervised methods are in general domain-independent and less expensive since they do not require building an annotated corpus.

Keyword extraction algorithms from both approaches have been successfully developed and implemented for documents in the European languages (Rose et al. 2010; Liu et al. 2009; Matsuo et al. 2004). However, despite the fact that Arabic is one of the major international languages making up about 4% of the Internet content, not many studies about extracting

Arabic keywords have been performed. El-Shishtawy and Al-Sammak (2009) presented a supervised method that uses linguistic knowledge and machine learning techniques to extract Arabic keywords. The system uses an annotated Arabic data set of 30 documents from a specific domain, compiled by the authors as a training data set. The keywords from the documents' data set used to evaluate their system were assigned manually.

An unsupervised keyphrase extraction system (KP-Miner) was proposed by El-Beltagy and Rafea (2008). This system was basically developed for the English language and then adapted to work with the Arabic language. Statistical analysis of the texts was conducted in order to determine the most weighted terms. Two main conditions are considered; the first states that a phrase has to have appeared at least n times in the document from which the keywords are to be extracted, and the second condition is related to the position where a candidate keyphrase first appears within an input document. The linguistic analyses performed on the texts are limited to stop word removal and word stemming.

The hypothesis defended in this work is that using the linguistic features of the Arabic language — mainly its rich and complex morphological structure — may present an attractive paradigm to improve the extraction of keywords. The proposed approach is designed to work on a single document without any prior knowledge about its content or domain. Typically, a generic unsupervised keyphrase extractor features two steps; the first is to extract as many candidate words as possible, and the second is to apply the linguistic knowledge of the text language to tune the final list of extracted keywords.

3. The Features of Arabic Language

Arabic is a Semitic language with rich morphology that is a combination of non-concatenative morphology and concatenative morphology. Regarding the concatenative aspect, an Arabic word is composed of a stem, affixes, and clitics. The affixes are concatenative morphemes that mark the tense, gender, and/or number of the word (Al-Sughaiyer and Al-Kharashi 2004). A clitic is a symbol consisting of one to three letters that can be attached to the beginning or the end of a word. It represents another part of speech, such as a preposition, a conjunction, the definite article, or an object pronoun (Habash 2010; Awajan 2007; Diab et al. 2007). In terms of their formation, most of the stems obey non-concatenative rules and are generated according to the root-and-pattern scheme. In general, an Arabic word may be decomposed in its components according to the structure shown in figure 1. For example, the word "والـلاعـبـون", or "and the players" in English, consists of the clitics "و" and "ال", the stem "لاعب", and the postfix "ون". Its stem is generated from the root "ل ع ب", according to the pattern "فـاعل". Figure 2 shows the steps for a word formation.

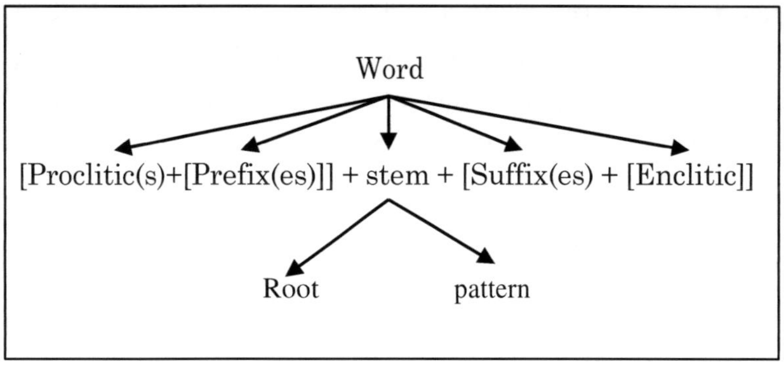

Figure 1. Arabic derivative word structure

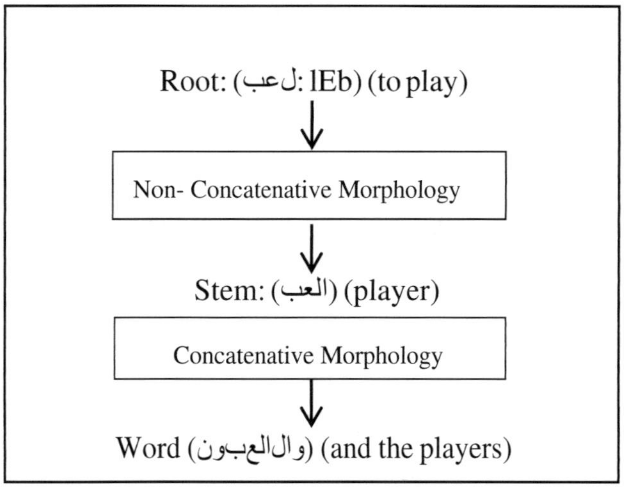

Figure 2. Arabic word formation (Example)

Arabic words are classified into two categories: derivative words and non-derivative words. The stems of derivative words are generated from the roots according to standard patterns or templates. These standard patterns represent the major spelling rules governing Arabic words. Based on the above, a derivative Arabic word can be represented by its root along with its morphological pattern, and its roots carry its basic conceptual meaning.

Non-derivative words include two sub- categories: fixed words and foreign words. Fixed words are a set of words that do not obey the derivation rules. These words are generally stop words, such as pronouns, prepositions, conjunctions, question words, and the like. The foreign words are nouns borrowed from foreign languages.

The combinatory nature of the Arabic language morphology creates an important obstacle for different natural language processing applications, including keyword extraction. This property, generally known as "data sparseness", results in a large number of words generated from the same root but with different stems (Benajiba et al. 2009). Consequently, the grouping of words according to their surface or stems cannot give keywords that accurately reflect the content of the document.

In order to tackle this problem, we need to conduct a deeper morphological analysis to extract the roots and to consider their properties in order to group related words and increase the weight of those representing the main ideas covered by the text. The linguistic analysis we are proposing will be applied at two different levels of the keyword extraction. The input text is preprocessed to assign each word with its POS in order to detect all the possible N-grams. The detected N-grams are then post-processed to extract the roots, and to group the N-grams generated from the same roots, and to accumulate their weights.

4. N-Gram Extraction

4.1 Part-of-Speech Tagging

This phase consists of several operations: sentence delimiting, tokenization, and POS tagging. The input text is processed to delimit sentences, following the assumption that no keyphrase parts are located separately in two or more different sentences (Pudota et al. 2010). Punctuation marks, such as commas, semicolons, and dots, are used to divide the input documents into sentences.

Tokenization aims at turning a text into a list of individual words or tokens (Manning et al. 2009). As the clitics attached to a word always refer to other entities, such as pronouns, prepositions, conjunctions, and the definite article, a tokenizer is applied to separate all the clitics except the definite article from the word. The tokenizer is repeatedly applied until the word stops changing.

We then assign a POS tag to each token using the Stanford Arabic parser (Green and Manning. 2010). The assigned POS tags are later used to select the possible N-grams, remove the verbs, and remove meaningless terms, such as the stop words.

4.2 N-gram Extraction and Filtering

A keyword is typically a combination of nouns and/or adjectives. Furthermore, the number of terms that are allowed in a keyword is often limited to three words. Thus, each sentence is processed to extract all the possible N-grams that constitute a sequence of adjacent words with a maximum length of three words. All the N-grams that contain verbs, stop words, or clitics are removed. Only the N-grams that have their members labeled with one of the POS tags marking nouns or adjectives are retained. In addition, the unigrams that are not labeled as nouns are removed from the N-gram list. Figure 3 shows the detected unigrams, bi-grams, and trigrams from a sentence.

Input Sentence in Arabic: ةيهشحلا ن يةالرد كةلمحلا الىإ زيارة كييالمرسئ يرلامقا

Input Sentence in English: The American president visited the Hashemite Kingdom of Jordan.

Tokenization: .ايةهشحلا | ن يةردال | كةلمحلا | الى | إيارةز | ب | كييموال | سئ يرلا |

Unigrams: كةلمحلا - يةمشهلا - ن يةردأل – كةلمحلا - يارةز - كييموال –

Bi-grams: كييالمرسئ يرلا سئ يرلا ةيهشحلا ن يةالرد - ن يةالرد

Tri-grams: ةيهشحلا ن يةالرد كةلمحلا

Figure 3. N-Grams Extraction

5. Keywords Selection

5.1 N-gram Normalization

Normalizing N-grams is the process of reducing the words of an N-gram into their base forms. This process will allow the clustering of N-grams carrying the same information, hence reducing the sparseness of the text's potential keywords. To achieve this objective, a word morphological analyzer is developed based on the Alkhalil Morpho-Syntactic System (Boudlal et al. 2010). It is applied individually to the words on the list of N-grams. The morphological structures produced by the analyzer are used to determine the category of words, derivative or non-derivative. The derivative words are represented by their root along with their morphological pattern, and the non-derivative words are represented by their stem, permitting different N-grams that have common base forms to reinforce each other in scoring and to reduce the number of redundant terms and concepts. Each N-gram is associated with its list of base forms called the normalized N-grams (NNG) at the end of this step.

5.2 N-gram Clustering and Weighting

All the N-grams generated from the same base forms are grouped together, their counts accumulated, and represented by their NNG. A vector representation of the text is produced where each detected NNG and its frequency are listed. In this work, we define the frequency of a normalized N-gram NGi noted Freq (NGi) as the sum of all the N-grams having the same base forms of NGi.

Each normalized N-gram should be assigned a weight that represents its relevance to be selected as a keyword. The keyword frequency and the keyword degree are generally considered for scoring potential keywords (Rose et al. 2010, Mihalcea and Tarau 2004). The weight of a normalized N-gram NGi is given by the following formula:

$$\text{Weight}(\text{NGi}) = \text{Freq}(\text{NGi}) / \sum_{j=1}^{m} (\text{Freq}(\text{NGj}))$$

where m is the number of Normalized N-grams.

As the unigrams are generally more frequent than the bi-grams and bi-grams are more frequent than tri-grams, we need to correct the weight of N-grams by introducing a new measure called score. The N-gram score takes into account the relevance of individual components forming the N-gram. The score of a unigram is equal to its weight since a unigram has one component. The score of other N-grams (bigrams, trigrams, ...) is given by the following formula:

$$\text{Score}(\text{NGi}) = \text{Weight}(\text{NGi}) + \sum_{j=1}^{N} (\text{Weight}(\text{Tj})),$$

where the T1, T2,..., TN represent the N roots/stems of the normalized N-gram NGi.

The degree of an N-gram is calculated as the sum of its Weight and the Weights of all the higher structures containing this N-gram. Thus, the degree favors terms occurring frequently in longer candidate keywords, and the score favors the frequent terms regardless of their co-occurrence with other terms.

5.3 Keywords Selection

The list of N-grams is reordered according to their scores since the highest scores determine the potential candidate keywords. The number of extracted keywords is set by the user. The selection of keywords is done according to the following rules.

- If two N-grams have the same score, the longer one will be selected.
- If two candidate keywords have the same number of components and the same score, we select the higher degree.
- If an N-gram is selected, all the possible combinations of its components will be removed from the list of N-grams to guaranty that an extracted keyword will not be included in another one.

The list of keywords is then built by replacing each selected normalized N-gram by the most frequent of its surface N-gram in the original text. Therefore, the list of keywords that will be associated with the document will have more readable form.

6. Experiments and Evaluation

In order to evaluate the performance of the proposed system, an experiment was carried out to test it by comparing the extracted keywords against the manually assigned ones. A collection of 70 journal articles and article abstract selected from six journals and covering different domains was used. The dataset is divided into three groups according to their size [table 1]. The average number of words per article is 3406. Each one of these articles was assigned a list of keywords. The number of keywords varies from 2 to 14, with an average of 5.14 keywords per document. The number of extracted keywords is set to the same number of keywords assigned manually to the documents, so the number of false positive detections and false negative detections will be equal, and the three measures P, R, and F will be identical.

Table 1 shows the main results of the conducted experiment. An average precision of 0.51 was achieved. Since the primary analysis of the dataset showed that only about 73% of the human-generated keywords appear in the document texts, this result can be considered as a good result. The results have shown also that better results are achieved with larger documents.

Table 1: Results

Dataset	Number of Documents	Average of words per article	Precision
1	22	6523	0.56
2	28	3238	0.54
3	20	212	0.41
All	70	3406	0.51

7. Conclusion

This paper proposed an unsupervised two-stage approach for keyword extraction from Arabic texts that avoids the necessity of annotated data. The conducted experiments showed that the proposed method can extract keywords from single documents in a domain-independent way. The linguistic analysis of the texts and the grouping of N-grams according to their linguistic features improve the quality of extracted keywords. An average precision of 0.51 was achieved in despite the fact that that only about 73% of the human-assigned keywords appear in the document texts.

Reference

Al-Sughaier, I., Al-Kharashi, I. (2004). Arabic morphological analysis techniques: A comprehensive survey. Journal of *The American Society for Information Science and Technology (JASIST)*, 55(3), 189-213.

Awajan, A. (2007). Arabic Text Preprocessing for the Natural Language Processing Applications. *Arab Gulf Journal of Scientific Research,* 25(4), 179-189.

Benajiba, Y., Diab, M., Rosso, P. (2009). Arabic Named Entity Recognition: A Feature-Driven Study. *IEEE Transactions on Audio, Speech, and Language Processing*, 17(5), 926-934.

Boudlal, A., Lakhouaja, A., Mazroui, A., Meziane, A., Ould Abdallahi, M., Shoul, M. (2010). Alkhalil Morpho Sys: A Morphosyntactic analysis system for Arabic texts, *International Arab Conference on* Information Technology (ACIT). Riyadh, Saudi Arabia.

Diab, M., Hacioglu, K., JURAFSKY, D. (2007). Automatic Processing of Modern Standard Arabic Text. *Chapter in Arabic Computational Morphology*. Springer Ed. 159-179.

El-Beltagy S., & Rafea A. (2008). KP-Miner: A keyphrase extraction system for English and Arabic documents, *Information Systems.* 34(1), 132-144.

El-Shishtawy, T., & Al-Sammak, A. (2009). Arabic Keyphrase Extraction using Linguistic knowledge and Machine Learning Techniques, In *Proceedings of the Second International Conference on Arabic Language Resources and Tools*, The MEDAR Consortium, Cairo, Egypt.

Frank, E., Paynter, G.W., Witten, I.H., Gutwin, C., Nevill-Manning, C.G. (1999). Domain-Specific Keyphrase Extraction. Proceedings of *the International Joint Conference on Artificial Intelligence*, Stockholm, Sweden, 668–673.

Green, S., and Manning, C. D. (2010). Better Arabic Parsing: Baselines, Evaluations, and Analysis. In *COLING*- Beijing. 394–402.

Habash, N. (2010). Introduction to Arabic Natural Language Processing. Morgan & Claypool Publishers, USA.

Hasan, K.S., NG, V. (2010). Conundrums in unsupervised Keyphrase Extraction: Making Sense of the State-of-the-Art. *COLING* 2010, 365-373.

Hulth, A. (2003). Improved automatic keyword extraction given more linguistic knowledge. In *Proceedings of the Conference on Empirical Methods in Natural Language Processing* , Sapporo, Japan,

Hulth, A. (2004). Combining Machine Learning and Natural Language Processing for Automatic Keyword Extraction. Doctoral dissertation. Department of Computer and Systems Sciences, Stockholm University.

Liu, Z., Li, P., Zheng, Y., Sun, M. (2009). Clustering to Find Exemplar Terms for Keyphrase Extraction. In *Proceedings of the Conference on Empirical Methods in Natural Language Processing*, Singapore. 257–266.

Manning, C. D., Raghavan, P., Schütze, H. (2009). Introduction to Information Retrieval. Cambridge University Press.

Matsuo, Y., Ishizuka, M. (2004). Keyword Extraction from a Single Document using Word Co-occurrence Statistical Information. International *Journal on Artificial Intelligence Tools,* 13(1), 157-169

Mihalcea, R., Tarau, P. (2004). TextRank: Brining order into texts. In Proceedings of *EMNLP 2004*, Association for Computational Linguistics, Barcelona, Spain. 404-411.

Pudota, N., Dattolo, A., Baruzzo, A., Tasso, C. (2010). A New Domain Independent Keyphrase Extraction System. *Digital Libraries: Communications in Computer and Information Science*, 91, 67-78.

Rose, S., Engel, D., Cramer, N., Cowley, W. (2010). Automatic keyword extraction from individual documents. *Text Mining: Applications and Theory* edited by Michael W. Berry and Jacob Kogan, John Wiley & Sons, Ltd. 3-20

Turney, P. D. (2000). Learning Algorithm for Keyphrase Extraction. *Information Retrieval*, 2(4), 303-336.

Turney, P. D., & Pantel, P. (2010). From Frequency to Meaning: Vector Space Models of Semantics. *Journal of Artificial Intelligence Research*, 37, 141-188.

The 2014 Conference on Computational Linguistics and Speech Processing
ROCLING 2014, pp. 185-192

Testing Distributional Hypothesis in Patent Translation

Hsin-Hung Lin* and Yves Lepage*

Abstract

This paper presents a wordlist-based lexical richness approach to testing distributional hypothesis for genre analysis in translation studies. In recent years, there has been continuing interest in patent translation. However, there are only a few lay their interests on comparison between native and non-native writing. The proposed approach to terms distrubution of technical words contained in United States Patent and Trademark Office (USPTO) and Japan Patent Office (JPO) in terms of lexical variation, lexical density and lexical sophistication, in brief, highlights distributional similarity of technical genre, and in particular, distibutional difference of academic and general genres.

Keywords: Patent Translation, Native Characterization, Corpus, Co-Occurrence.

1. Introduction

As globalization has resulted in rapid greater economic growth, the challenges of interdisciplinary interaction in pursuit of precise patent writing have incredibly increased.

In Lin and Hsieh (2010a), English patent documents were statistically extracted and computationally examined from LexisNexis Academic, a database for legal professionals. They compiled a reference corpus of independent claim texts and lay the focus on their collocation features. Mutual information is attainable with the help of selectional collocation features underlining specific clausal types represented in natural language processing of patent specification.

While their work appears to fill a niche in the ESP (English for Specific Purposes) field (and particularly in the English for Occupational Legal Purposes), Lin and Hsieh (2010b) further compiled a modern patent language technical term list with statistical-retrieval methodologies as a mandatory

* Graduate School of Information, Production, and Systems, Waseda University, Japan.
E-mail: nobuhiro602@toki.waseda.jp; yves.lepage@waseda.jp

approach. The research content and statistical investigations assist patent attorneys expand the vocabulary size for the advancement of patent writing at an international level.

Lin and Hsieh (2011) proposed a mixed-method approach to detecting scholarly discourse in patent technical documents. The Patent Technical Word Corpus (hereafter PTWC), containing 16 million word tokens, was compiled to elucidate the underpinning principles in identifying discourse elements, text-structure components, and the location of references. Whereas most existing IPR (intellectual property rights) databases accessible for information retrieval, the creation of PTWC, based on corpus-statistics and text-processing technology, refines more decisive characteristics of terminological knowledge as potential contribution for evaluation of technical documents.

To characterize technical genre in translation studies, we use lexical richness based on technical wordlist to test distributional hypothesis.

2. Technical Terms Distribution

We firstly conduct a quantitative survey based on USPTO Glossary to rank the distribution of technical terms used in United States Patent and Trademark Office (USPTO) and Japan Patent Office (JPO) within the time period from year 2010 to 2013. Table 1 below presents the statistical results.

'Comprising', a term of art used in claim language which means that the named elements are essential in describing the invention, ranked the first in USPTO. According to USPTO Glossary, it is a transitional phrase that is synonymous with "including," "containing" or "characterized by;" is inclusive or open-ended and does not exclude additional, unrecited elements or method steps. On the contrary, 'consisting of', a transitional phrase that is closed and excludes any element, step, or ingredient not specified in the claim, ranked the 6th.

To characterize transitional phrases of technical genre in translation studies, we retrieved co-occurring information of 'comprising' and 'consisting of' to compare it with academic and general genres.

Table 1. Distribution of patent technical words in USPTO

Rank	Term	Frequency	Rank	Term	Frequency
1	comprising	3785213	11	specification	854667
2	scope	2459656	12	continuation	738785
3	patent	1603882	13	dependent claim	625886
4	Group	1306808	14	composed of	617353
5	element	1245265	15	independent claim	587926
6	consisting of	1165427	16	representative	518762
7	drawing	1015261	17	benefit claim	437599
8	disclosure	919881	18	person	383784
9	application (patent)	884470	19	priority claim	381352
10	patent application	884470	20	interference	341173

We give the survey of terms used in JPO in Table 2. It is noted that "comprising" ranked the first in distribution of USPTO and JPO, whereas "consisting of" ranked the 6th.

Table 2. Distribution of patent technical words in JPO

Rank	Term	Frequency	Rank	Term	Frequency
1	comprising	629750	11	applicant	60293
2	composed of	371852	12	drawing	53469
3	element	272496	13	person	48893
4	POWER	272088	14	IDS	24946
5	Group	176103	15	Control No.	22905
6	consisting of	136992	16	interference	22445
7	PAIR	122746	17	RE	19777
8	representative	72519	18	specification	18102
9	Request (PCT)	70606	19	classification	16977
10	application (patent)	62027	20	independent claim	15513

3. Methodology

3.1 The Distributional Hypothesis

Sahlgren (2008:33) maintains that distributional approaches to meaning acquisition utilize distributional properties of linguistic entities as the building blocks of semantics. This hypothesis is often stated in terms like words which are similar in meaning occur in similar contexts (Rubenstein & Goodenough, 1965). In other words, words that occur in the same contexts tend to have similar meanings (Pantel, 2005).

3.2 Corpus Preparation

Transitional phrases in patent application were used to specify whether the claim is limited to only the elements listed, or whether the claim may cover items or processes that have additional elements. The most common transitional phrase used is the open-ended phrase "comprising". However, many claims use closed-ended language such as "consisting of".

In this regards, we retrieve co-occurring information containing "comprising" and "consisting of" from LexisNexis Academic for corpus preparation. Table 3 shows the structure for the corpus creation.

Table 3. Genre-based co-occurrence corpus of transitional phrases

Genres	Native Writing	Non-Native Writing
Technical (Patent)	USPTO	JPO
Academic (Law Journal)	Canadian Legal Journals	HK Law Journal
General (Newspapers)	US Newspapers	Non-US Newspapers

3.3 Lexical Richness

Lexical richness is a concept about one's lexical uses, which can be measured by lexical density, sophistication, and variation (Kao and Wang, 2014:54).

Kojima and Yamashita (2014:23) suggest that lexical richness measures primarily assess learners' vocabulary use. Lexical variation, the proportion between different words (types) and the total number (tokens) of words used in the text, is known as the type-token ratio (TTR).

Lexical density is defined as the percentage of lexical words in the text, for example, nouns, verbs, adjectives, and adverbs (Laufer and Nation, 1995:309). Since only content words carry semantic meanings, a greater lexical density indicates more semantic information conveyed in a text.

Read (2000: 200) distinguishes dimensions of lexical richness, and one of these is lexical sophistication, which he defines as 'the use of technical terms and jargon as well as the kind of uncommon words that allow writers to express their meanings in a precise and sophisticated manner'. The proportion of words used at different frequency levels, in terms of K1, K2, AWL (Academic Word List), and off-list words, in the text. K1 and K2 words are the most commonly used first 1000 and 1001 to 2000 words, respectively, in English. Words beyond these K1, K2, and AWL are placed into the off-list level, where proper nouns, rare words, special terms, acronyms, abbreviations, incompletions, and even misspellings may be found.

4. Results and Discussion

In terms of lexical density, non-natives employed more semantic information than the natives, among all genres. In terms of lexical variation, non-natives employed more lexical diversity than the natives in technical and academic genres.

Academic Genre, in particular, HK Law Journal, containing most semantic information (83%), among the all, whilst general genre, Non-Us Newspapers, containing least lexical diversity, as we excluded technical genre for analysis.

4.1 Technical Genre

In technical genre, in particular, JPO (Patent Abstract of Japan), containing least advanced words (15.03%) in the texts, among all.

Table 4. Lexical sophistication of "comprising" in technical genre

Word Level (%)	USPTO	JPO
K1 Words	50.35	50.37
K2 Words	2.61	3.61
AWL Words	23.74	21.78
Off-List Words	23.31	24.24

Less vocabulary knowledge in K2, AWL, and Off-list words were employed in "consisting of", compared with that of "comprising". The natives employed more academic words in Table 4, more off-list words in Table 5.

Table 5. Lexical sophistication of "consisting of" in technical genre

Word Level (%)	USPTO	JPO
K1 Words	62.37	64.89
K2 Words	0.29	0.34
AWL Words	19.43	19.74
Off-List Words	17.92	15.03

4.2 Academic Genre

In academic genre, HK Law Journal, containing most advanced words (33.28%) in the texts, among all.

Table 6. Lexical sophistication of "comprising" in academic genre

Word Level (%)	Canadian Legal Journal	HK Law Journal
K1 Words	59.02	51.02
K2 Words	5.88	3.07
AWL Words	13.47	12.63
Off-List Words	21.63	33.28

As shown in Table 6 and Table 7, non-natives employed more off-list words in academic legal genre, whereas the natives employed more K1 and K2 words in academic legal genre.

Table 7. Lexical sophistication of "consisting of" in academic genre

Word Level (%)	Canadian Legal Journal	HK Law Journal
K1 Words	59.74	50.74
K2 Words	6.12	2.97
AWL Words	13.07	14.24
Off-List Words	21.07	32.05

4.3 General Genre

As can be seen in Table 8 and Table 9, the non-natives employed more K2, AWL, and Off-list words but less K1 words in general genre.

Table 8. Lexical sophistication of "comprising" in general genre

Word Level (%)	US Newspapers	Non-US Newspapers
K1 Words	63.34	51.97
K2 Words	3.69	5.47
AWL Words	11.66	16.73
Off-List Words	21.30	25.84

Table 9. Lexical sophistication of "consisting of" in general genre

Word Level (%)	US Newspapers	Non-US Newspapers
K1 Words	63.37	53.48
K2 Words	4.03	7.71
AWL Words	12.61	16.42
Off-List Words	19.99	22.09

In short, K1 words were employed more by the natives in academic and general genres, whilst less used in technical genres.

5. Conclusion and Future Work

There is a correlation between distributional similarity and meaning similarity, which allows us to utilize the former in order to estimate the latter (Sahlgren, 2008:33). In terms of distribution statistics, the technical genre reveals more distributional and meaning similarity.

In summary, lexical richness is a valid and reliable measure to characterize genres. For future research, we seek to investigate the origin differences between syntagmatic and paradigmatic relations to further refine the preliminaries of the present study.

References

Kao, S. M, & Wang, W. C. (2014). Lexical and organizational features in novice and experienced ELF presentations. *Journal of English as a Lingua Franca, 3*(1), 49-79.

Kojima, M., & Yamashita, J. (2014). Reliability of lexical richness measures based on word lists in short second language productions. *System, 42*, 23-33.

Laufer, B., & Nation, P. (1995). Vocabulary size and use: Lexical density in FL written production. *Applied Linguistics, 16*, 307-322.

Lin, H. H., & Hsieh, C. Y. (2010a). Collocation Features of Independent Claim in US Patent Documents: Information Retrieval from LexisNexis. *ROCLING XXII: Conference on* Computational Linguistics and Speech Processing, pp. 296-310. Taiwan: Academia Sinica.

Lin, H. H., & Hsieh, C. Y. (2010b). The Specialized Vocabulary of Modern Patent Language: Semantic Association in Patent Lexis. *PACLIC 24: Pacific Asia Conference on Language, Information, and Computation*, pp. 417-424. Japan: Waseda University Press.

Lin, H. H., & Hsieh, C. Y. (2011). Characteristics of Independent Claim: A Corpus-Linguistic Approach to Contemporary English Patents. *International Journal of Computational Linguistics and Chinese Language Processing, 16*(3-4), 77-106.

Pantel, P. (2005). Inducing ontological co-occurrence vectors. In *Proceedings of the 43rd Conference of the Association for Computational Linguistics*, pp. 125–132). Morristown, NJ, USA: Association for Computational Linguistics.

Read, J. (2000). *Assessing vocabulary*. Cambridge: Cambridge University Press.

Rubenstein, H., & Goodenough, J. (1965). Contextual correlates of synonymy. *Communications of the ACM, 8* (10), 627-633.

Sahlgren, M. (2008). The distributional hypothesis. *Italian Journal of Linguistics, 20*(1), 33-53.

The 2014 Conference on Computational Linguistics and Speech Processing
ROCLING 2014, pp. 193-203

Spectrum Analysis of Cry Sounds in Preterm and Full-Term Infants

Li-mei Chen[1], Yu-Hsuan Yang[1], Chyi-Her Lin[2], Yuh-Jyh Lin[2], Yung-Chieh Lin[2]

Abstract

Long-time average spectrum (LTAS) was used to analyze the cry phonations of 26 infants under four months old; 16 of them are full-term and the other 10 infants are preterm. The results of first spectral peak, mean spectral energy, spectral tilt, high frequency energy were used to compare the cry phonatory between full-term and preterm infants. In addition, cry duration and percent phonation is also compared. According to previous studies, full-term and preterm infants' crying behavior show significant differences because immature neurological development of preterm infants. Major findings in this study are: (1) There was no significant difference in unedited cry phonation across groups; (2) There was no significant difference in percent phonation across groups; (3) There was no significant difference in first spectral peak across groups, and no significant difference within groups could be found. However, full-term infants have higher first spectral peak than that of preterm infants; (4) There was no significant difference in mean spectral energy across groups, yet there was a significant main effect for partition; (5) There was no significant difference in spectral tilt across groups. Post hoc comparisons identified higher spectral tilt in P2 than in P3 in the full-term infants; (6) There was no significant difference in high frequency energy across groups. Significant differences were observed across partition, and in both groups, P1 had higher HFE than P3. The differences in the measures of crying behavior between full-term and preterm infants can help to estimate health condition of infants who are under 4 months old.

Keywords: Long-time average spectrum, Infant cry, Preterm infants

1. Introduction

Previous studies show that preterm infants are prone to immaturity of neurological development which leads to their sensitiveness toward pain stimulation, and the greater pain they suffer would reflect on crying behavior. If a set of distinctive measures can be identified, it might be possible to differentiate infant cries in the spectrum of normative behavior and cries due to organic pathology. The measures

[1] Department of Foreign Languages, National Cheng Kung University
[2] Department of Pediatrics, Medical College, National Cheng Kung University

would be helpful for doctors and caregivers to identify if the unknown cries are caused by just infant colic or other more complicated factors. Long-time average spectrum (LTAS) of crying behavior were analyzed in two groups of newborn infants in this study. LTAS was used to analyze the infant's non-partitioned crying episode (NP), as well as the 3 equal-length partitions (P1, P2, P3). First spectral peak (FSP), mean spectral energy (MSE), spectral tilt (ST), and high frequency energy (HFE) were measured.

Colic strikes infants who are under four months old, and it makes the infants cry in the evening on a daily bases or at the moment of waking up (Lester, Boukydis, Gracia-Coll, & Hole, 1990). The cause of this pain is still unknown (Zeskind & Barr, 1997). Colic occurs when infants are around one month old and it often disappears without a reason when infants are older than three months (Clifford, 2002). It is a universal and commonly-seen phenomenon which is the cause for excessive cry behavior. Though previous studies have suggested that higher fundamental frequency and a larger percentage of dysphonation in crying behavior can be found in the pain cries of infants who suffer from colic, no standard acoustic features in cry vocalization of infants with colic was established (Zeskind & Barr, 1997). Long-time average spectrum might provide an option to see if there are any significant variations in the cries of infants with colic and those who are healthy from first spectral peak, mean spectral energy, spectral tilt, and high frequency energy.

Though infants are not able to talk, they can express their feelings and emotions through crying, facial expression, and body movements. Diseases are able to be discovered by some characteristics in crying behavior (Radhika, Chandralingam, Anjaneyulu, & Satyanarayana, 2012). For example, different pain stimuli would lead to different fundamental frequencies in infant cry vocalization (Radhika et al., 2012). If more specific characteristics are found in certain diseases, it would be more effective in prescribing and curing. Sometimes parents can differentiate why their babies cry by their various crying behavior (Soltis, 2004). As for the way of eliciting cries, Johnston, Stevens, Craig, & Grunau (1993) had proposed two different ways: the heel-stick procedure and injection. In this current study, injection was used as the only standard method of eliciting cries to avoid any nuances that might caused by the different types of pain stimuli. However, even though there are some scientific ways of detecting the pain intensity infants endure, the experience of pain is quite subjective and is not merely related to physiological but also psychological factors (Qiu, 2006). Moreover, since infants use crying to arouse caregivers' attention, it can be expected that infants' crying behavior differs with and without their caregivers around them (Green, Gustafson, Irwin, Kalinowski, & Wood, 1995). Usually, the responses from caregivers bring cry behaviors to a halt (Green et al., 1995). Thus, crying is regarded not only an independent behavior but also plays an important role in social interactions between infants and their caretakers (Green et al., 1995). Furthermore, crying is a way of drawing other people's attention to help infants get rid of the uncomfortable situation or meet their needs (LaGasse, Neal, & Lester, 2005).

Because of the immature development of nervous systems caused by premature birth, preterm infants' crying behavior is believed to reveal different characteristics from that of full-term infants whose nervous systems are comparatively well-developed (Goberman & Robb, 1999). Premature infants are reported to have higher *fo* in their cry phonation, and it might be due to the immature, shorter vocal folds (Johnston et al., 1993). Or as Zeskind (1983) stated that high-risk infants are not able to perfectly control their crying behavior and that they tend to react more intensely towards pain stimuli than low-risk infants. Infants react differently to the same stimulus pain whether they are healthy or born at risk. However, while some studies have shown that preterm infants are more sensitive to pain stimuli, others found that some premature infants have less intense reactions towards pain than normal infants (Qiu, 2006).

The main objective of this current study is to find out how the crying behavior between full-term and preterm infants differs from each other. The findings might help in detecting infants' health conditions. Moreover, if the differences of the crying behavior can be systematically characterized, the measurements can be further applied to identify features in neonate cries due to infant colic.

2. Method

2.1 Participants

Previous studies indicated that gender did not lead to significant differences in first spectral peak, mean spectral energy, spectral tilt, and high frequency energy (Goberman & Robb, 1999; Goberman, Johnson, Cannizzaro, & Robb, 2008). Therefore, gender was not controlled in this study. There were 26 infant participants; 16 were full-term infants and the other 10 were preterm infants. The infants were all under four months old for both full-term infants and preterm infants according to their gestational ages. All of the infants in this study were considered to have normal hearing according to interview with parents.

2.2 Data Collection

For data collection, TASCAM wave recorder and RODE uni-directinal microphone were used while recording the cry phonation of both preterm and full-term infants. The microphone was held near the infants' mouth. All infants were in the supine position while receiving the injection because acoustic properties (e.g. fundamental frequency) might be influenced by postures of infants (Lin & Green, 2007). Data were collected in the hospital. The cry phonation of both groups of infants was recorded during and after they receive the injection. The pain stimulus was the same in both groups of infants.

2.3 Acoustic Analysis

Based on Goberman and Robb (1999), a crying episode of infants was defined as the duration of the continuous crying activity, beginning with the first audible cry sound after the pain stimulus, and an episode was completed as soon as the infants stopped crying. The non-voiced parts of a crying episode were first edited out in the cry vocalization, making a "non-partitioned crying episode" (Goberman & Robb, 1999). In this current study, all the inspiratory cry was eliminated from pain stimulus, only the phonatory parts were analyzed. Then, a non-partitioned episode was divided into three partitions with the same length of durations (P1, P2, P3). P1, P2, P3 are regarded as the early, middle, and late sections of the crying episode, respectively, corresponding to the attack, cruise, and subdual phases of a crying episode as suggested by Truby and Lind (1965). First spectral peak, mean spectral energy, spectral tilt, and high frequency energy were measured. First spectral peak was identified as the first amplitude peak across the LTAS display. Mean spectral energy was measured with the mean amplitude value from 0 to 8000 Hz. Spectral tilt was the ratio of energy between 0-1000 Hz, and 1000-5000 Hz. High frequency energy was the sum of amplitudes from 5000 Hz to 8000 Hz.

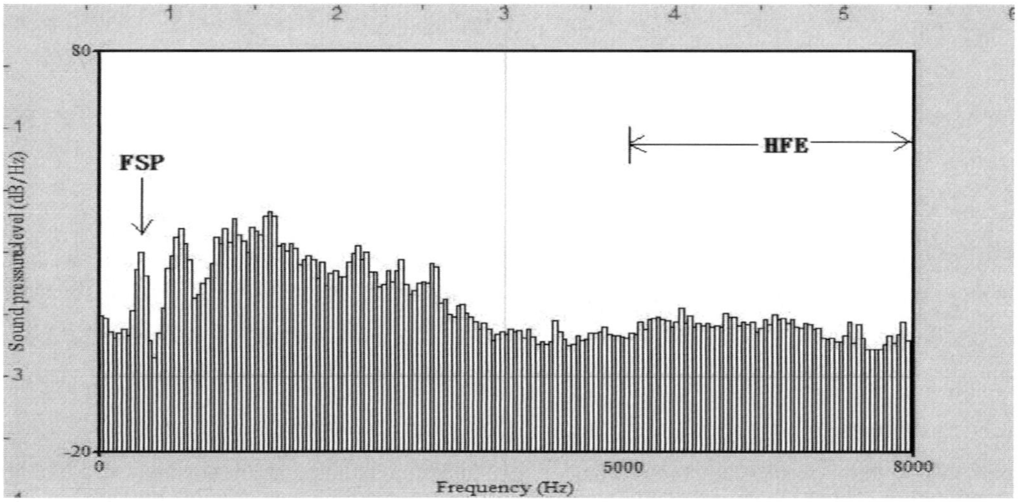

Figure 1. *Typical LTAS display showing the location of the first spectral peak (FSP) and high frequency energy (HFE) between 5000Hz and 8000Hz.*

3. Results & Discussion

3.1 Unedited Cry Duration

The average duration of crying episodes for the 16 full-term infants was 43.26s (SD=31.27), and for the 10 preterm infants was 36.21s (SD=30.93). Although full-term infants have longer average duration of crying episodes, there are no significant differences between the two groups, $t(24) = 0.48$, two-tailed, $p > .05$. The result is the same as that of Goberman and Robb (1999).

3.2 Percent Phonation

The percentage of cry phonation in a long-term non-partitioned, unedited crying episode was calculated. The average percent phonation across the crying episodes of the 16 full-term infants and the 10 preterm infants was 67% (SD=17.04) and 67% (SD=13.98) respectively. That is, 67% of the unedited crying episode contained cry phonation. Like what was found in Goberman and Robb (1999), there is no significant differences across groups in the percentage of cry phonation, $t(24) = 0.39$, two-tailed, $p > .05$.

3.3 First Spectral Peak (FSP)

The non-partitioned and partitioned first spectral peak values of the 16 full-term and the 10 preterm infants are listed in Table 1. A two-way analysis of variance (ANOVA) was performed to check if there were significant differences in FSP values between the two groups, and whether there was significant variation between the three equal-length cry durations (P1, P2, P3) in each group. The results indicated no significant term by partition interaction ($p > .05$), no significant main effect for term status ($p > .05$), and no significant main effect for partition ($p > .05$). Despite the fact that there were no significant differences in statistical tests, we found that full-term infants have higher non-partitioned FSP (182.07Hz) than that of preterm infants (130.44Hz). From overall observation, full-term infants demonstrated higher FSP in non-partitioned and the three partitioned episodes. Full-term and preterm infants displayed different trends of FSP in P1, P2, and P3.

While the infants were receiving injections, the sharp pain stimulated them and all the infants burst out crying. According to the previous studies (Johnston et al., 1993), preterm infants are expected to have higher FSP because preterm infants were thought to be more sensitive and would react more intensely to pain. Intensive crying behavior causes the increase of the subglottal pressure and the stiffness of the vocal folds. However, in this current study, the mean FSP of the full-term infants turned out to be higher than that of the preterm infants, in both the non-partitioned episode and the three equal-length episodes. Moreover, full-term infants' crying episode involved more distinct phases with decrease of FSP in P3. In preterm infants, FSP kept increasing from P1 to P3.

Table 1. *First spectral peak from the non-partitioned episodes (NP) and three partitioned crying episodes with equal length (P1, P2, P3) from the full-term and preterm groups of infants*

	FSP (Hz)				
Group		NP	P1	P2	P3
Full-term	M	182.07	135.88	184.79	149.46
	SD	139.06	113.24	142.45	119.31
Preterm	M	130.44	104.35	117.40	139.14
	SD	71.74	52.06	67.36	82.11

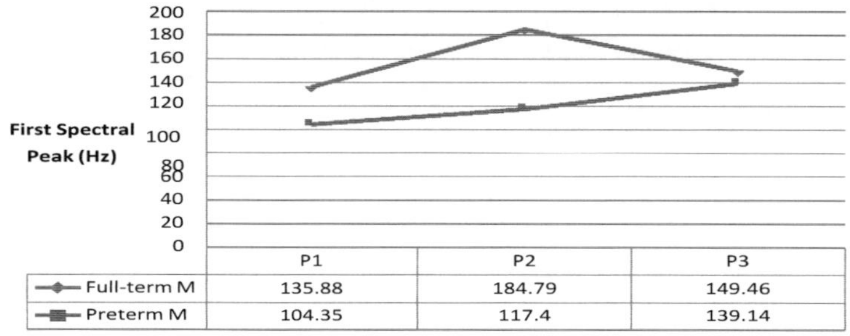

***Figure** 2. First spectral peak of full-term and preterm infants over time (P1, P2, and P3 are three equal-length partitioned crying episodes.)*

3.4 Mean Spectral Energy (MSE)

The mean spectral energy of non-partitioned and partitioned episodes of the 16 full-term and the 10 preterm infants are compared and listed in Table 2. A two-way analysis of variance (ANOVA) was performed to investigate if there was significant variation between the two groups, and whether there was significant variation between the three equal-length cry durations (P1, P2, P3) in each group. No significant term by partition interaction ($p > .05$) was found. There was a significant main effect for partition ($F = 6.47$, $p < .05$), yet there was no significant main effect for term, $p > .05$. One-way ANOVA tests were then performed in each group to check the changes in MSE (in P1, P2, P3). In full-term infants, P2 was significantly higher than P3. In preterm infants, P1 showed significantly higher energy than P2 and P3. The changes are illustrated in Figure 3.

Premature infants, compared to full-term infants, are reported to have higher *fo* in their cry phonation, and it might be due to tension of the larynx (Johnston et al., 1993). Greater pain stimulus makes laryngeal muscles tighten. In this current study, although no significant differences could be identified, preterm infants showed higher mean of MSE in non-partitioned episode and the three equidurational crying episodes. This shows that during the cry duration, the preterm infants' laryngeal muscles are tighter and they have a more severe reaction toward pain stimulus. The tighter laryngeal muscles suggest a more intense cry behavior. Moreover, a decrease in MSE could be observed in both full-term and preterm infants. This might suggest that the laryngeal muscles of both groups of infants loosen by phase, especially in preterm infants. There is sharper decrease of MSE from P1 to P3 in preterm infants.

Table 2. Mean spectral energy from the non-partitioned episodes (NP) and three partitioned crying episodes with equal length (P1, P2, P3) from the full-term and preterm groups of infants

		MSE (dB)			
Group		NP	P1	P2	P3
Full-term	M	19.368	19.982	19.507	14.323
	SD	9.627	9.523	11.158	11.266
Preterm	M	22.801	25.201	18.695	15.628
	SD	5.785	6.409	7.963	6.153

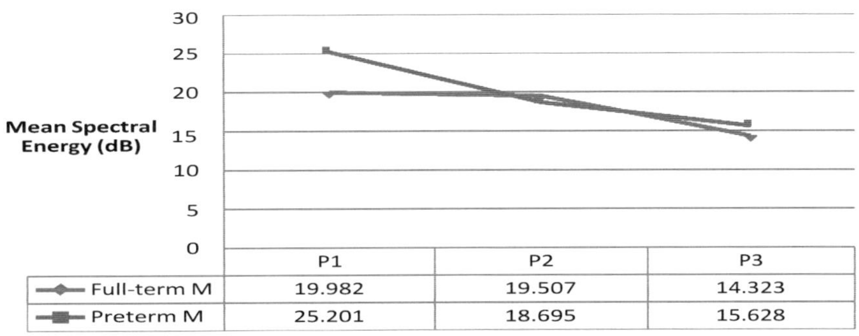

Figure 3. *Mean spectral energy of full-term and preterm infants over time (P1, P2, and P3 are three equal-length partitioned crying episodes.)*

3.5 Spectral Tilt (ST)

The spectral tilt of non-partitioned and partitioned crying episodes of the two groups are compared and listed in Table 3. In order to identify if there was significant differences of ST between the two groups and whether there was significant variation between the three equal-length cry durations (P1, P2, P3) in each group, a two-way analysis of variance (ANOVA) was performed. There were no significant term by partition interaction ($p > .05$), no significant main effect for partition, and no significant main effect for term. To investigate changes in ST across partitions within each group, separate one-way ANOVA tests were performed for full-term and preterm infant groups. In full-term infants, post hoc comparisons identified a significantly higher ST for P2 than for P3 ($p < .05$), but no significant differences in ST across partitions for the preterm infants ($p > .05$). Overall, the full-term infants showed higher ST values at the onset of crying vocalization which decreased over time; whereas the preterm infants had lower ST values at the onset, which increased over time. The changes are demonstrated in Figure 4. For full-term infants, higher P2 than P3 in ST was observed. The ST of full-term infants does not increase over time as mentioned in Goberman and Robb (1999); on the contrary, the ST of full-term infants decreases over time. However, the increase of ST can be found in preterm infants.

The variation of ST of full-term and preterm infants is shown in table 3. Preterm infants have a slightly higher ST than full-term infants. ST refers to how quickly the amplitude of the harmonics decreases. A higher ST value was related to hypoadduction of the vocal folds (Mendoza, Munoz, & Naranjo, 1996). In this current study, hyperadduction is observed in the decrease ST of full-term infants, whereas, hypoadduction is observed in the increase ST of preterm infants.

Table 3. *Spectral tilt from the non-partitioned episodes (NP) and three partitioned crying episodes with equal length (P1, P2, P3) from the full-term and preterm groups of infants*

	ST				
Group		NP	P1	P2	P3
Full-term	M	1.381	2.242	1.423	1.118
	SD	0.307	3.207	0.387	0.300
Preterm	M	1.839	1.935	2.811	3.218
	SD	0.685	0.659	2.795	5.326

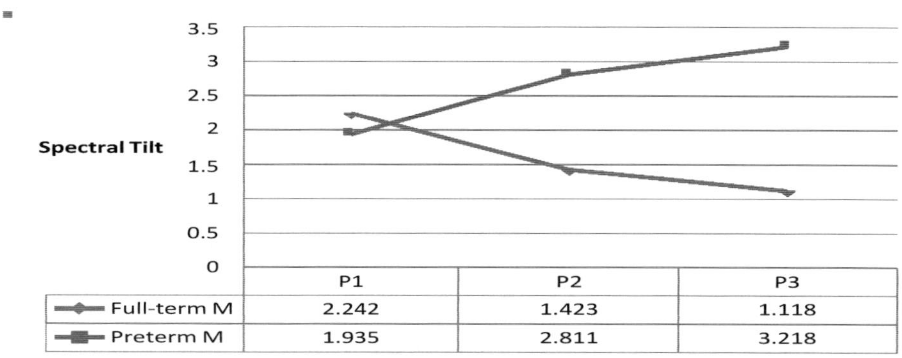

Figure 4*. Spectral tilt of full-term and preterm infants over time (P1, P2, and P3 are three equal-length partitioned crying episodes.)*

3.6 High Frequency Energy (HFE)

The high frequency energy of non-partitioned and partitioned crying episodes of the two groups are compared and listed in Table 4. In order to identify if there was significant variation between the two groups, and whether there was significant variation between the three equal-length cry durations (P1, P2, P3) in each group, a two-way analysis of variance (ANOVA) was performed. No significant term by partition interaction ($p > .05$) was found. There was no main effect for term ($p > .05$), stating that there were no significant differences in HFE across the two groups. There was significant main effect for partitions ($F = 8.29$, $p < .05$). Furthermore, one-way ANOVA tests were performed to check changes in HFE across partition within each group. Significant differences in HFE were found across partition for both full-term infants (F = 3.91, $p < .05$) and for preterm infants (F = 4.57, $p < .05$). There was a significantly higher P1 in HFE than P3 in both infant groups ($p < .05$). In both groups, HFE decreases over time. The HFE of full-term infants does not change drastically over time; however, in preterm infants, the HFE shows a steep descent. The changes are demonstrated in Figure 5. HFE in both full-term infants and preterm infants decreases overtime. However, HFE of preterm infants has a wider range, crossing from 1225 to 1807, while the range HFE of full-term infants is about 300.

Table 4. *High frequency energy from the non-partitioned episodes (NP) and three partitioned crying episodes with equal length (P1, P2, P3) from the full-term and preterm groups of infants*

		HFE (dB)			
Group		NP	P1	P2	P3
Full-term	M	1672	1703	1543	1272
	SD	582	552	720	590
Preterm	M	1737	1807	1511	1227
	SD	469	514	546	509

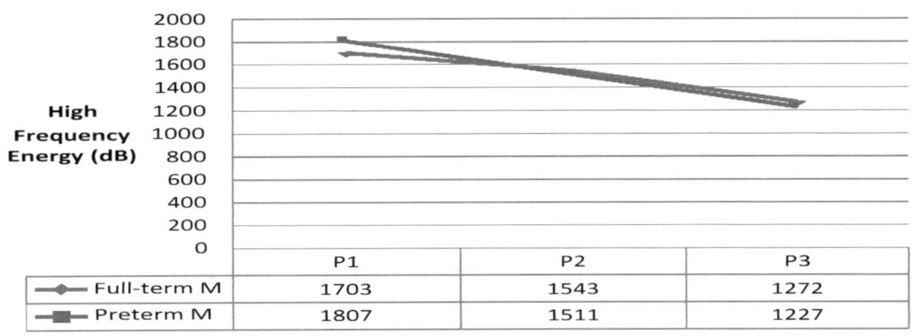

Figure 5. *High frequency energy of full-term and preterm infants over time (P1, P2, and P3 are three equal-length partitioned crying episodes.)*

Some of the results in this current study did not match the findings in previous studies. The differences could be due to a few discerning variables. First, although the uni-directional microphone was used in this study, the environmental noises could not be completely controlled because the nurses were required to explain the procedure to the caregivers. Moreover, there was unavoidable overlapping from noises of other infants' cry sound. Once the infant's cry vocalization was overlapped with adults' voice or other infants' cry sound, the partition could no longer be used for further analysis. Second, all the infants receiving injections had their caregivers around them. This caused inevitable interaction between adults and infants, bringing unexpected nuances to the results. Both full-term and preterm infants might use more strength in crying, hoping their caretakers would alleviate their pain. Third, some caretakers tended to soothe the infants as soon as they started crying, which would significantly change the natural cry episode since the soothing and consolation from the caretakers might influence their cry phonation. The infants might feel safe and stopped crying. This might cause incomplete early, middle, and late sections in a cry episode, as Goberman and Robb (1999) mentioned. In further studies, the interaction of infants and their caregivers is probably one of the variables that should be strictly controlled. Moreover, video recording should be implemented in order to identify whether the infants stopped crying spontaneously or their attention was drawn by other things. Lacking complete three sections of cry episode might be the main reason of the discrepancy in the findings of this current study and previous studies.

4. Summary

Cry phonations of neonates from 16 full-term infants and 10 preterm infants were analyzed with long-time average spectrum (LTAS). Major findings were: (1) Full-term infants had higher first spectral peak than that of preterm infants; (2) Mean spectral energy in both groups of infants decreased over time; (3) Spectral tilt in full-term infants decreased, but increased in preterm infants over time; (4) High frequency energy in both full-term and preterm infants decreased over time. In further study, the environmental noise (e.g., from nurses, parents, and other infants around) should be controlled in order to acquire sufficient data to identify more systematic distinctions in the patterns of cry phonation between full-term and preterm infants.

Acknowledgements

This research was supported by a grant from National Science Council (NSC102-2410-H-006 060) and the Ministry of Education, Taiwan, R.O.C. The Aim for the Top University Project to the National Cheng Kung University. We thank the infant participants and their families for their time and cooperation.

References

Clifford, T. (2002). Infant colic: A prospective, community-based Examination (Unpublished doctoral dissertation). The University of Western Ontario, Canada.

Goberman, A. M., Johnson, S., Cannizzaro, M. S., & Robb, M. P. (2008). The effect of positioning on infant cries: Implications for sudden infant death syndrome. *International Journal of Pediatric Otorhinolaryngology, 72*, 153-165.

Goberman, A. M. & Robb, M. P. (1999). Acoustic examination of preterm and full-term infant cries: The long-time average spectrum. *Journal of Speech, Language, and Hearing Research, 42*, 850-861

Green, J. A., Gustafson, G. E., Irwin, J. R., Kalinowski, L. L., & Wood, R. M. (1995). Infant crying: Acoustics, perception, and communication. *Early Development and Parenting, 4(4)*, 161-175.

Johnston, C., Stevens, B., Craig, K., & Grunau, R. (1993). Developmental changes in pain expression in premature, full-term, two- and four-month-old infants. *Pain, 52*, 201-208.

LaGasse L. L., Neal A. R., & Lester B. M. (2005). Assessment of infant cry: Acoustic cry analysis and parental perception. *Mental Retardation and Development Disabilites, 11*, 83-93.

Lester, B., Boukydis, C., Gracia-Coll, C. & Hole, W. (1990). Colic for developmentalists. *Infant Mental Health Journal, 11(4)*, 321-333.

Lin, H. C., & Green, J. A. (2007). Effects of posture on newborn crying. *Infancy, 11(2)*, 175-189.

Mendoza, E., Munoz, J., & Naranjo, N. (1996). The longtime average spectrum as a measure of voice stability. *Folia Phoniatrica, 48*, 57–64.

Qiu, J. (2006). Does it hurt? *Nature, 444*, 143-145.

Radhika, R. L., Chandralingam, S., Anjaneyulu, T. & Satyanarayana, K. (2012). A suggestive diagnostic technique for early identification of acyanotic heart disorders from infant's cry. *International Journal of Electrical and Electronics, 1(3)*, 32-38.

Soltis, J. (2004). The signal functions of early infant crying. *Behavioral and Brain Sciences, 27*, 443-458.

Truby, H., & Lind, J. (1965). Cry motions of the newborn infant. In J. Lind (Ed.), *Acta Paediatrica Scandanavica: Newborn Infant Cry* (Suppl.163), 7–58.

Zeskind, P. (1983). Production and spectral analysis of neonatal crying and its relation to other biobehavioral systems in the infant at-risk. In T. Field & A. Sostek (Eds.), *Infants born at-risk: Physiological and perceptual processes*. New York: Grune & Stratton.

Zeskind, P. & Barr, R. (1997). Acoustic characteristics of naturally occurring cries of infants with "colic". *Child Language Development, 68*, 394-403.

The 2014 Conference on Computational Linguistics and Speech Processing
ROCLING 2014, pp. 204-213

Web-Based Recording and Visualization Framework for Moving Trajectories

Po-An Yang[1] LiJung Chi[1] Kun-Ta Chuang[1]
Seth Chen[2] Jonathan Tsai[2] Yung-Chung Ku[2]

[1]Dept. of Computer Science and Information Engineering
National Cheng Kung University
Tainan, Taiwan, R.O.C.
ktchuang@mail.ncku.edu.tw

[2]Innovative DigiTech-Enabled Applications & Services Institute, IDEAS
Institute for Information Industry
Taipei, Taiwan, R.O.C.
{seth, jonathan, piperku}@iii.org.tw

Abstract

隨著智慧型手機的普及，個人軌跡資料的收集越來越方便，有關軌跡的應用也越來越多，像是 Foursquar [1]、Human [2]等 app 已陸續成為最火紅的手機應用。不過這些應用通常都只有很簡單的呈現打卡地點或軌跡，讓資料以靜態的出現，並沒有進一步的將資料視覺化，即使有，通常也要等到官方自行整合後釋出資料。我們提出的 Web-based 的系統架構，不僅可以即時動態呈現軌跡，更能跨平台，不受限於裝置環境，使用者可以透過瀏覽器來記錄自己的軌跡。軌跡儲存後，我們也提供一個即時呈現大家軌跡的移動動態呈現機制，不僅可以看見自己的軌跡，也可以看見他人的軌跡。另外有關於個人軌跡紀錄，通常使用者會有個人隱私的擔憂，在我們的架構中，會給每個使用者 UUID，透過 UUID 模糊了使用者與個人軌跡之間的連結，只有使用者的 UUID 及軌跡會留在 Database 中，系統不會知道使用者的 identity 資訊。最後我們也實作一些資料視覺化的技術，讓軌跡得以動態方式呈現。

Keywords: Trajectory, GPS, Data Visualization.

1. Introduction

有關於地圖軌跡的應用，已經是現在人不可缺少的一環，但多數的系統都偏向做導航或 打卡等，鮮少有系統像世界迷霧 [3]一樣，讓使用者以地圖為日誌，記錄自己的軌跡。而即使有這些系統，通常這樣的應用程式都無法跨平台，包含 iOS 及不同的 android 等作業系統，均須特別撰寫不同的應用程式。在本文中，我們提出並實作了一個 Web-based 的軌跡擷取及呈現的系統架構，讓使用者可以簡單的透過瀏覽器或手機 app 記錄自己的軌跡，並且以資料視覺化的技術將軌跡呈現。

我們實作的平台是 Github Pages [4]，透過 Github Pages，在此設計中，我們完全使用現在熱門的雲端服務，完全不用架設自己的 server，只要將 code 放到指定的 branch，使用者就能很方便的使用我們的服務，並且讓未來需要這個系統架構的開發者或研究員，可 以很方便的fork我們的作品，增加他們需要的功能。

另外在記錄軌跡的部份，有些裝置沒有 GPS 定位的晶片，因此我們的系統支援 HTML5 的技術透過 wifi 或行動網路來定位；如果裝置有 GPS，我們的系統會用 GPS 來定位較精準的位置。有關軌跡資料的儲存，我們系統用 Firebase [5]當作資料庫。Firebase 是目前矽谷很熱門的雲端資料庫系統，Firebase 讓我們可以專注在前端的開發，透過 Firebase 簡便的 API，我們的系統可以很容易的存取使用者的軌跡資料。在軌跡呈現的部份，地圖是用 Open Street Map [6]，OSM 是一個 Crowdsourcing 平台，由於圖資較其他開放式地圖完整，所以我們系統選用 Open Street Map 當底層地圖；軌跡是用 Leaflet [7]，這是一套 Open-source JavaScript Library，除了有很方便的 API 可以在地圖上畫路徑，更可以讓開發者在他們的架構下，增加自己需要的套件，以疊圖層的方式，將資料呈現在地圖上， 我們會有兩層的 layer，一層是靜態的路線，一層是動態的路線移動。

以下我們將分別介紹系統的整體架構以及實作的細節，最後也會探討一些未來的加值應 用。

2. Framework Overview

在 Framework Overview 中會介紹我們系統架構的流程，如下圖(一)。我們全部的架構都是以 Web 為基礎，如此可以很容易的跨平台。

首先使用支援 HTML5 的瀏覽器或是手機 app 來取得使用者的位置，由於現今瀏覽器大多支援 HTML5，所以可以方便我們跨平台做定位。接下透過我們系統架構中的 GPS-Logger[1] 記錄使用者的軌跡，當使用者按下 Save 後，GPS-Logger 會把軌跡傳至 Firebase。將 Firebase 獨立出來，可以很清楚的切割我們的架構，透過 Firebase 連結前面的 GPS-Logger 收集軌跡資料，及後面的 Trajectory Visualization 軌跡呈現，Firebase 讓我們不需要任何伺服器編碼，就能將整套系統即時呈現。最後使用者進入 Trajectory Visualization，便能馬上看到自己動態的軌跡。

在 Part3 中，我們會介紹 GPS-Logger 如何運作，如何記錄使用者的軌跡。在 Part4 中，我

[1] GPS-Logger : http://frankyang0529.github.io/gps-log/

們會介紹資料儲存的格式為何，以及如何存入跟讀取軌跡。在 part5 中，我們會介紹 GPS-Path-View[2] 如何以新穎的方式，將軌跡資料呈現。在 Part6 中，我們提出一些未來展望，會介紹幾個有潛力的研究方向，除了前端的 Data Visualization 還有後端的 Data Mining，讓 Trajectory 的應用更豐富。最後在 Part7 中，我們會對我們的系統下結論，並且提出我們對未來LBS 應用趨勢的看法。

圖(一) Our Framework

3. Implementation of GPS-Logger

在 GPS-Logger 中，我們定位是使用 HTML5 Geolocation API [8]，這是由 World Wide Web Consortium(W3C) [9]所訂定的標準，由於這套 API 的支援度很廣泛，所以可以滿足我們跨 平台的需求。定位前會先詢問使用者是否願意讓我們的系統存取位置資料，如果使用者同 意，Geolocation API 會透過 IP address、Wi-Fi、Bluetooth MAC address、radio-frequency identification(RFID)、Global Position System(GPS)或 GSM/CDMA cell ID 去查詢使用者的位 置，並且回傳精準度最高的位置資訊。目前多數瀏覽器都有支援這套 API，像是 Internet Explorer 9、Firefox 3.5、Chrome、Safari 5 及 Opera 10.6 以後的版本都有支援這套標準。Geolocation API 有很多細節可以操作， 可以讓使用上更為靈活， 像是有個參數是 enableHighAccuracy，讓開發者可以選擇是否取得較精準的位置，如果選擇 true，定位上會 比較久，但位置資訊較為精準。

使用者進入我們系統架構的當下，系統就會透過 random 函數製造一個長度為 36 的 Universally Unique IDentifier(UUID)，UUID 是通訊唯一識別碼，藉此來隱藏使用者的真實資訊，達到匿名的效果，當使用者重新開啟GPS-Logger時，都會重新分配UUID，讓使用

[2] GPS-Path-View : http://chilijung.github.io/gps-path-view/

者資訊更不容易被查詢。UUID包含了32個十六進位數字，並且用'-'區分成5組，個數分別是 8, 4, 4, 4, 12，像是 523512e4-7b50-ee94-9475-f5dac6fe1cca，UUID全部大約有 $3.4*10^{38}$ 個，由於數量級龐大，所以有心人士並不容易透過我們的系統找到使用者的真實身份，即 使每奈秒(10^{-9}秒)生產一兆個 UUID，也要百億年才用的完。

當使用者取得 UUID 並且同意讓網站取得位置資料後，我們將會在地圖上標示出使用者的位置，如下圖(二)。如果點選了 GPS Information 則會顯示現在的經緯度、移動速度、位置誤差及高度資訊，其中經緯度的單位是 degree，位置誤差及高度是 meter，移動速度則是 meter/second。

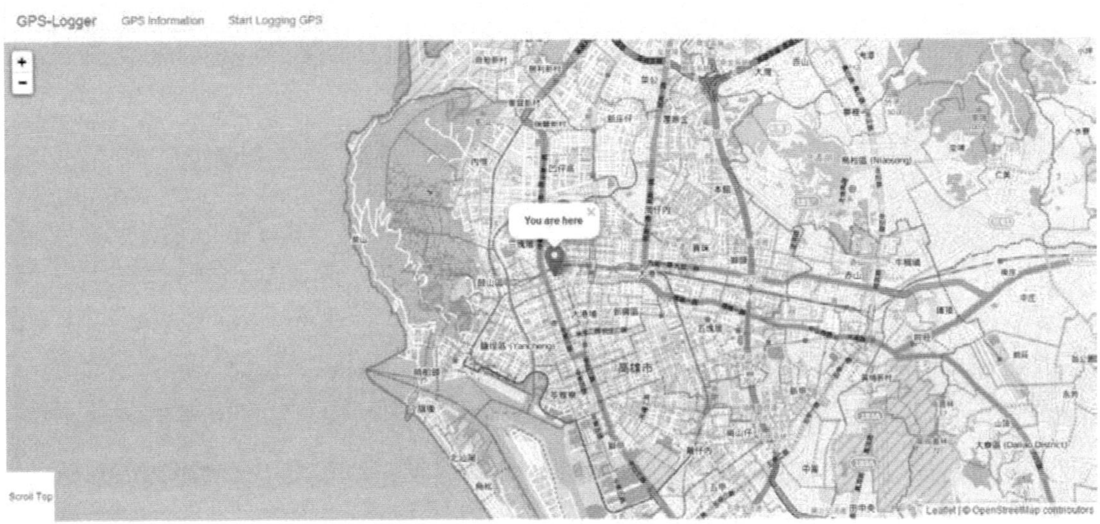

圖(二) GPS-Logger

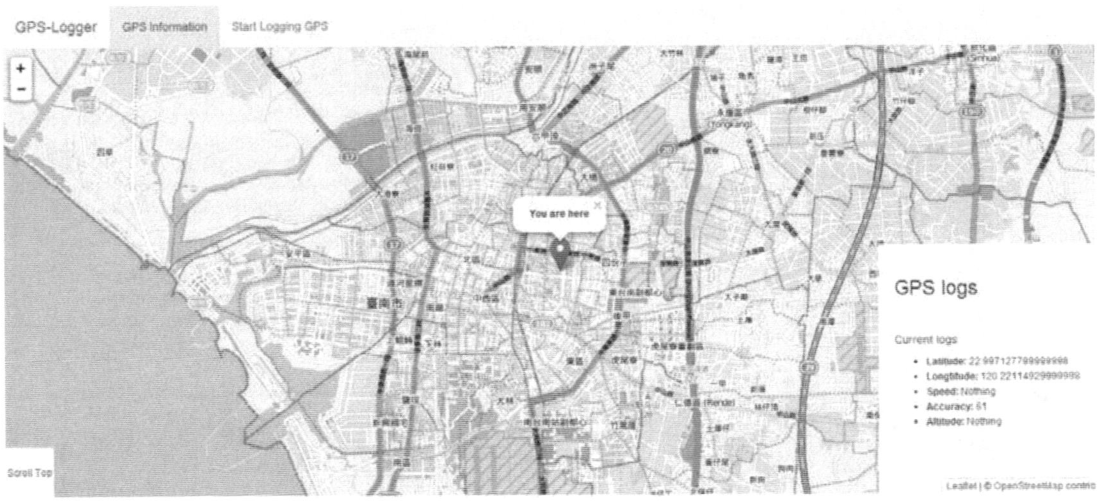

圖(三) GPS-Information

當使用者按下 Start Logging GPS，會跳到另一頁面，如下圖四。按下 Start Logging 後，則會紀錄下每秒 GPS 的資訊，使用者也可以在頁面上看到自己的即時定位，此時資料都還沒上傳到 Database，所有記錄都還只是在本地端，當使用者按下 Save 後，資料才會上傳到我們的 Database；如果使用者不希望我們存取資料，也可以選擇 Draw in map，GPS-Logger 也會以動態的方式將資料呈現再本地端。

圖(四) Start Logging GPS

手機版的 app，我們是透過 phonegap [10]把 HTML、CSS 及 JavaScript 轉成 Android app，運作情況如下圖五及圖六。

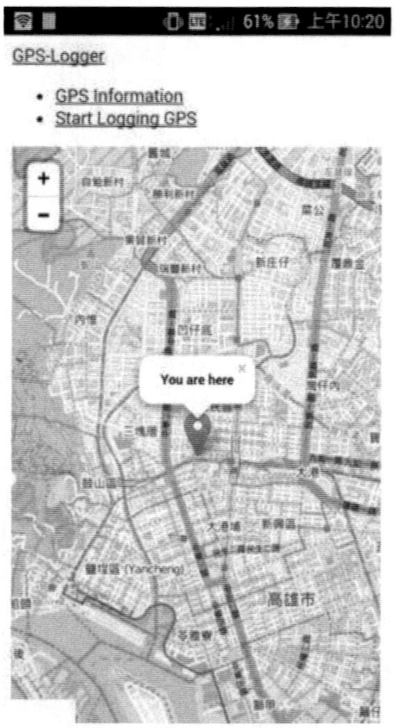

圖(五) GPS-Logger app

圖(六) GPS-Logger app Start Logging

4. Trajectory Database

Firebase 是目前矽谷最熱門雲端資料庫系統，有很多新興的即時(real-time)應用程式都以 Firebase 當資料庫，Firebase 讓開發者不用分心於 server 架設，就能同時容納數萬人上線，使開發人員可以專注於前端的開發，而不用擔心後端或是資料庫的狀況，即使是免費的方案，也能擁有 5GB 的流量及 100GB 的儲存空間，這項服務最好的地方就是，將資料存取和資料轉換在單一系統內合併，以前，資料傳送和存取原本是兩件分開的事，但現在兩者已結合成資料同步。

透過 Firebase，我們可以很方便的存取資料，GPS-Logger 每秒記錄一個點，當使用者按下 Save 後，我們會將本地端的資料都存入 Database，同時也將本地端的資料都清除，所以當使用者下次按下 Save 時，並不會存入一樣的資料，但是 UUID 是相同的，每次 Save 都會獨立成一條軌跡。

傳送到 Database 的資料是 array of json objects，json object 中包含了 id、lat、lng 及 time，id 是使用者的 UUID，lat 是緯度，lng 是經度，time 是時間資料，是由 javascript 的 Date object 轉成 string，當這些資料以 json object 儲存後，在往後的 Data Visualization 或是分析都可以很方便的擷取資料。當使用者每次儲存資料在 Firebase 時，Firebase 會亂數給一個編碼，像是-JQ8Fqz3OgNd-9hhIi5n，而此編碼底下就是使用者存入的資料。在 Firebase 的網站，也可以很容易的察看資料庫中的資料，如下圖七。

圖(七) Firebase 資料庫查詢介面

5. Trajectory Visualization

在 Data Visualization 中，我們使用的地圖是 Open Street Map，OSM 是目前圖資最豐富，

且更新最快的開放式地圖，顯示軌跡的圖層是 Leaflet，Leaflet 是很輕的 JavaScript Library，擁有豐富的畫圖 API，可以在地圖上畫 path、circle、polygon 等等，並且也有廣大的社群開發許多 Leaflet 套件，讓 Leaflet 功能更為廣泛，路徑上的箭頭與動畫即是 Leaflet 的插件，分別是 Leaflet.TextPath [11]及 Leaflet.AnimatedMarker [12]，點擊路徑時，會彈出一個對話框，告訴使用者路徑編號，而對話框也是 Leaflet 本身的 API。

在實作上，首先，我們會從 Firebase 取得全部資料，依序讀取 Firebase 隨機編號下的資料存入本地端的變數，再來將同一隨機編號底下的 Trajectory 集合成一條路徑，並加上包含 UUID 的對話框，最後會把路徑加上箭頭、做成動畫並產生 checkbox，讓使用者選擇是否把該路徑繪在自己的地圖上。Checkbox 的預設都是不勾選的，當使用者勾選某一條路徑時，系統會將地圖畫面移至該條路徑的起點。

在網頁的左上角有 START 跟 RESTART，按下 START，則地圖上的藍色標籤會開始沿著有勾選的路徑跑，當標籤在移動時，checkbox 會鎖起來，不能再新增或取消勾選，所以路徑無法從地圖上新增或移除；當使用者按下 RESTART，則會解鎖 checkbox，並將座標移回該條線的起點。

我們使用的 Trajectory 除了從 GPS-Logger 中收集的之外，還有從 Microsoft Research - GeoLife GPS Trajectories [13]取得軌跡，並且也能使用 My tracks[3]記錄軌跡，在透過我們的 kml 轉換器[4]，將軌跡上傳 Firebase。下圖八是 GPS-Path-View 的整個介面，下圖九跟十是部份 GeoLife GPS Trajectories 的 Data Visualization。

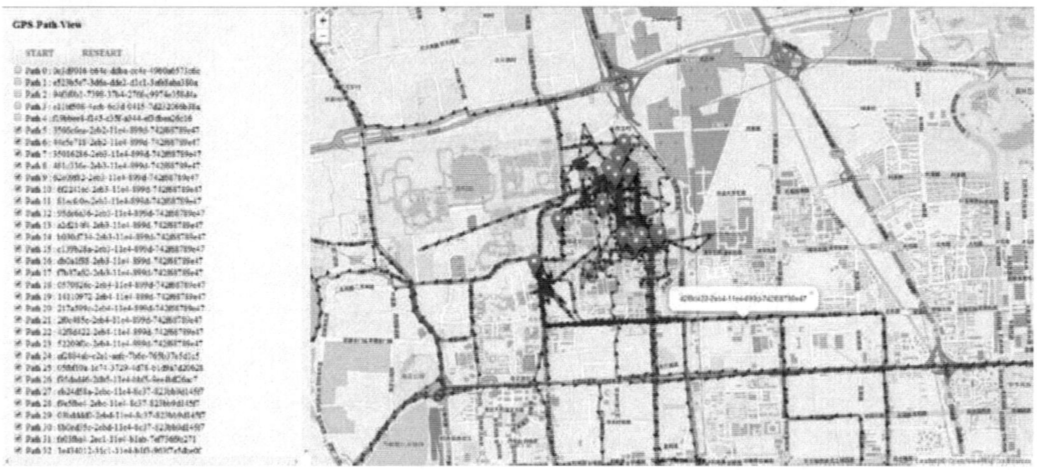

圖(八) GPS-Path-View with 170 Trajectories in Microsoft Research – GeoLife GPS Trajectories

---

[3] My Tracks: https://play.google.com/store/apps/details?id=com.google.android.maps.mytracks

[4] Kml 轉換器: http://kml-parse.herokuapp.com/kmz/

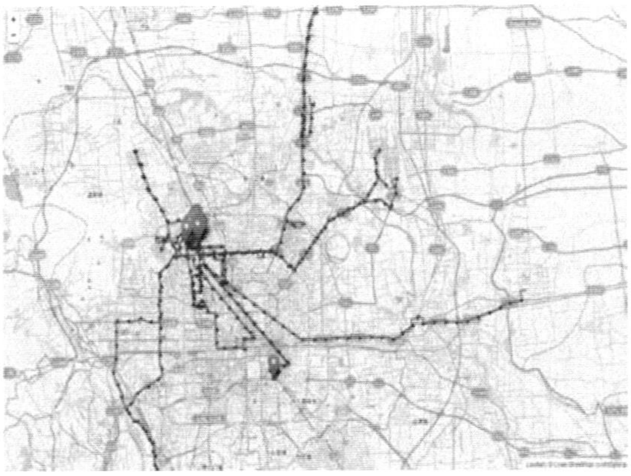

圖(九) GPS-Path-View Zoom out

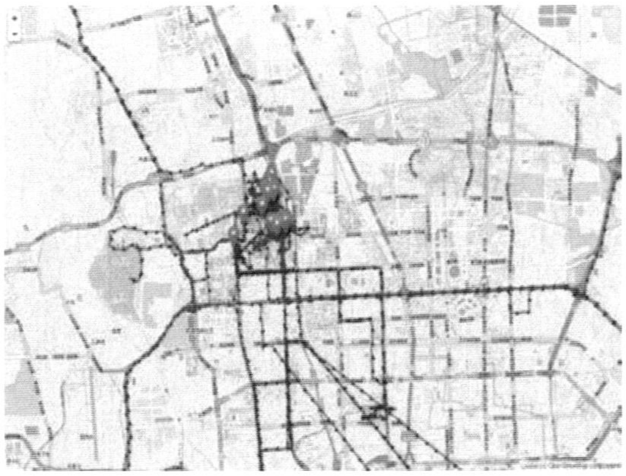

圖(十) GPS-Path-View Zoom in

6. Future Work

使用者軌跡記錄及分析近年來已經普遍用於運動、健康等應用中。例如 NIKE+ RUNNING [14]，即為一個很熱門的運動路徑記錄 APP。然而目前這類軟體均為 APP-based 的架構而非 Web-based，在使用上多少會因為作業系統版本間的差異，而有系統更新的困難。我們認為，我們提出利用 Web-based 架構能克服平台差異造成的問題，並且我們使用的服務平台 Github Pages 及 Firebase 都是免費的，可以減輕開發者或研究員的負擔。後續利用我們所提出的軌跡記錄架構，除了能做為相關運動健康應用，我們正著手於以下應用上的開發。

首先，我們將針對 Open Street Map 的推廣跟便利度這方面來著手，加大 Open Source 平台的編輯便利度。OSM 是一個 Crowdsourcing 的平台，由於地圖的資料均由熱心的圖客們(Mapper)貢獻完成，如何讓圖客們很容易的了解某個地方可能有新的道路更新，包含道路新增，是一個很重要的課題。舉例來說，下圖十一是還沒加上路徑的 Open Street Map，下圖十二是標上路徑以後的 Open Street Map，我們發現本來地圖上沒有的路，但是卻有車子走過，表示這個地方可能有路，細察之後，我們發現這是北京市望京北路及廣澤路的交叉路口，配合比對 Google Map (下圖十三)，則會發現該地區路況已經變了，廣澤路在 Open Street Map 上只有一條道路，但在 Google Map 上卻有兩條道路，由此現象可以觀察到，未來我們可以將路徑資料與地圖資料做比對，當有一定數量的車子從原本地圖上沒有路的地方走過時，表示該地區有可能道路已經變更，如此可以增進 Open Street Map 改善的速度，讓 Open Street Map 的圖資更為完整。

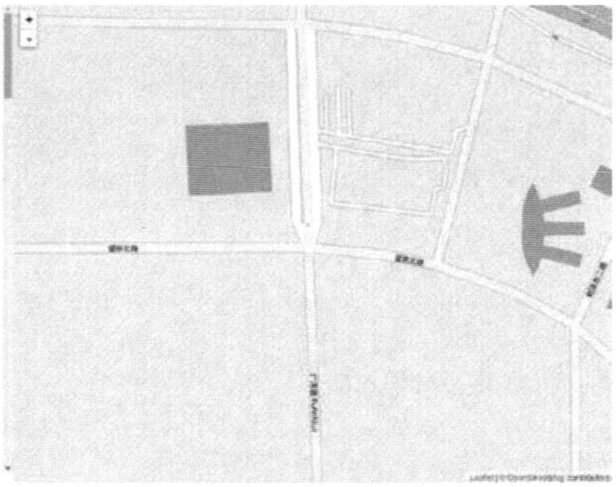

圖(十一) Open Street Map

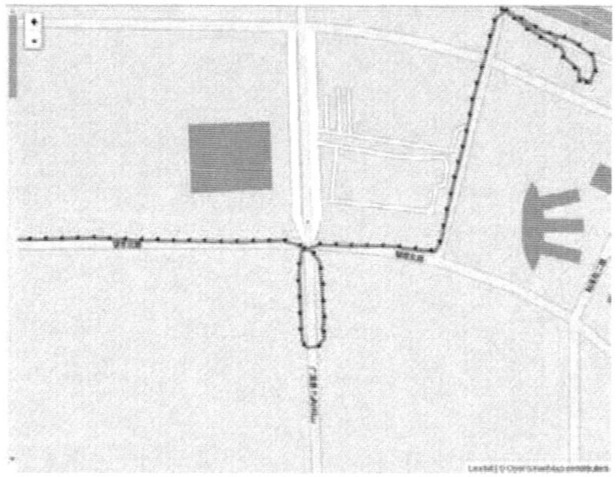

圖(十二) OSM with Trajectory

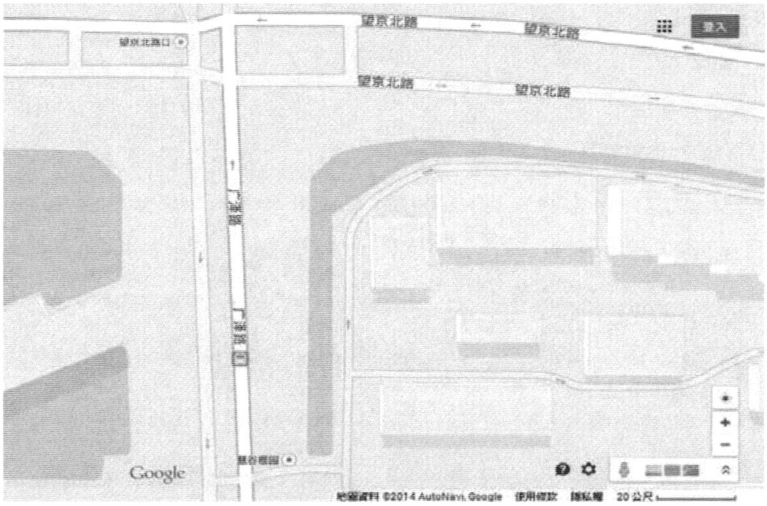

圖(十三) Google Map

此外，軌跡探勘技術已經被視為下一個階段的重要研究課題。研究上通常會透過評量軌跡 之間的相似度來作為下一步應用的先備知識，然而要完成這項評量是非常困難的，因為軌 跡的長度及空間上的關聯十分難用傳統的尤拉距離計算來評斷。我們正進行將軌跡轉換為 使用者行動的 POI 的方式來提供研究人員進行 semantic 上的分析。例如一個使用者的軌 跡，我們能轉換為"孔廟停留 30 分鐘"->"安平古堡停留 30 分鐘"。如此我們將更能提供研 究技術人員提出更容易使用者個人化行銷或推荐等應用。此兩方面將是我們接下來著手的 挑戰。

7. Conclusion

在本文中，我們提出了一個 Web-based 的軌跡擷取及資料即時呈現的雲端架構。透過現有的雲端服務，使用者可以不受限於手持式裝置的作業系統，均可便利的記錄其移動的細節。我們認為，軌跡加值應用將是未來十分重要的一個 LBS 應用趨勢，透過資料的呈現及分析，可以提供個人化加值服務。我們也提出了一些未來的實作細節，包含將使用者的停 留資訊擷取出來的方法，以便後續的 data mining 分析過程，可以用 semantic 的角度來進行分析動作，我們預期能顯著的提高應用服務的精準度。

Acknowledgments

The authors especially thank the Taiwan Ministry of Economic Affairs and Institute for Information Industry for financially supporting this research : "Plan title : Fundamental Industrial Technology Development Program (2/4)".

Reference

[1] "Taipei | Food, Nightlife, Entertainment." Available: https://foursquare.com/.

[2] "Human - Activity Tracker: track walking, running, and biking." Available: http://human.co/.

[3] "世界迷霧 | 去實現你環遊世界的夢想吧!" Available: http://zh-hant.fogofworld.com/.

[4] "GitHub Pages," 15-Aug-2014. Available: https://pages.github.com/.

[5] "Firebase - Build Realtime Apps." Available: https://www.firebase.com/.

[6] "OpenStreetMap." Available: http://www.openstreetmap.org/#map=5/51.509/-0.088.

[7] "Leaflet — an open-source JavaScript library for interactive maps." Available: http://leafletjs.com/.

[8] "Geolocation API Specification." Available: http://dev.w3.org/geo/api/spec-source.html.

[9] "World Wide Web Consortium (W3C)." Available: http://www.w3.org/.

[10] "PhoneGap | Home." Available: http://phonegap.com/.

[11] "makinacorpus/Leaflet.TextPath," *GitHub*. Available: https://github.com/makinacorpus/Leaflet.TextPath.

[12] "openplans/Leaflet.AnimatedMarker," *GitHub*. Available: https://github.com/openplans/Leaflet.AnimatedMarker.

[13] "GeoLife GPS Trajectories." Available: http://research.microsoft.com/apps/mobile/download.aspx?p=b16d359d-d164-469e-9fd4-daa38f2b2e13.

[14] "Nike Running," *Nike.com*. Available: http://www.nike.com/tw/zh_tw/c/running.

Association for Computational Linguistics
209 N. Eighth Street
Stroudsburg, Pennsylvania 18360

CURRAN ASSOCIATES INC
proceedings
.com

Fachtagung Bauwerksdiagnose (Bauwerksdiagnose 2018)

Praktische Anwendungen Zerstorungsfreier Prufungen and Zukunftsaufgaben

Berichtsband BB 165

Berlin, Germany
15-16 February 2018